Shaping and Reshaping Chinese American Identity

Shaping and Reshaping Chinese American Identity

New York's Chinese during the Depression and World War II

Jingyi Song

LEXINGTON BOOKS
A division of
ROWMAN & LITTLEFIELD PUBLISHERS, INC.
Lanham • Boulder • New York • Toronto • Plymouth, UK

Published by Lexington Books
A division of Rowman & Littlefield Publishers, Inc.
A wholly owned subsidiary of The Rowman & Littlefield Publishing Group, Inc.
4501 Forbes Boulevard, Suite 200, Lanham, Maryland 20706
http://www.lexingtonbooks.com

Estover Road, Plymouth PL6 7PY, United Kingdom

British Library Cataloguing in Publication Information Available

Library of Congress Cataloging-in-Publication Data

Song, Jingyi, 1950–
Shaping and reshaping Chinese American identity : New York's Chinese during the Depression and World War II / Jingyi Song.
p. cm.
Includes bibliographical references and index.
ISBN 978-0-7391-4307-0 (cloth : alk. paper) — ISBN 978-0-7391-4309-4 (electronic)
1. Chinese Americans—New York (State)—New York—History—20th century. 2. Chinese Americans—New York (State)—New York—Social conditions—20th century. 3. Chinese Americans—New York (State)—New York—Economic conditions—20th century. 4. Chinese Americans—Societies, etc. 5. Chinese Americans—Ethnic identity. 6. Depressions—1929—New York (State)—New York. 7. World War, 1939–1945—Chinese Americans. I. Title.
F128.9.C5S67 2010
305.895'10747109043—dc22 2009053701

™ The paper used in this publication meets the minimum requirements of American National Standard for Information Sciences—Permanence of Paper for Printed Library Materials, ANSI/NISO Z39.48-1992.

Printed in the United States of America

To my father, Professor Jingying Song, who encouraged me to fulfill my goal but never got the chance to see my work

Contents

Acknowledgments

Many people have contributed to the completion of this project and I would like to acknowledge my gratitude to them.

I am immeasurably indebted to Dolores Greenberg for her intellectual guidance and constructive suggestions when the project started. I would like to express my sincere appreciation to Thomas Kessner for his critical comments. I also want to extend my thanks to Pyong Gap Min for his helpful advice and inspiration.

I am grateful to other professors and to my friends for their knowledgeable suggestions and emotional support, particularly Susan Newman, Duane Tananbaum, Hans Trefousse, Carol Gee, Binita Mehta, Pia Mukherji, Lori Lohman, and Kathy Johnson. I am indebted to the librarians and staff at the Mina Rees Library of the Graduate School of CUNY for their professional assistance in my research. I also owe special gratitude to the archivists at the Union Theological Seminary, the Municipal Archives of New York City, and the Museum of Chinese in America in New York's Chinatown, who made it possible for me to explore the materials needed for my research.

My gratitude also goes to my colleagues who offered advice and constructive suggestions when the project was being transformed into the book. I would like to express my heartfelt thanks to James Llana for his generous support. The project could never have been completed without those who provided help. My thanks also go to the anonymous reviewers, who endorsed the manuscript enthusiastically while making useful suggestions. I am deeply grateful to Julie E. Kirsch, editorial director, and Joseph Parry of Lexington Books for their efficiency and editorial suggestions.

My deepest thanks and appreciation go to my family and relatives and for their support, especially my daughter, Jie, and her husband, Adam Cataldo, whose academic achievements inspired me in a special way.

Introduction

According to the most recent historical scholarship, the emergence of a "new" Chinese immigrant community in New York City dates from the federal immigration law of 1965, which lifted restrictive quota provisions.[1] College graduates and technical personnel comprised a large portion of the influx of new Chinese immigrants.[2] Their educational sophistication and technical skills, it is said, enabled them to adapt themselves to modern American society and to inject a dynamic element that significantly changed the community they found in New York City.[3] Few studies have investigated the Chinese community of the 1930s and 1940s, when the groundwork for the dramatic transformation of the 1960s and 1970s was actually laid.

Shaping and Reshaping Chinese American Identity: New York's Chinese during the Depression and World War II focuses on the remaking of the Chinese community in New York City from the Depression years to the end of World War II. Daniel J. Elazar suggests that community "is an exceedingly complex organism. It is not a highly integrated structure but a loosely knit system of institutions, organizations, groups, families, and individuals whose roles and areas of concerns are relatively specialized, often overlapping, and not infrequently shifting."[4] Benjamin B. Ringer and Elinor R. Lawless believe that the formation of an ethnic community is a distinctive societal phenomenon. These scholars see community as a consequence of the interplay of power, polity, and policies of the larger society imposed upon racial minorities. Membership in an ethnic group is "primarily a function of birth—a matter of ascription rather than of voluntary choice."[5] Emphasizing the shared belief system and common national origin, Ringer and Lawless apply the theories of "we-ness" and "they-ness" to analyze the dynamics within an ethnic community and the impact of the political-economic order of society upon ethnic communities.

I find these theories useful as I am particularly interested in exploring the diversity of experiences among different interest groups of the Chinese in New York City and how their changing perspectives contributed to transformations in the attitudes of the larger non-Asian community. Among the questions I will address, for example, are: What changes and continuities occurred within the city's Chinese community in the years of the Depression and World War II contributing to its transformation? How did different groups of Chinese react in these years to the persistent discrimination perpetuated in American society? Racism was rooted in the Anglo-Saxon white supremacist culture of the United States. Social scientists have shown how it penetrated the life of Americans. Like other racial minorities, the Chinese in New York experienced sanctions, segregation, prejudice, and discrimination. They were racially labeled as Mongolians, a yellow menace, and heathens. However, they did not passively accept the stamp of racial inferiority. Instead, they resisted.

Shaping and Reshaping Chinese American Identity investigates the experiences of Chinese New Yorkers in their varied struggles for racial equality. It also examines the development of institutions created by the Chinese to integrate themselves into mainstream activities as a means of claiming their rights as American citizens. This institutional analysis will demonstrate how second-generation immigrants' conscious decisions regarding their future in a hostile environment helped to form a new dual identity for themselves and change the way other New Yorkers saw them.

The Chinese community in New York City has been a social mosaic since its formation in the 1840s. Sailors and merchants, together with a labor force that either came from Cuba, Peru, and Canada or remained after the completion of the first transcontinental railways in the 1860s, made up a large part of the pioneer generation. Scholars and professionals constituted the gentry that provided community leadership as they had at home.

Seeking opportunities and a better life, these people worked hard to attain their goals. However, the hostile political and social climate, specifically the 1882 Chinese Exclusion Law that barred Chinese immigrants from entering this country and prohibited their naturalization on the basis of race, made it difficult, sometimes impossible, for them to achieve their goals. Excluded by society, many preferred to stay in their own ethnic enclave for self-protection.

For decades after the enforcement of the exclusion law, New York's Chinese, like the Chinese in cities in the West, fought for their survival as well as for legal recognition of equality in this country. They filed civil suits against the unequal treatment. They participated in demonstrations to ensure that their protests would be publicly heard. The shared experience of being Chinese and living under the shadow of the Chinese Exclusion Law brought Chinese of different ages and classes together to fight for racial equality.

Before the 1930s, struggles for justice had traditionally been confined within the frame of the elite in the Chinese community. When the Great Depression plagued the country, demands for change took a completely different course. Traditionally, New York's Chinese had turned to charitable organizations and local district associations for help during hard times. The Great Depression was so severe and persistent that traditional ethic institutions could not meet the needs of thousands of people who had lost their businesses and jobs. Instead, desperate unemployed laborers, restaurant workers, and self-employed laundrymen organized to protect their interests. The formation of labor organizations such as the Lien Yi Society and the Chinese Unemployed Council and small business associations such as the Chinese Hand Laundry Alliance and the Chinese American Restaurant Association of Greater New York were new to the Chinese community. Independent of elite control and local district affiliations, these groups challenged longstanding Chinese community authorities.

In their efforts to survive, these new organizations integrated their activities into the larger society. The creation of labor alliances with other American labor unions and the demands of Chinese small businessmen for equality demonstrated their desire for change. The activities of New York's Chinese labor organizations, in particular, resulted in the development of a new class consciousness. As important, the Chinese in New York called for government relief during the Depression, indicating a growing awareness of both the government's role in aiding the needy and their own right as citizens to request such assistance.

New York's Chinese had been forced to withdraw into their own community to protect themselves from unnecessary risks since the enforcement of the Chinese Exclusion Law of 1882. Their reactions and activities in the Depression demonstrated shifting attitudes toward society. In coping with prejudice and hostility, the 1930s marked a turning point from isolation to involvement.

Shaping and Reshaping Chinese American Identity points to the importance of a politically mature second generation. The younger generation of Chinese Americans saw the United States as "the land of the free and the home of the brave," but the realities of racial intolerance intruded upon their dreams and efforts to improve their lives. They were stereotyped, lumped together as opium smokers, cheap labor, and filthy heathens who ate rats and cats. The Depression made it even more difficult for them to survive.

After repeated rejection of their status as Americans, the young increasingly turned to political participation as a means of protection against discrimination. Growing political consciousness accounts for such organizations as the New York Chinese American Voting League and the Chinese American Citizens Alliance and their significant participation in local and national political activities. Their involvement in both the 1932 and the 1936 presidential campaigns demonstrated their insistence on political democracy and their intention to be included in the system.

Recent publications about Chinese American identity in the 1930s such as Wayne Hung Wong's book and Gloria H. Chun's article concluded that racism alienated Chinese Americans and reinforced their identity as Chinese rather than American.[6] Yet the experiences of Chinese New Yorkers demonstrated a complexity in search of identity with a desire for racial equality as they pursued recognition as Americans. In addition to participating in mainstream politics, young Chinese New Yorkers also involved themselves in social and educational activities as a means of self-expression and a way of shaping their Chinese American identity. Evidence of their growing self-awareness can be found in the cultural and educational activities of clubs such as the Ging Hawk Club and the Chinese Athletic Club, as well as essay contests, musical performances, art exhibitions, and bilingual Chinese- and English-language learning programs. Team sports, especially those that required opponents, provided a new mode of contact between Chinese American youths and other ethnic groups. The principle of "play to win" encouraged both pride in their Chinese heritage and confidence in integrating themselves into society as Americans.

Identity gained as Chinese Americans during the Depression paralleled international events of the 1930s that also contributed to a newly found sense of Chinese American identity. Identification with their ethnic heritage escalated in 1937 when Japan invaded China. Calling their support "American spiritual and material help," New York's Chinese contributed $56 million to civilian relief work in China during the nine years from 1937 to 1945. Advocating for China's military defense, Chinese New Yorkers established military personnel training institutions such as the New York Chinatown Naval Academy and the Association of Chinese American Youth to Support China and the War, and Chinese American volunteers went to the war front.

In the studies on the Chinese American search for identity, Him Mark Lai and Shih-shan Henry Tsai maintain that the enthusiastic support for China's defense came out of the desire to have a strong nation to back overseas Chinese.[7] However, evidence reveals the need for a different, more inclusive perspective. We need to take into account that Chinese Americans joined the American military to defend the United States. A Chinese American identity is a more accurate explanation of support for both China and the United States. After two and three generations, the Chinese in the United States developed strong patriotic feelings for the land where they lived and worked. War activities for both the United States and China also contributed to the cohesion of New York's Chinese community, exemplified in the work of organizations such as the New York Overseas-Chinese Anti-Japanese Association and the Chinese War Relief Association of America.

World War II provided the opportunity to intensify efforts to repeal the exclusion laws and legalize the status of all Chinese immigrants. Chinese American women, stereotyped as passive and obedient, played an important role. They took the lead in intensified lobbying efforts. Their organization, the Chinese Women's Association of New York, initiated a campaign to lobby Congress for the repeal of the Chinese Exclusion Law. During the war, they assumed nontraditional roles; in addition to their activities to raise money in support of both the Chinese and American war efforts, Chinese women joined the American army.

In 1943, Congress passed the repeal bill that terminated the sixty-one years of Chinese exclusion legislation. Scholars generally agree that the repeal bill of 1943 was a consequence of American war considerations to combat Japanese war propaganda and to keep China as America's war ally.[8] This book explores the efforts of New York's ordinary Chinese Americans. Their commitment to racial equality and their dedication to the American war effort also contributed to the repeal, and in the process changed the attitude of Americans. American organizations such as the Citizens Committee in New York were established to support the Chinese. When the war was over, New York's Chinese were no longer viewed as docile, apolitical, or uncommunicative. Instead, they had established themselves as loyal and valuable members of society and altered mainstream perception.

The Great Depression and World War II provided a tremendous impetus for the Chinese in New York to realize their goals of integrating themselves into mainstream American life as citizens. But it was the Chinese themselves who finally brought change.

Shaping and Reshaping Chinese American Identity consists of six chapters. The first chapter provides background information. It examines the formation and experiences of the Chinese community in New York prior to the Chinese Exclusion Law of 1882. It also investigates how racism created and perpetuated the isolation of New York's Chinese. It details how segregation and discrimination were inextricably linked in their experience from the 1880s to the 1930s.

Chapter 2 describes Chinese unemployment in New York in the years of the Great Depression. It also discusses the responses of New York's Chinese, particularly the newly founded labor unions and small businessmen's associations, to the devastating situation. One of the consequences of their efforts was the decline of the traditional structure of the Chinese community as people took more responsibilities for the welfare of their own.

Chapters 3 and 4 seek to understand the impact of the Depression on the second generation of Chinese immigrants. Economic hardship intensified racial discrimination. As a consequence, they found it difficult to get jobs in a society where they were stereotyped as aliens. The findings of these two chapters demonstrate their awareness of the intensified racial discrimination and how they were actively involved in mainstream political and cultural events as a means of protesting racial inequality. Chapter 3 focuses on their organized cultural activities in search of Chinese American identities, while chapter 4 emphasizes their growing political consciousness demonstrated in their active participation in federal and local elections as a means of claiming their rights as American citizens.

Chapters 5 and 6 examine the experiences of New York's Chinese in the war years before and after Pearl Harbor. New York's Chinese support of China in wartime reflected their identity of being both Chinese and Americans. Like other ethnic groups, Chinese Americans appealed for support of their country of origin. As we will see, they participated in varied organized activities in support of China's military defense and they raised money for civilian relief. As Chinese Americans, they joined American military forces to defend this country. *Shaping and Reshaping Chinese American Identity* also examines their participation in wartime production. It argues that their contributions to the war front and to the home front eventually brought up the issue of the Chinese exclusion laws for reconsideration. The book concludes by relating the active participation of the Chinese in New York during the war years to the national movement for racial equality that resulted in new federal legislation.

The conclusion summarizes the themes based on the findings of the ways in which the Depression and World War II created the momentum for Chinese Americans to break down the barriers of exclusion. Engagement rather than disengagement in American society became a major shift in the political behavior of Chinese Americans in New York. This political strategy assisted the growing consciousness of Chinese Americans and brought them together to improve the life of the Chinese community in New York.

The reader should keep in mind that New York's Chinese lived in different geographic locations such as Brooklyn and Queens, not just in "Chinatown" in Lower Manhattan, as is sometimes implied. Therefore, I use the term "Chinese community" in discussing this ethnic group. For the "second-generation Chinese immigrants," I mean the generation born in the United States around the 1910s and 1920s, to distinguish them from foreign-born Chinese.

Many of the primary sources for my research were in Chinese and I have used Pingyin, a popular phonetic system for the translation of names and geographic locations. But I also keep some popular names as they were translated according to the Wade-Giles phonetic system more familiar to English readers.

Notes

1. Hsiang-Shui Chen, *Chinatown No More* (Ithaca, N.Y.: Cornell University Press, 1992); Bill Ong Hing, *Making and Remaking Asian America through Immigration Policy 1850–1990* (Stanford, Calif.: Stanford University Press, 1993); Jan Lin, *Reconstructing Chinatown: Ethnic Enclave, Global Change* (Minneapolis: University of Minnesota Press, 1998); Sucheng Chan, *Asian Americans: An Interpretive History* (Boston: Twayne Publishers, 1991); Franklin Ng, *Asian American: Re-conceptualizing Cultures, History, and Politics* (New York: Routledge, 2002); Huping Ling, *Chinese St. Louis: from Enclave to Cultural Community* (Philadelphia: Temple University Press, 2004).

2. Shih-shan Henry Tsai, *The Chinese Experience in America* (Bloomington and Indianapolis: Indiana University Press, 1986), 195; Bernard Wong, "The Chinese: New Immigrants in New York's Chinatown," in *New Immigrants in New York*, ed. Nancy Foner (New York: Columbia University Press, 1987), 246; Pyong Gap Min, *Asian Americans Contemporary Trends and Issues* (New York: Sage Publications, 1995).

3. Sue Fawn Chung, "Fighting for Their American Rights," *Claiming America: Constructing Chinese American Identities during the Exclusion Era*, ed. K. Scott Wong and Sucheng Chan (Philadelphia: Temple University Press, 1998), 119; also see Herbert R. Barringer, Robert W. Gardner, and Michael J. Levin, *Asians and Pacific Islanders in the United States* (New York: Russell Sage Foundation, 1993), 37–38; Leon F. Birvoer and Anthony J. Agresta, "The Future Asian Population of the United States," in *Pacific Bridges: The New Immigration from Asian and the Pacific Islands*, ed. James T. Fawcett and Benjamin V. Carino (Staten Island, N.Y.: Center for Migration Studies, 1987).

4. Daniel J. Elazar, *Community and Polity: The Organizational Dynamics of American Jewry* (Philadelphia: The Jewish Publication Society of America, 1980), 9.

5. Benjamin B. Ringer and Elinor R. Lawless, *Race-Ethnicity and Society* (New York and London: Routledge, 1989), 5.

6. Wayne Hung Wong, *American Paper Son: A Chinese Immigrant in the Midwest* (Urbana and Chicago: University of Illinois Press, 2006); Gloria H. Chun, "'Go West . . . To China': Chinese American Identity in the 1930's," in *Claiming America: Constructing Chinese American Identities during the Exclusion Era*, ed. K. Scott Wong and Sucheng Chan (Philadelphia: Temple University Press, 1998), 174.

7. H. M. Lai, *The Chinese of America: 1785–1980* (San Francisco: Chinese Cultural Foundation, 1980); Shih-shan Henry Tsai, *The Chinese Experience in America* (Bloomington: Indiana University Press, 1986).

8. John W. Dower, *War without Mercy: Race and Power in the Pacific War* (New York: Pantheon Books, 1986); Fred Riggs, *Pressures on Congress: A Study of the Repeal of Chinese Exclusion* (Westport, Conn.: Greenwood Press Publishers, 1950)

CHAPTER ONE

New York's Chinese Community before the 1930s

It has been over 170 years since Chinese immigrants first settled in New York City. This chapter provides background information on the early settlement of Chinese immigrants and the establishment of an ethnic community in New York City. It examines, in brief, the period from the 1840s to the Chinese Exclusion Act of 1882 to demonstrate the diversity of Chinese migration from such places as the American West, Canada, and South America, as well as from southern areas in China. This chapter aims to refute and undermine enduring historical stereotypes. The Chinese who came to New York City were searching for economic opportunities. They were not coolies, cheap laborers, opium smokers, or gangsters, as they have often been depicted. This chapter contends that, especially after the passage of the Chinese Exclusion Act of 1882, the prevailing atmosphere of racism in the broader American society engendered and perpetuated the isolation of New York's Chinese. However, in contrast with traditional portrayals of the Chinese as victims, this chapter chronicles their strategies for resistance against segregation and discrimination from as early as 1882.

Community Building in the Nineteenth Century

People from many lands have settled in the United States. New York City, with its cosmopolitan population, has been a symbol of the nation as a land of immigrants. By the middle of the nineteenth century, it had become a preeminent American manufacturing, commercial, and financial center with an increasingly diverse population.[1]

Immigrants to New York City from the world outside brought with them varied hopes and expectations, diverse skills, and cultural heritages. As newcomers, they tended to stay close to their own ethnic groups for mutual support in an unfamiliar environment. The Chinese, like the early Irish, Germans, and Italians, founded their community in a three-block area along Doyer, Cherry, and Mott Streets on Manhattan's Lower East Side in the 1840s.[2]

Unlike farmers from Guangdong, China, who migrated to the West Coast, the pioneer Chinese immigrants to New York City were sailors, indentured laborers who had escaped from Cuba and Peru, and merchants who had lived in other places in the United States before coming to New York. Scholars and professionals also figured among these early settlers.[3]

In 1850, the *New York Times* estimated that some 150 Chinese lived around Cherry Street.[4] Three decades later, five hundred Chinese were reported to live in New York.[5] The 1868 Burlingame Treaty between the United States and China allowed legal status for those Chinese who wanted to stay and change their "home and allegiance," whether from "curiosity, for trade, or to become permanent residents," thus opening up the door for the Chinese to come to the United States freely. The completion of the transcontinental railroads accounted for the growth of the Chinese population. The hostile situation in the West that forced the Chinese to move to the East to look for safer places was also an important factor for the influx of Chinese immigrants into New York, especially after the passage of the Chinese Exclusion Act. The *Sonora Democratic Banner* reported that to escape the pogrom fever in Truckee, in winter of 1885–1886 alone, "many Chinese le[ft] for New York City on the overland train."[6]

The growth of New York's economy provided Chinese immigrants with opportunities. They worked as cooks, street peddlers, merchants, farmers, and domestic servants. The Chinese Consolidated Benevolent Association (CCBA) was established to meet the needs of the larger population and to settle disputes and conflicts over business and personal issues as more Chinese settled in New York. Prominent merchants and elite scholars assumed leadership of the association. The CCBA became known as "the government of Chinatown" in the 1870s since its principles and policies dominated social, economic, and political life within the ethnic community.[7]

New York's Chinatown reflected the growth of the early small retail food and notions stores. In 1878, Yuet Sing opened his grocery store at 10 Chatham Square, selling Chinese wines, dried vegetables, preserved sugared fruits, and grains shipped from China to meet the needs of the growing Chinese population.[8] Wo Kee opened its door for business at 8 Mott Street in the same year to sell assorted articles of daily use. The *New York Tribune* in 1885 told a story of Ah Sue, a Chinese resident at 62 Cherry Street, who started a small tobacco and candy store.[9] Around the same time Ah Ken opened a little cigar store on Chatham Street.[10]

In addition to retail stores, service trades also emerged to serve the needs of the increasing number of Chinese residents in New York. In 1885, An Ken started a small boardinghouse for the convenience of Chinese sailors who stopped in New York.[11] A number of barber shops and restaurants opened for business as well.[12] Lee Yun came to New York City in 1880 from China and invested $1,000 to be one of twenty-three partners in the Bond Wah Restaurant.[13] By the mid-1890s, the former narrow and curving Mott Street became a popular commercial area. An American journalist recalled that, along the street, "the lower floor of every building houses a business of some sort."[14] "Numerous novelty shops, with all sorts of Chinese . . . embroidered wares . . . robes . . . chop-sticks, dishes, tea-sets, dolls" became an attraction to visitors from sightseeing buses.[15]

While it is true that early Chinese immigrants lived within the area of Chatham Square and Mott, Doyer, and Pell Streets, by the 1890s most lived elsewhere. In 1890, only twenty-five hundred of thirteen thousand Chinese lived in Chinatown, while four thousand out of eighteen thousand Chinese lived there in 1898.[16] By 1900, the number rose to six thousand, but an estimated thirteen thousand lived in other areas of the city.[17] These statistics indicate that the majority of the Chinese did not live in an ethnic enclave. Even though the proportion of Chinese living in Chinatown increased from 19 percent in 1890 to 22 percent in 1898, it remained less than one-quarter of all the Chinese in the New York City area.

The first-generation Chinese immigrants were mainly young, single males. They were not bond or contract coolies, but came of their own free will. They might not have brought any preconceived plans or even wanted to settle permanently upon their arrival. But they were open to possibilities for a better life and showed evidence of a more permanent acculturation. After years of living in New York, some Chinese married Irish girls;[18] others took Anglo-Christian names and became naturalized United States citizens. A bank identification record showed that the Chinese had their accounts at Seamen's Bank for Savings, indicating they had settled in New York.[19] Observers described the Chinese residents in New York City as friendly and hardworking people.

However, in only two years between 1898 and 1900, the percentage of Chinese living within Chinatown increased to 32 percent. The rapid upward trend in the proportion of Chinese living within Chinatown suggests the severe influence of the anti-Chinese exclusion laws on demographic patterns. Increasing hostility forced the Chinese to stay close to each other for mutual support and protection.

In the Years of Exclusion Laws

On May 6, 1882, Congress enacted the Chinese Exclusion Act, which legally prohibited the Chinese from freely entering the United States. The Chinese Exclusion Act became the first national legislation that banned immigrants based on race. For decades after the 1882 Chinese Exclusion Act, more laws and regulations were imposed to bar the Chinese from freely entering the United States and to deny the right of naturalization to those already in the country. The 1888 Scott Act prohibited over twenty thousand Chinese from reentering the United States, because their certificates of identity had been declared null and void when they had temporarily departed to visit their families in China. The 1892 Geary Act extended the 1882 act for another ten years, thereby continuing to prohibit the Chinese from entering the country. Moreover, it required the Chinese in the United States to register for certificates of residence that had never applied to other ethnic groups. The Cable Act of 1922 requiring an American woman who married a foreigner to take the nationality of her husband made it impossible for a Chinese to get citizenship through marriage. The quota system of the 1924 immigration law declared ineligible for citizenship those Chinese already in the United States.

Restrictive state and local legislation across the country also excluded the Chinese from participating in social and economic activities. In Albany, the New York State Workingmen's Convention voted to boycott all Chinese labor and all citizens who "may in any manner assist the Chinese."[20] Trade unions in New York City and Brooklyn declared boycott of Chinese laundrymen. Ninety hotels discharged their Chinese employees in Los Angeles. In some areas, the Chinese were segregated in schools and theaters. Barber shops, hotels, restaurants, and other public facilities refused to provide services. Property owners signed restrictive covenants to keep the Chinese from buying homes or moving into certain neighborhoods. In a number of states, such as California, Arizona, and Washington, legislation forbade Chinese from buying land. Local laws prohibiting the Chinese from marrying "whites" were also enforced.

Roundups and purges took place in many states. Chinese residents were given twenty-four hours to leave their home in Eureka, California. The Knights of Labor began to boycott Chinese labor throughout Kansas in 1884.

In some places, innocent Chinese immigrants were killed in anti-Chinese riots. During an attack on the Chinatown area in Rock Springs, Wyoming, in 1885, twenty-eight Chinese were killed and another fifteen were wounded. Others suffered tremendous losses at the hands of rampaging mobs.[21] In 1886, rioters set fires in Tacoma and Seattle, forcing the Chinese from their homes.[22] Immigration officials in New York City raided the Chinese community. At one time, twenty-seven Chinese were arrested and deported. Lon Thom, born in New York City's Chinatown, was stripped of her citizenship when she married a Chinese student from China in 1922.[23]

Many Chinese immigrants left the United States as riots continued. The U.S. Bureau of Census reported that 10,366 Chinese left the United States in 1882 alone.[24] There was no indication of arrivals that year. In the years following 1882, Chinese immigrants continuously departed in larger numbers: 12,157 left in 1883; 14,145 in 1884; 19,655 in 1885.[25] Enforcement of the restrictive legislation sharply reduced the Chinese population in the United States from 104,455 in 1880 to 89,863 in 1900.[26]

For almost a century, historians and scholars have been seeking explanations of the causes and consequences of restrictive immigration legislation. Mary R. Coolidge suggested in 1909 that cultural ignorance and prejudice distorted the possibility of an American understanding of the Chinese, which eventually resulted in antagonism.[27] Later works of John Higham on nativism,[28] and Stuart C. Miller's books about the stereotyped images of Chinese immigrants, also present a cultural explanation of the causes of the exclusion laws.[29] Both Gunther Barth and Alexander Saxton seek economic explanations, suggesting that economic crisis and the panic that ensued contributed significantly to the rejection by American labor of the Chinese. The myth of coolies, they believe, also helped bring about the restrictive legislation.[30]

Historians, such as Delber L. Mckee and Alexander Saxton argue that racial prejudice and racist views of "debased Mongolian" and "heathen Chinese" that were deeply rooted in the culture of white supremacy in the United States played an important role in Americans' hostile reception of the Chinese.[31] Robert G. Lee and Krysten R. Moon demonstrated in their research that media and advertisements created images of heathenish Chinese that shaped the unequal treatment of the Chinese.[32] Political corruption in American government, scholars concur, contributed to the passage of the Chinese exclusion legislation as well. Politicians who were scrambling for power used anti-Chinese sentiment to push for the passage of the exclusion act.[33]

Despite the social hostility and political antagonism, most Chinese immigrants remained.[34] How did the Chinese survive hardship in these years of exclusion and what efforts did they make to enable them to survive? My research demonstrates that although those who chose to stay suffered from hostility, they did not distance themselves from society. Instead, they denounced the discriminatory legislation and fought to regain their constitutional right to live and to work in their adopted land.

Fighting in Court

One important campaign in the Chinese immigrants' struggle for justice was fought in court. Like other Americans, they pursued racial equality through the judiciary process. They hired lawyers and used the courts to affirm the rights of Chinese immigrants, merchants, and their families, and returning laborers. Over 9,200 Chinese immigrants filed cases against the exclusion laws in the years between 1882 and 1905.[35] A lawsuit, *Wing Hing vs. City of Eureka*, became the first to file for reparations by the Chinese in Eureka, California, in the Supreme Court for their lost property and being forced from their homes by mob violence.[36] Though a legal failure, this case became a political triumph as the filing of the lawsuit was a courageous and bold act of the Chinese taking a collective stand against enforced deportation.[37]

Individual Chinese men and women also took actions to file lawsuits to protect their legal rights against discrimination. For example, in 1886, Yick Wo, a small laundry businessman in San Francisco, filed his case in the U.S. Supreme Court against the San Francisco Laundry Ordinance, arguing that the ordinance prohibited him from practicing his job and violated his civil rights.[38] In 1887, Chae Chaping brought his case to the Supreme Court, charging that the American immigration agency's refusal to let him reenter the United States after his short visit to China was unconstitutional, because he had resided in the United States for a dozen years from 1875 to 1887 before he left for China.[39]

In 1892 Congress passed an identification bill initiated by Democratic congressman Thomas Geary to seize on anti-Chinese sentiment and it was quickly signed into law by President Benjamin Harrison. Being indignant over the new legislation, the Chinese protested. In 1893, only a few months after the passage of the Geary Act, three Chinese immigrants—Fong Yue Ting, Lee Joe, and Wong Quan—challenged the restrictive law, which required Chinese laborers in the United States to register and to obtain certificates of lawful residence.[40] They charged in the Supreme Court that the requirement for Chinese immigrants to carry an identity certificate was unconstitutionally selective. They lost their cases as the Court upheld the constitutionality of the registration law. Yet it aroused the Chinese all over the country. Calling it "the Dog Tag Law," the Chinese in the United States committed mass civil disobedience against humiliation.[41]

Chinese women participated in the legal fight against racial discrimination. They defied exclusion and proved to be resourceful in taking cases to the courts. In 1900, Mrs. Gue Lim sued the United States, arguing that American refusal of her entry into the United States as the wife of a Chinese merchant violated the American protection of Chinese merchants in the United States provided by the 1880 treaty. After years of persistent struggle, she won her case and was granted permission to join her husband.[42]

The Supreme Court rulings were both supportive and suppressive, as we have seen in the Gue Lim case and the Fong Yue Ting case. Early Chinese immigrants engaged in fierce battles against restrictive laws and the ways these laws were enforced through the judiciary system charged the U.S. government with racial discrimination and injustice. Seeking court decisions to assure equal treatment of the Chinese like other recent immigrants became an important measure of the Chinese to protect their civil rights in the United States. It revealed a fundamental belief of the Chinese in the promises of American righteousness and justice.

Rallies, Petitions, and Organizations

Court actions for justice clearly demonstrated Chinese immigrants' determination in their pursuit of racial equality and freedom. In addition to court cases, Chinese immigrants also expressed their opposition to restrictive legislation publicly. Yung Hen, a San Francisco poultry dealer, denounced the discriminative law by questioning a newspaper reporter openly about "Why do they not legislate against Swedes, Germans, Italians, Turks and others?" A Chinese woman persisted that the Chinese had "as much right to land in America as the Irish."[43]

In New York City, the Chinese participated in mass demonstrations and rallies demanding equal treatment for Chinese immigrants. The *New York Tribune* reported one such event on its front page: on June 15, 1901, fifteen thousand Chinese rallied in Chinatown to condemn the restrictive laws.[44] By the end of the rally, it reported, the participants were in such high spirits that most of them signed a petition directed to the federal government demanding the immediate repeal of exclusion acts. During the rally, the participants also urged a joint effort of all Chinese in the United States to protest the violation of Chinese civil rights. A petition was drawn up to send to other Chinese communities east of the Mississippi River.[45]

In this event, prominent merchants and scholars of the elite class of the Chinese community provided both strong support and leadership.[46] The elite class of gentry and merchants were exempt from restrictive laws, since the 1882 exclusion legislation allowed for "teachers, students, merchants, or travelers for pleasure or curiosity" to come to the United States. However, these exempted classes, as named in the law, did not escape from anti-Chinese harassment. Efforts were still made to block them from coming to the United States. Members of the exempted classes had to be approved by the Chinese government in certificate form, and by an American consul. In 1899, when Yee Ah Lum and thirty other merchants applied for permission to enter the United States, they were denied entrance on the grounds that their certificates in English lacked some of the information required. Efforts were also make to bar members of the exempted group from returning to the United States, unless they presented legal documents proving that they had a wife, child, or parents in the country.

The constant and arbitrary disregard of the rights of members of elite classes spurred them to advocate racial equality, and they took on their traditional responsibility of leading the struggle. They frequently petitioned American authorities for equitable treatment on behalf of the Chinese in the United States. They sponsored court cases against restrictive laws toward Chinese in the United States. They wrote letters to congressmen, a quintessential American practice, denouncing the violence directed at Chinese. They demanded government compensation for the Chinese victims who lost their property in riots and for the relatives of those who were killed by anti-Chinese mobs, arguing that their demand was not simply a matter of asking for payment for lost property and lives; rather, it was to force the government to protect the civil rights of Chinese immigrants.[47]

In addition, political organizations were formed to oppose the Chinese exclusion laws. The Chinese Equal Rights League was one of the first such organizations established in New York City in the early 1890s. Its membership increased to 150 in a short time. Members of this organization were merchants and professionals, and most of them had lived in the United States for more than ten years, some since their childhood. Committing itself to "the people of this great Republic to deliver their fellow countrymen from the outrageous persecution," the league declared that "we claim a common manhood with all other nationalities" that should be recognized according to the principle of American democracy and freedom. By claiming a "common manhood" with other American immigrants, the Chinese Equal Rights League sought to dissolve images of differences in culture, religion, language, and race that "saturated American editorials, broadsheet, advertisements, and cartoons and shaped the unequal treatment of the Chinese under immigration laws."[48]

Soon after its establishment, the Chinese Equal Rights League organized a mass meeting at Cooper Union requesting public support of justice for the Chinese on September 22, 1892.[49] Two hundred Chinese merchants and laborers, joined by more than one thousand New Yorkers, participated in the rally. They condemned the idea that the Chinese were sojourners in the United States and appealed for an "equal chance in the race of life in this our adopted home," declaring that their interest was in the United States, because their "homes, families and our all" were here. "America is our home through long residence," they contended.[50]

The General Society of Chinese Residing in the United States for the Opposition of the Exclusion Treaty was another important organization that was formed as a united front of Chinese immigrants in New York. It drew support from Chinese mercantile associations and Chinese Christian societies, as well as political organizations such as the Baohuanghui and the Zhigong Party (*Chee Kung Tong*) across the United States.[51] Reflecting a new national spirit that transcended the usual class and local barriers, members of this organization participated in support of the 1905 boycott movement in China, which was launched directly to oppose the unequal treatment of Chinese immigrants in the United States.

Activities in Support of the 1905 Boycott

The 1905 boycott movement was initiated by Chinese merchants in Shanghai to protest against the restrictive American policies toward Chinese immigrants in May. It spread first to other coastal cities in southern China and soon became a national movement as teachers, students, doctors, workers, and housewives in major cities participated.

The 1882 Chinese Exclusion Law and other restrictive laws that followed humiliated the Chinese in the United States. They also offended the Chinese across the Pacific. Protests against the racial discriminatory laws spread over the country in China, especially when the Supreme Court in the United States decided to surrender authority and let Congress hand over immigration decisions to the Bureau of Immigration. Chinese immigrants were devastated in a series of lawsuits, especially in *Ju Toy vs. United States* in 1905, when federal district courts were barred by the Supreme Court from hearing Chinese admission cases. The anger and frustration of the Chinese in China over the exclusion policy reached a climax when the Chinese in the United

States joined them to boycott American trade and business to press the American government to repeal the unjust laws.

The Chinese in Shanghai quit working for American companies, moving their homes and businesses out of American-owned buildings, and pulling their children out of American schools. In June, a month after it began, 350 Chinese teachers and students at the Anglo-Chinese College in Fuzhou wrote to President Roosevelt to petition against American mistreatment of overseas Chinese in America.[52]

At the height of the boycott, medical doctors in Beijing, Shanghai, and other cities across China refused to prescribe American medicines. Cigarette smokers rejected American brand cigarettes. Housewives boycotted American-imported flour. In Guangdong, boatmen resolved not to ferry American goods across the Pearl River. Bankers agreed not to do business with the International Banking Corporation of America. Chinese press rejected any advertisements placed by the Americans. The movement aroused Chinese from all walks of life. An American traveler reported while visiting a mountaintop monastery in China that "even the old monks" talked about it.[53]

The boycott movement lasted a year.[54] It sent a strong message to the United States of Chinese opposition to racial inequality. "The whole nation of China," remarked Kang Youwei, a prominent Chinese scholar, had become "indignant" over the unfairness of the exclusion policy against the Chinese as a national group. The goal of the boycott, he told President Theodore Roosevelt, was to prevent the exclusion of any Chinese from the United States.[55] The boycott, as Jonathan D. Spence describes, was the first national protest movement against American anti-Chinese legislation by means of concerted economic sanction.[56] More significantly, the 1905 boycott movement stimulated a new kind of popular nationalism that strengthened linkages between the Chinese at home and abroad. A historian, Yong Chen, describes it as a newfound trans-Pacific Chinese nationalism.[57]

New York's Chinese community strongly supported the boycott, saying that their "brothers in China only acted to echo" their wishes. Boycott advocates launched fundraising campaigns to assist their fellow Chinese in China and Chinese New Yorkers donated to the campaigns from their savings. By the end of 1905, more than $15,000 in cash had been collected in New York and in other places in the United States.[58]

Besides fundraising, mass meetings and rallies were organized to support the boycott. Political organizations such as General Society of Chinese Residing in the United States for the Opposition of the Exclusion Treaty and the New York Chinese Equal Rights League were among the most active organizations to support the boycott. They organized mass rallies such as the one at Cooper Union in July 1905 particularly for the purpose of supporting the boycott.[59] The shared grievance and collaboration in the boycott, as Guanhua Wang pointed out, demonstrated the dynamic relationship between the Chinese across the Pacific.[60]

The boycott affected American business with China. It devastated many American businesses and deprived the United States of approximately $30 million to $40 million worth of trade.[61] The Standard Oil Company in Guangdong reported that its sales plummeted from about ninety thousand cases of fuel monthly to nineteen thousand.[62] The Del Monte Milling Company suffered great losses as Chinese merchants cancelled their purchase orders.[63] Reverend J. M. W. Farnham, a missionary of the American Presbyterian Church in Shanghai, wrote to President Roosevelt in late 1905 that "this boycott . . . will drive out every American" from China.[64]

President Theodore Roosevelt became alarmed. He responded to the protest against the harsh enforcement of the policy cautiously. He wrote that "in the effort to carry out the policy of excluding Chinese laborers . . . grave injustices and wrongs have been done to this nation and the people of China."[65] In order to protect the American business interests in China, he urged a cautious American immigrant policy toward Chinese. In his 1905 annual message to Congress, the president proposed a revision of laws and treaties as the only way to solve the boycott conflict. "As a people, we have talked much of the open door in China, and we expect . . . justice being shown to us by the Chinese,"[66] indicating that the United States should also show respect to China. In order to reduce the tension, the president issued an executive order, calling for the courteous behavior of Americans toward Chinese students, merchants, and others.[67] Accordingly, the U.S. government shortened delays in processing arrivals and discarded a proposal for a new round of Chinese registrations. The 1903 humiliating Bertillon system of identification that required detailed measurements of the nude body was terminated.

However, President Roosevelt's concern proved too weak to change congressional policy. Certain policy modification was a totally inadequate solution to racial exclusion. American immigration officials continued to deny legal immigrants permission to enter the United States. Commissioner-General Frank P. Sargent charged that the boycotters were simply "interested in the importation of coolies" and warned that any relaxation of immigration policy would result in "emasculation, if not repeal of the exclusion policy."[68] By 1906 the policy of Chinese exclusion was firmly entrenched in American immigration law with the opening of a new immigration detention center on Angel Island.

Nonetheless, the 1905 boycott had made its point by pushing the improvement of the abusive policy against Chinese immigrants. In 1905, immigration authorities had rejected 29 percent of the certificates approved by American consuls in China; in 1906, after the boycott, they rejected only 6 percent.[69] The struggle for racial equality continued and it required a new path to be achieved.

Activities in Support of a Strong China

The 1905 boycott sent a strong message to the American government of the determination of the Chinese for racial equality. It also demonstrated the close relationship between Chinese on both sides of the Pacific. Chinese immigrants differed from other immigrants in relating to their home country. Because of the Chinese Exclusion Law, they developed a dual allegiance often more complicated than that of other ethnic groups. Convinced that their unequal treatment in the United States was a reflection of the ineptness of China and that a strong China could help them improve their status in the United States, they supported efforts to modernize China.

Endorsement of their homeland's self-strengthening movements was an example of such support. The self-strengthening movements were the responses to China's defeat in the Opium Wars. Oriented in its purpose to be militarily strong, China soon expanded reforms to include projects in transportation (shipping and railways), communication (telegraph), mining, and light industry. Chinese immigrants made important contributions of money and technology. Among others, Huang Bingchang from San Francisco went back to China in 1890 and started the first electricity generating station in Guangzhou. In 1905, Chin Gee Hee from Seattle started a campaign to raise capital from Chinese immigrants in the United States and Canada to finance the construction of the Sunning Railroad, the first railroad that ran from Taishan District to Xinhui District in Guangdong province.[70] In 1911, Fong Joe Guey went to China to start the Guangdong Aviation Company. A resident of Oakland, California, Fong was considered the first Chinese aviator in the world. Others included Tom Gunn, the first Chinese American licensed pilot, who also went back to his ancestral land in 1912. J. K. Choy left Honolulu for China and later became head of the Chinese Merchants Navigation Company.[71]

Chinese New Yorkers also provided strong support in the effort to strengthen China. Chen Heqin, among others who decided to go back to their ancestral country to assist modernization projects, went to China to "serve his Fatherland" with his science degree from Columbia University in 1919.[72]

In addition to their support for China's technological advancement, Chinese New Yorkers also advocated political reforms, even revolution. In the years of supporting the self-strengthening movements, New York's Chinese urged a constitutional monarchy and an end to the absolute imperial rule. After the failure of the One Hundred Days Reform that petitioned for the replacement of Qing court, they allied with the Baohuanghui, a political party established in the United States, to continue agitation for a constitutional monarchy and other political reforms. An important community association, the Chinese Consolidated Benevolent Association, announced their affiliation with the party and many individuals became party members.[73]

Merchants provided financial support for the party's newspaper, the *Chinese Reform News*, to spread reform ideas. On March 10, 1904, its inaugural issue in Chinese appeared in New York, and it became the first Chinese newspaper published in the United States. Published every Wednesday and Saturday, it reported the development of Chinese national industries and enterprises. The newspaper also kept close watch on Japanese expansion in Asia. News on local political reforms, as well as rebellions against the Qing court, appealed to readers in the United States.

New York's Chinese were enthusiastic supporters of armed rebellions against the Qing court, which they believed held responsibility for their unequal treatment in the United States. By 1907, radical Chinese New Yorkers had joined with the Chinese across America to raise $58,813 for a military school in New York, the *Ganchen Xuexao* (The Vanguards), to train young men to fight in China.[74]

New York's Chinese remained an important source of moral and financial support in the years when republic revolution spread over China. They were inspired by the radical movements in China to topple the Qing Manchu rule. They condemned the Qing court for the humiliation that Chinese on both shores of the Pacific suffered since the middle of the nineteenth century because of the defeat of China by foreigners under its rule. Believing in the ideal "Three Principles of People of nationalism, democracy, and the people's livelihood," they became enthusiastic for the 1911 revolution and a republic in China.

New York's Chinese had switched their political affiliation from the Baohuanghui to Sun Yat-sen (Sun Zhongshang) and his party, the Tongmenghui (Chinese United League), as it had a clear agenda to "Expel the Manchus, Restore Chinese rules, and Establish a republic."[75] When Sun came to New York to raise funds for his party, he received the endorsement of New York's Chinese. Duanfang, a high Qing court official, reported that wherever Sun Wen (Sun Zhongshan) went during his trips, thousands of Chinese would go to hear him speak. "Nobody could change the trend," as Sun and his cause "[were] in accordance with the will of the people."[76] During his second trip to New York, Sun collected the $20,000 needed for a military uprising to overthrow imperial rule.[77]

New York's Chinese felt rewarded when a republic was declared in China in 1911. They sent congratulatory telegrams to the new government. Festive rallies were organized. On December 30, two thousand Chinese New Yorkers participated in a mass parade organized by the Young China Association in New York to celebrate the victory of the republican revolution.[78] They lined Mott, Pell, and Doyer Streets hailing the establishment of the new republic. Many of New York's Chinese rushed out to buy the new Chinese national flags. The *Young China* reported that hundreds of new national flags were sold in one day.[79] Celebrations of the new republic lasted for several days. During this time, barber shops stayed open day and night to cut men's queues, a sign of Chinese national humiliation.[80] Proud and elated, and with their queues gone, New York's Chinese expected support for the improvement of their status in the United States.

However, the reversion of Yuan Shikai to imperial rule soon after the revolution disappointed these expectations. In the years that followed the revolution, China suffered from warlords' wars as well as political chaos. Believing that "the only way to save China was to make certain that China adhered to democracy,"[81] New York's Chinese condemned Yuan and continued to support the Republic as China's legitimate government. A *Chinese Reform News* article denounced emperors as felons and predicted that anyone who attempted to restore the old feudal system would eventually be doomed.[82] Dare-to-die corps were organized in several Chinese communities across the United States to commit themselves to the cause against warlords.[83]

Activities in Support of Chinese Sovereignty

The efforts of New York's Chinese to support a strong China were also demonstrated in their endorsement of Chinese territorial integrity. The establishment of concessions and extraterritoriality by foreign powers in China as consequences of the Opium Wars humiliated the Chinese in the United States. They strongly supported efforts to regain Chinese territories as a means of preserving national dignity and strengthening their demands for racial equality in the United States. Their petition to President Woodrow Wilson for Chinese territorial integrity during the Paris Peace Conference once again demonstrated the dual sense of nationalism felt by the Chinese in America.

Chinese New Yorkers resented the Treaty of Versailles for leaving Shandong, a former German concession in China, under Japanese control without considering China's claim of sovereignty after World War I. The Chinese

Consolidated Benevolent Association (CCBA) sent a telegram to President Wilson, urging the president to adhere to the principles of his Fourteen Points for national self-determination, equality, and democracy in dealing with Chinese territories.[84] It also sent a telegram to Lu Zhengxiang, Wang Zhengting, and Gu Weijung, Chinese delegates to the conference, to encourage them to seek justice for China.[85] In May 1919, New York's Chinese invited Kong Xiangke and Xu Zonghan, two delegates from Shandong province to the conference, to New York after they refused to sign the Treaty of Versailles.[86]

New York's Chinese students also participated in activities to demand justice for China during the Versailles Convention. Their organization, the New York Chinese Students Patriotic Association, released four pamphlets relating to the Shandong issue in a short period of time between February and July 1919, condemning the unequal treaty and asking the Chinese to continue their struggle for the dignity of their mother country.[87] At the same time, it lobbied the U.S. Senate, a common American political practice, to pressure the American government to reconsider its policy on the Chinese territorial issue.[88]

The Chinese American Citizen Alliance in New York also expressed its opposition to the Treaty of Versailles.[89] Clearly identifying themselves as Chinese Americans, members of this organization sent a telegram to Congress:

> We, the Chinese Americans, joined the American army and navy to fight for the Chinese Republic. We are determined to fight until our last blood to regain Shandong with its rich natural resources from [the] Japanese.[90]

The strong opposition of New York's Chinese played an important role in bringing the Shandong issue to the Washington Conference for reconsideration in 1921. To ensure that justice would be done for China, the New York Chinese Student Patriotic Association sent representatives to the conference, where a resolution to deny the right of Japan to acquire Shandong was upheld.[91]

The victory at the Washington Conference was a consequence of the New York Chinese's continuous support for a strong China. Their demand for China's sovereignty and their support for a modern China also served the desire of Chinese immigrants to be treated equally. At both the Versailles Convention and the Washington Conference, New York's Chinese sent a strong message to the international community about their requirement for racial equality while supporting China's demand for territorial integrity. In an April telegram to the Versailles Convention, they urged the repeal of all laws and regulations discriminating against overseas Chinese.[92] Thus their demand for justice for China supported their request for racial equality in the United States.

Conclusion

Chinese immigrants settled in New York more than a century and a half ago. They gradually started their businesses, and worked hard to achieve their goal of living a better life. The Chinese exclusion laws jeopardized their American dreams. Throughout the years of exclusion, they opposed racial discrimination through legal processes, petitions to the government, and mass demonstrations. Their resistance efforts received support from their compatriots in China. In their efforts to regain their constitutional right to live and work in the United States, New York's Chinese also endorsed reforms and revolution for a strong China as a means of strengthening their demands for racial equality in the United States. These dual obligations demonstrated not only the close tie between New York's Chinese and their motherland but also their desire to live in the country where they had lived and worked.

Efforts of Chinese immigrants for justice and equality, as we will see, continued, even though they took a different course when the Great Depression hit the United States. In order to survive the Depression, I show the degree to which they participated in activities to redefine themselves and their relationship to American society.

Notes

1. For the early history of New York City, see Edwin Burrows and Mike Wallace, *Gotham: A History of New York City to 1898* (New York: Oxford University Press, 1999); Thomas Muller's *Immigrants and the American City* (New York: New York University Press, 1993) is an informative history book about immigrants in American cities. Tyler Abider's book, *Five Points: The 19th-Century New York City Neighborhood That Invented Tap Dance, Stole Elections, and Became the World's Most Notorious Slum* (New York: A Plume Book, 2001), provides a vivid picture of the diversity of Lower East Manhattan in the nineteenth century.

2. Historical findings indicate that as early as in the 1830s Chinese sailors and peddlers were seen in New York City. See Judy Young, Gordon H. Chang, and Him Mark Lai, ed., *Chinese American Voices: From the Gold Rush to the Present* (Berkeley: University of California Press, 2006). Historical findings of early New York's Chinese immigrants can be found in number of scholars' publications from the late nineteenth century through the present. See Louis J. Beck, *New York's Chinatown: An Historical Presentation of Its People and Places* (New York: Bohemia Publishing Company, 1898); Alvin F. Har-

low, *Old Bowery Days* (New York: D. Appleton and Company, 1931); and S. W. Kung, *Chinese in American Life: Some Aspects of Their History, Status, Problems, and Contributions* (Seattle: University of Washington Press, 1962). *Sons of the Yellow Emperor: History of the Chinese Diaspora* by Lynn Pan (New York: Kodansha International, 1994) also covers some information on early New York's Chinese experiences. *New York City's Chinese Community* by Josephine Tsui Yueh Lee (Charleston, S.C.: Arcadia Publisher, 2007) presents New York's Chinese community with historical photos.

3. Loren Fessler, *Chinese in America: Stereotyped Past, Changing Present* (New York: Vantage, 1983), 6; Mike Berger, "New York Chinatown," in *Chinese Chamber of Commerce of New York, 50th Anniversary Issue* (New York: Chinese Chambers of Commerce of New York Inc., 1957), 28; John Kuo Wei Tchen, "New York Chinese: The Nineteenth-Century Pre-Chinatown Settlement," in *Chinese America: History and Perspectives* (San Francisco: Chinese Historical Society of America, 1990), 3; Judy Young, Gordon H. Chang, and Him Mark Lai, ed., *Chinese American Voices: From the Gold Rush to the Present* (Berkeley: University of California Press, 2006), 429.

4. Hsian-shui Chen and John Kuo Wei Tchen, "Towards a History of Chinese in Queens," in *Asian/American Center Working Papers* (New York: Asian/American Center, Queens College, City University of New York, 1989), 2.

5. *New York Tribune*, June 21, 1885.

6. *Sonora Democratic Banner*, Dec. 25, 1885, and Jan. 22, 1886. Jean Pfaelzer, *Driven Out: The Forgotten War against Chinese Americans* (New York: Random House, 2007), 263. By 1892, thousands of Chinese had escaped from enslaved labor in the Caribbean and from the violence of the roundups in the West. They were seeking respite in New England, New York, and the South. Ibid., 293.

7. The Chinese Consolidated Benevolent Association (CCBA) is also known as the Chinese Six Companies. It was the umbrella organization for the large kinship and mutual benefit organizations established in the United States to serve Chinese immigrants and preserve order in the community.

8. Mike Berger, "New York Chinatown," in *Chinese Chambers of Commerce of New York Inc., 50th Anniversary* (New York, 1957), 30.

9. Ah Sue moved to New York in 1847. A year later, he met an Irish girl named Murphy and married her. He had a small tobacco and candy store to make a living. *New York Tribune*, June 21, 1885.

10. Alvin Harlow, *Old Bowery Days* (New York: D. Appleton and Company, 1931), 392. Other stores were also opened during this period. For example, the Lee family opened a Chinese grocery, "Chinaware Shop," at 32 Mott Street in 1891. Soy Dee opened a little store at 7-9 Mott Street. Ann, "Chinatown," *New York City Guide: Chinese in New York, Racial Groupings in New York*, Mar. 16, 1936, WPA Federal Writers' Project, Folder #50, New York's Municipal Archives, Microfilm.

11. Ann, "Chinatown," *New York City Guide: Chinese in New York, Racial Groupings in New York*, Mar. 16, 1936, WPA Federal Writers' Project, Folder #50, New York's Municipal Archives, Microfilm.

12. Ibid.

13. Josephine Tsui Yueh Lee, *New York City's Chinese Community* (Charleston, S.C.: Arcadia Publisher, 2007), 14.

14. Konrad Bercovici, *Around the World in New York* (New York: The Century Co. 1921), 105.

15. Ibid.

16. "The Chinese in New York City," in *Description: Present Distribution in New York*, NYC Unite, Racial Groups in New York, WPA Federal Writers' Project Roll #66, Folder #50, File 1635, 1, 1936, Microfilm; Emanual Kanter, "Earliest Colonization and Original Habitat, Etc. of Chinese in New York," WPA Federal Writers' Project, Folder #50, 2, 1936, Microfilm; Nathan Ausubel, "The Chinese in New York City," WPA Federal Writers' Project, Folder #50, File 409181, 1, Microfilm.

17. *Report of the Office of Immigrant Affairs and the Population Analysis Division in New York City*, 1900, Chantham Square Public Library, Chinatown.

18. George W. Walling, the New York chief of police, estimated that there were "15 Chinamen who had married to American women" by 1887. According to him, these Chinese were of "the progressive class . . . who have learned English and have abandoned all idea of returning to the Flowery Kingdom. . . . The women in most cases have made excellent wives." George W. Walling, *Recollection of a New York Chief of Police: An Official Record of 38 Years as Patrol, Detective, Captain, Inspector and Chief of the New York Police* (New York: Caxton Book Concern Limited, 1887), 428.

19. For more information, see John Kuo Wei Tchen's article, "New York Chinese: The Nineteenth-Century Pre-Chinatown Settlement," in *Chinese America: History and Perspectives* (San Francisco: Chinese Historical Society of America, Asian American Studies, San Francisco State University, 1990), Vol. 4, 177.

20. Jean Pfaelzer, *Driven Out: The Forgotten War against Chinese Americans* (New York: Random House, 2007), 274.

21. The sufferings of Chinese immigrants in the United States during the riots are well presented in Jack Chen, *The Chinese of America* (San Francisco: Harper and Row, 1980); Him Mark Lai, *The Chinese of America 1780–1980: An Illustrated History* (San Francisco: Chinese American Organization, 1980); Jean Pfaelzer, *Driven Out: The Forgotten War against Chinese Americans* (New York: Random House, 2007).

22. S. W. Kung, *Chinese in American Life* (Seattle: University of Washington Press, 1962), 90; Jean Pfaelzer, *Driven Out: The Forgotten War against Chinese Americans* (New York: Random House, 2007), 219.

23. Lon Thom remained in the country of her birth, the United States, as a noncitizen for eighteen years before she regained her American citizenship after Congress amended some of the provisions of the Cable Act in 1940. Kathryn M. Fong, "Asian Women Lost Citizenship," *San Francisco Journal*, Dec. 19, 1976, 12; Sucheng Chan, "Exclusion of Chinese Women, 1875–1943," in *Entry Denied: Exclusion and the Chinese Community in America, 1882–1943* (Philadelphia: Temple University Press, 1991), 128–29; Erika Lee, *At America's Gates: Chinese Immigration*

during the Exclusion Era, 1882–1945 (Chapel Hill: University of North Carolina Press, 2003), 238.

24. U.S. Bureau of Census, *Historical Statistics of the United States, 1789–1945*, Washington D.C., 1949; Shih-shan Henry Tsai, *The Chinese Experience in America* (Bloomington and Indianapolis: Indiana University Press, 1986), 194.

25. Ibid.

26. Betty Song, *Mountain of Gold: The Chinese in America* (New York: The Macmillan Company, 1967), 320.

27. Mary Coolige, *Chinese Immigrants* (New York: H. Holt and Company, 1909, 1968).

28. John Higham, *Strangers in the Land: Patterns of American Nativism 1860–1925* (New Brunswick, N.J.: Rutgers University Press, 1963).

29. Stuart C. Miller, *The Unwelcome Immigrants: The American Image of the Chinese 1785–1882* (Berkeley and Los Angeles: University of California Press, 1969).

30. Gunther Barth, *Bitter Strength: A History of Chinese in the United States 1850–1870* (Cambridge, Mass.: Harvard University Press 1964); Alexander Saxton, *The Indispensable Enemy: Labor & the Anti-Chinese Movement in California* (Los Angeles: University of California Press, 1977).

31. Delber L. McKee argues that the exclusion laws had been a national racial policy toward Chinese as the laws excluded all Chinese rather than only laborers. See McKee, *Chinese Exclusion versus the Open Door Policy 1900–1906: Clashes over China Policy in the Roosevelt Era* (Detroit: Wayne State University Press, 1977), 24; Alexander Saxton, *The Indispensable Enemy: Labor & the Anti-Chinese Movement in California* (Los Angeles: University of California Press, 1977).

32. Robert G. Lee, *Orientals: Asian Americans in Popular Culture* (Philadelphia: Temple University Press, 1999); Krysten R. Moon, *Yellowface: Creating the Chinese in American Popular Music and Performances, 1850s–1920s* (New Brunswick, N.J. Rutgers University Press), 2005.

33. Him Mark Lai, *The Chinese of America 1780–1980: An Illustrated History and Catalog of the Exhibition* (San Francisco: Chinese American Organization, 1980), Erika Lee, *At America's Gates: Chinese Immigration during the Exclusion Era, 1882–1945* (Chapel Hill: The University of North Carolina Press, 2003).

34. At the same time Chinese continued to enter into the United States by taking advantage of the established smuggling network and using false papers and identities to evade the exclusion laws. See Erika Lee's book, *At America's Gates: Chinese Immigration during the Exclusion Era, 1882–1945* (Chapel Hill: The University of North Carolina Press, 2003) and Wayne Hung Wong's *American Paper Son: A Chinese Immigrant in the Midwest* (Urbana and Chicago: University of Illinois Press, 2006).

35. Shih-shan Henry Tsai, *The Chinese Experience in America* (Bloomington and Indianapolis: Indiana University Press, 1986), 79.

36. Judge Lorenzo B. Sawyer struck out all sections of the complaint that held Eureka responsible for the mob actions, the loss of Chinese businesses, and driving

out of the Chinese. Only the claims for property losses due to the city's negligence remained.

37. Wing Hing, a twenty-five-year-old merchant, acted as "assignee" for fifty Chinese men and two Chinese women to sue Eureka and demanded a total of $75,245 for lost property in the riots in 1885. Ibid., 199.

38. The U.S. Supreme Court ruled that the San Francisco Laundry Ordinance violated the civil rights of a Chinese laundryman by denying him equal protection under the law in the case of *Yick Wo vs. Hopkins*. This was the first time that a law's application rather than a law itself was ruled to be discriminatory under the Fourteenth Amendment. Jean Pfaelzer, *Driven Out: The Forgotten War against Chinese Americans* (New York: Random House, 2007), 282.

39. Chae Chaping's case was settled in 1889 by the U.S. Supreme Court. He was denied the right of reentry into this country because the Supreme Court held that the Scott Act was constitutional.

On September 3, 1888, Mr. William L. Scott of Pennsylvania, chairman of the National Democratic Campaign Committee, introduced a bill to the House of Representatives to further ban Chinese immigrants. On October 1, this bill was signed into law. It provided that Chinese laborers who left the United States were not permitted to return and that all certificates of identity for temporary visits abroad were declared null and void. The Scott Act effectively excluded over twenty thousand Chinese who had temporarily departed to visit their families or relatives in China.

40. On May 5, 1892, a restrictive law, the Geary Act, was passed in Congress. The new law was more restrictive than anything preceding it. It had the effect of bearing heavily upon Chinese Americans. It not only extended the 1882 act for another ten years, but also required the Chinese in the United States to carry a certificate as proof of their lawful residence. Imprisonment and deportation were the penalties for those who failed to have or carry a certificate. This law had never applied to other ethnic immigrant groups. The enforcement of the restrictive legislation sharply reduced the Chinese population in the United States from 104,455 in 1880 down to 89,863 in 1900.

41. Jean Pfaelzer, *Driven Out: The Forgotten War against Chinese Americans* (New York: Random House, 2007), 291.

42. In the case of *Mrs. Gue Lim vs. United States*, the Supreme Court ruled that the wives and minor children of Chinese merchants in the United States were permitted to enter this country because the 1880 treaty protected them.

In 1880, the United States and China modified the Burlingame Treaty of 1868. Article V of the Burlingame Treaty remained in the modified 1880 treaty. See Shih-shan Henry Tsai, *The Chinese Experience in America* (Bloomington and Indianapolis: Indiana University Press, 1986), 7.

43. Erika Lee, *At America's Gates: Chinese Immigration during the Exclusion Era, 1882–1945* (Chapel Hill: The University of North Carolina Press, 2003), 123.

44. *New York Tribune*, June 15, 1901, 1.

45. Ibid.

46. The *New York Tribune* reported that the most powerful and wealthy Chinese merchants in New York were leaders in the protest movement. See Delber L. Mckee, *Chinese Exclusion versus the Open Door Policy 1900–1906: Clashes over China Policy in the Roosevelt Era* (Detroit: Wayne State University Press, 1977), 37.

47. As a result of the effort, the American government conveyed its regret over the consequences of the anti-Chinese riots, but refused to take responsibility for the compensation payment. See Shih-shan Henry Tsai, *China and the Overseas Chinese in U.S. 1868–1911* (Fayetteville: University of Arkansas Press, 1983), 61; Erika Lee, *At America's Gates: Chinese Immigration during the Exclusion Era, 1882–1945* (Chapel Hill: The University of North Carolina Press, 2003), 123.

48. Jean Pfaelzer, *Driven Out: The Forgotten War against Chinese Americans* (New York: Random House, 2007), 293.

49. *New York Times*, Dec. 17, 1892; S. W. Kung, *Chinese in American Life* (Seattle: University of Washington Press, 1962), 84; Ibid.

50. Chinese Equal Rights League, "The New and Monstrous Anti-Chinese Bill: The Geary Registration Act," in *Appeal of the Chinese Equal Rights League to the People of the United States for Equality of Manhood* (New York: Chinese Equal Rights League, 1892). See also Jean Pfaelzer, *Driven Out: The Forgotten War against Chinese Americans* (New York: Random House, 2007).

51. The Baohuanghui was a political party established in the United States to continue agitation for reforms after the failure of the One Hundred Day Reform in China. The Zhigong Party (*Chee Kung Tong*) affiliated with Sun Yat-sen and his party, Tongmenghui, advocating revolution in China.

52. Delber L. Mckee, *Chinese Exclusion versus the Open Door Policy 1900–1906: Clashes over China Policy in the Roosevelt Era* (Detroit: Wayne State University Press, 1977), 114.

53. Iris Chang, *The Chinese in America: A Narrative History* (New York: Viking, Penguin Groups, 2003), 142.

54. The Chinese government issued an imperial edict to crush the boycott under the pressure of the American government to put it down. At the time in 1906, the boycott was directed against foreigners, including the Qing court ruled by Manchus in China. The Chinese government decided to crush the movement as it was afraid that the movement might turn into domestic revolution to topple the throne.

55. Kang's conversation with the president in June 1905: *New York Tribute*, June 28, 1905, 3; June 29, 1905, 8; Delber L. Mckee, *Chinese Exclusion versus the Open Door Policy 1900–1906: Clashes over China Policy in the Roosevelt Era* (Detroit: Wayne State University Press, 1977), 131.

56. Jonathan D. Spence, *The Search for Modern China* (New York and London: W.W. Norton and Company, 1990), 238.

57. Yong Chen, *Chinese San Francisco, 1850–1943: A Trans-Pacific Community* (Stanford, Calif.: Stanford University Press, 2002), 148–61; Erika Lee, *At America's*

Gates: Chinese Immigration during the Exclusion Era, 1882–1945 (Chapel Hill: The University of North Carolina Press, 2003), 125.

58. New York's Chinese also participated in fundraising campaigns across the United States, particularly in the campaigns organized by the Resist Treaty Committee of San Francisco. By the end of 1905, the Resist Treaty Committee had raised more than $15,000 in cash across the country and secured many new pledges for 1906. Unfortunately, the funds were burned by the devastating fire that resulted from the earthquake in San Francisco on April 18, 1906. The *Chung Sai Yat Po* (*China Daily*), Apr. 6, 1906; Shih-shan Henry Tsai, *China and the Overseas Chinese in the United States, 1868–1911* (Fayetteville: University of Arkansas Press, 1983), 114.

59. S. W. Kung, *Chinese in American Life* (Seattle: University of Washington Press, 1962), 84.

60. Guanhua Wang, *In Search of Justice: The 1905–1906 Chinese Anti-American Boycott* (Cambridge, Mass.: Harvard University Press, 2001).

61. Iris Chang, *The Chinese in America: A Narrative History* (New York: Viking, Penguin Groups, 2003), 143.

62. Ibid.

63. Delber L. Mckee, *Chinese Exclusion versus the Open Door Policy: 1900–1906: Clashes over China Policy in the Rooservelt Era* (Detroit: Wayne State University Press, 1977), 134.

64. Ibid., 114.

65. *Annual Repots of the Commissioner-General of Immigration* (Washington, D.C., 1907), 143–44; Erika Lee, *At America's Gates: Chinese Immigration during the Exclusion Era, 1882–1945* (Chapel Hill: The University of North Carolina Press, 2003), 126.

66. Delber L. McKee, *Chinese Exclusion versus the Open Door Policy 1900–1906: Clashes over China Policy in the Roosevelt Era* (Detroit: Wayne State University Press, 1977), 141.

67. Ibid., 121.

68. Erika Lee, *At America's Gates: Chinese Immigration during the Exclusion Era, 1882–1945* (Chapel Hill: The University of North Carolina Press, 2003), 125.

69. Iris Chang, *The Chinese in America: A Narrative History* (New York: Viking, Penguin Groups, 2003), 144.

70. This was the first railroad entirely financed by Chinese Americans. Him Mark Lai, *The Chinese of America 1780–1980: An Illustrated History* (San Francisco: Chinese American Organization, 1980), 65; Judy Young, Gordon H. Chang, and Him Mark Lai, ed., *Chinese American Voices: From the Gold Rush to the Present* (Berkeley: University of California Press, 2006), 125–28.

71. Him Mark Lai, *The Chinese of America 1780–1980: An Illustrated History* (San Francisco: Chinese American Organization, 1980), 67.

72. *Chinese Reform News*, June 4, 1919.

73. L. Eve Armentrout Ma, *Revolutionaries, Monarchists & Chinatowns: Chinese Politics in the Americas & the 1911 Revolution* (Honolulu: Hawaii University Press, 1990), chapter 6.

74. Xianzi Wu, *Zhong guo min zhu xian zhen dang dang shi* (San Francisco, 1952), 85–91; Shih-shan Henry Tsai, *China and the Overseas Chinese in the United States, 1868–1911* (Fayetteville: University of Arkansas Press, 1983), 92.

75. Many New York Chinese switched their political affiliation from the Baohuanghui to Tongmenghui because the Baohuanghui continued to support the Manchu's legacy to govern. In an interview with the *New York Times* in 1904, Liang Qichao, a former member of the party, claimed that he felt little attachment to Emperor Guangxu anymore. Lian also believed that the Baohuanghui was no longer interested in reform as a national politics. It became more conservative. See L. Eve Armentrout Ma's book, *Revolutionaries, Monarchists & Chinatowns: Chinese Politics in the Americas & the 1911 Revolution* (Honolulu: Hawaii University Press, 1990), for details. The Tongmenghui took roots in the United States in 1906 with the support of anti-Qing secret societies, such as the Hungmenjiao (The Religious League of Hungmen), the Zhigong Party (*Chee Kung Tong*), and the Xingzhonghui (The Revive China Society), which was established in Honolulu with an initial membership of 112 in 1894.

76. *Materials on Xinhai Revolution*, Vol. 4, 41–44; Shen Hu, *Ya Pian Zhan Zheng Dao Wu Si Yun Dong (From the Opium War to the May Fourth Movement)* (Beijing: People's Publisher, 1980), 714.

77. L. Eve Armentrout Ma, *Revolutionaries, Monarchists & Chinatowns: Chinese Politics in the Americas & the 1911 Revolution* (Honolulu: Hawaii University Press, 1990), 131.

78. *Young China*, Dec. 30, 1911.

79. *Young China*, Nov. 30, 1911.

80. *Young China*, Nov. 29, 1911.

81. *Young China*, Dec. 28, 1911.

82. *Chinese Reform News*, Aug. 29, 1917.

83. *Young China*, Dec. 8, 1911.

84. In the telegram, the CCBA also asked the president to bring the Twenty-One Requests to the international negotiation table, and demanded the repeal of the unequal treaty. *Chinese Reform News*, Feb. 8, 1919.

85. Ibid.

86. *Chinese Reform News*, May 21, 1919; July 23, 1919.

87. The four pamphlets were "Chinese vs. Japanese," "China's Claims at the Peace Table," "The Kiao Chau Settlement," and "Why China Refused to Sign the Peace Treaty." *Chinese Reform News*, July 23, 1919.

88. Ibid.

89. The Chinese American Citizen Alliance in New York was founded in 1916. Located at 6 Mott Street, this organization played an important role in assisting American-born Chinese to feel more a part of America.

90. *Chinese Reform News*, June 4, 1919. A number of New York's American-born Chinese joined the American military forces during the Great War. According to the *Chinese Reform News*, April 6, 1919, ten out of one thousand soldiers recruited from New York were Chinese Americans. Tan Xing, Tan Quan, and Li Benzi were among those who were the first to be recruited into the American army and fought in the war. When the war was over, New York's Chinese community held parades and meetings to welcome those who came back from the war and honored them as Chinese American soldiers. The New York Chinese contributions to the war were rewarded. After the war, a few Chinese American soldiers were promoted. Huie Dongyong, Huie Kin's son, was one of those who received promotion to a higher military position after the war. *Chinese Reform News*, May 7, 1919.

91. The Chinese government accepted the association's application for sending its representatives to be part of the government delegation to the conference. Five students presented themselves as delegates. Weili Ye, "Crossing the Cultures: The Experience of Chinese in the U.S.A., 1900–1925," Ph.D. dissertation, Yale University, 1989, 67.

92. *Chinese Reform News*, Apr. 6, 1919.

CHAPTER TWO

The Great Depression and Economic Organizations

The Great Depression plagued the United States in one form or another for more than a decade from 1929 onward. It was a traumatic experience for Americans who faced unemployment, the loss of land and business, and, in some cases, homelessness and starvation. This chapter describes the Great Depression and its impact on the New York Chinese community. It focuses on New York's Chinese labor unions and small business associations, and to see how organizational activities helped Chinese New Yorkers survive the Depression. However, the emergence of the grassroots organizations was not simply an economic response to the Depression. Instead, the newly established institutions reflected the rise of the class consciousness of Chinese New Yorkers. Their engagement in the American labor movement at large also demonstrated a new culture and desire for their acceptance by American society. The formation of diverse interest groups' organizations shook the infrastructure of Chinatown. Their activities fundamentally challenged the governance of the Chinese community in New York. Their move to integrate themselves into society as Americans became a milestone in the history of New York's Chinese.

The Economic Impact of the Depression

Historians have argued for more than a half century about the causes of the Depression. However, most of them agree that the lack of diversification of the American economy, the maldistribution of purchasing power, the failure of the credit structure, and the crash of the stock market were major problems that eventually contributed to the economic crisis. Observers also agree that it is not remarkable that the crisis occurred. Periodic recessions are normal features of capitalist economics. The significance of the crisis lies in its severity and length.[1]

During the Depression, economic grievances and suffering extended into every area of society. During the first three years of the Depression, more than five thousand banks failed. Unemployment climbed to twelve million in 1932. In an industrial city like Cleveland, half of the working people were out of a job by that year.

The Great Depression battered almost every New Yorker. Unemployment escalated in New York City as the economic crisis penetrated. The 1929 collapse of the stock market brought the financial center of the world to its knees. The fifteenth census reported that the population of New York in 1930 was 6,930,416.[2] About one-fourth of its workers were unemployed by 1933.[3] Two hundred thirty-two thousand New Yorkers were reported unemployed and 16 percent of the population was dependent on relief.[4] Without income, people could not pay the rent or buy food. Accordingly they slept in subways or built makeshift shelters in vacant lots. "Hoovervilles" were clusters of common shacks for the homeless in Central Park. Bread lines stretched for blocks outside Red Cross and Salvation Army kitchens. One historian reported that on a single day during the early Depression, eighty-five thousand New Yorkers waited for free meals at eighty-one locations in front of churches and other charitable institutions.[5] Across the country, nearly two million people took to the roads, riding freight trains from city to city, in search of jobs.

The Depression hit the American economy severely. As a part of the American economic structure, Chinese communities in the United States suffered great losses during the Depression. There were approximately 74,954 Chinese living in the United States in 1930.[6] By 1931, 25 percent of the Chinese in the United States were jobless. Over a thousand Chinese merchants lost their savings, worth hundreds of thousands of dollars, in bank failures. Many small proprietors went bankrupt.[7] Laundries, a major concentration of small business in Chinese communities, collapsed in many cities such as St. Louis, Missouri.[8]

Chinese New Yorkers suffered greatly as the economic crisis continued. More than a hundred and fifty out of three hundred Chinese restaurants went out of business in the year 1930. As a consequence, New York's Chinese groceries and stores closed. Other enterprises were also severely affected.[9] Restaurant and laundry workers found themselves in the swollen ranks of the unemployed due to business closures. Approximately three thousand Chinese labors in New York City had lost their jobs by 1932.[10]

Out of the total New York population of 6,939,446, 1930 census figures recorded the New York Chinese population as 8,414.[11] The discriminatory and exclusionist legislation had a permanent adverse effect upon the Chinese in the United States. As they were barred from entering the United States and denied the right of naturalization, the Chinese remained a very small population. Great differences exist between the number of the Chinese listed in the U.S. census and the estimates given by observers and the Chinese themselves. Both Leong Gor Yun, a Chinese American journalist, and Thomas Chow, a Chinese American in the Federal Writers' Project, estimated that thirty thousand Chinese were living in New York in 1930.[12] Bendiner, another Chinese American in the Federal Writers' Project, reported that eighteen thousand were living in New York.[13] According to a condensed report for the years of 1932–1936 by Theodora Chan Wang, president of the Chinese Women's Association in New York, there were almost ten thousand Chinese living in New York City in 1932.[14] Part of the reason for the disparity was due to the nature of New York as a port of entry and departure, which made it difficult to collect accurate statistics. Chinese immigrants, like other ethnic groups, moved around looking for jobs after a temporary stay in New York when they first arrived. The great Depression made the situation worse. In addition, because of Chinese exclusion laws and the harsh enforcement of the legislation, many Chinese hid from census takers to avoid deportation.

According to the U.S. Bureau of the Census data, New York's Chinese population grew from 1920 to 1940, due partly to an increase in American native-born Chinese. There were only 710 native-born Chinese in New York in 1910. By 1920, 1,084 native-born Chinese New Yorkers were recorded. There was a big jump in the New York Chinese population in 1930 when

Table 2.1: New York's Chinese Population Estimates and Total Population in New York City

	Census Data	Leong Gor Yun	Bendiner	NYC Total
1900	6,321	N.A.	N.A.	3,437,202
1910	4,614	N.A.	N.A.	4,716,883
1920	5,042	N.A.	N.A.	5,620,048
1930	8,414	30,000	18,000	6,939,446
1940	12,753*			7,454,995*

* Source: U.S. Bureau of the Census Data, in Ira Rosenwaike, *Population History of New York City* (Syracuse, N.Y.: Syracuse University Press, 1972), 141.
N.A.= Not Available

1,926 native-born New York Chinese were recorded. By 1940, 4,745 native-born Chinese New Yorkers were recorded.[15] The Depression accounted for the increase in New York's Chinese population, as many Chinese from other states moved to the East: a major reason for the move arose from a "dream" of potential opportunities.[16]

The Depression and Traditional Chinese Aid Associations

During the Depression, New York's traditional Chinese community organizations assumed their charitable responsibilities. The most important, the Chinese Consolidated Benevolent Association (CCBA), quickly established relief agencies to distribute food and clothing to the needy and the desperate. The CCBA was originally formed in 1874 to settle disputes and conflicts over business and personal issues in the New York Chinese community. Membership in this association extended to different social stratifications. Prominent merchants and elite scholars constituted the leadership of the association. Representatives of various organizations, such as business and district associations, comprised a large part of the CCBA. The CCBA had judiciary power over most aspects of the lives of New York Chinese. Both the Chinese and American society considered the CCBA the representative body for all Chinese in New York. During the Depression, the CCBA used its resources revenues collected from business firms and its membership fees to provide emergency aid to its people.

Other Chinese community organizations, such as the Chinese Merchants Association in New York City, and various district associations also contributed to the relief efforts. The Chinese Merchants Association in New York City was a business association. In 1931, this organization filed a petition in the New York Supreme Court, asking permission to mortgage its clubhouse property at 41 Mott Street for $45,000 to be spent for the relief of the needy.[17]

District associations, known as Hui Guan, also set up emergency programs to assist the community. Many Chinese immigrants to New York originally came from various geographic districts in Guangdong and Fujian provinces in China. Not long after they settled in New York in the early 1890s, those from the same geographic district established associations to seek mutual assistance and support as they spoke the same dialect and shared similar customs. The Ning Yang Hui Guan (Ning Yong Association), for example, was organized by immigrants from Taishan (Toishan) in New York in 1890.[18]

During the Depression, each district association established a special fund for those who were in financial difficulty. Members of the district associations contributed to the fund whenever they could afford it. In addition, district associations provided temporary room and board for those who could not afford to pay their rent.[19]

Mutual assistance among individual Chinese immigrants operated during the Depression too. Workers split full-time jobs with their fellows. Landlords gave tenants a month's concession on rent. Children brought friends home after school to share what food they had.[20] Adults adopted orphans in order to save their lives.[21]

However, traditional charitable organizations and mutual aid among individuals could not meet the needs of so many people who had lost their businesses and jobs during the Depression. Because of the unpredictable economic crisis and prolonged unemployment, local Chinese newspapers reported that tenants evicted for nonpayment of rent and people starving to death were not rare phenomena in New York's Chinese community during the Depression. The suicide rate increased as the long-time unemployed felt hopeless.[22] The Chinese work ethic was so important that the unemployed Chinese preferred death to the shame of being out of work.

Labor Unions and Small Business Alliances

As the Depression continued, and the hardships became more unpredictable, neither the political authorities nor the traditional charitable organizations in the Chinese community could provide sufficient aid to the devastated people in their community. Overwhelmed, New York's Chinese turned to other alternatives for survival. In the midst of the Depression, the emergence of different kinds of labor organizations and small business associations such as the Chinese Unemployed Council, the Chinese Maritime Union, the Chinese Hand Laundry Alliance, and the Chinese American Restaurant Association of Greater New York illustrated the transformations taking place within the Chinese community in the 1930s.

Instead of looking for assistance from traditional organizations, Chinese laborers and small businessmen moved toward self-reliance and organization to survive the economic crisis. The formation of labor organizations and small business alliances during the Depression challenged the authority of the CCBA and fundamentally shook the traditional social structure of the New York Chinese community. As the newly organized alliances turned away from depending on the network of traditional institutions within the New York Chinese community, the traditional organizations lost their power and influence.

The 1930s saw the emergence of a powerful American labor union movement. Inspired by the collective bargaining provisions of the National Industrial Recovery Act (NIRA), workers became more organized than before and they challenged employers, demanding recognition of their rights to exist and the rights to claim their benefits.

Influenced by the American labor movement, Chinese workers and small businesses undertook new strategies to cope with economic difficulties. They began to form their own organizations and seek support from American labor unions to protect their interests. Their efforts to take part in the 1933 citywide pro-NIRA parades and in the 1937 National Maritime Union strike are good examples of the movement toward integrating Chinese immigrants into society through active engagement in American mainstream activities. In their struggle for survival during the Depression, New York's Chinese small businessmen sought American government assistance and legal protection. Their demand for municipal government relief, like their legal battles against the New York City Laundry Ordinance and the license codes in the 1930s, significantly challenged the legitimacy of existing American discrimination against the Chinese.

The Depression of the 1930s was harsh to the Chinese in New York. The hard times fostered in them a desire for equal rights and legal protection as minority citizens. In their effort to survive the economic crisis, New York's Chinese became actively involved. Driven by a legacy of racist exclusion, they developed a new set of attitudes reflecting their desire for change.

The Chinese Exclusion Law of 1882 made it almost impossible for the Chinese to find jobs in the industrial sectors of the larger society, because it became extremely difficult for them to document legal status necessary for such work. The Chinese exclusion not only barred the Chinese from freely entering the United States, but also denied the right of naturalization to those already in the United States.[23]

Strong antiforeign sentiment that led to the passage of a series of New York State laws restricting alien employment opportunities also resulted in the reduction of the number of Chinese workers in manufacturing.[24] For example, the New York State legislature passed a law in 1884 that excluded all aliens (not just those who had not yet declared their intention to become citizens) from jobs in state and local public works.[25] The 1885 *New York Tribune* report counted three hundred cigar makers in New York's Chinatown. Three decades later, Chinese cigar makers had almost disappeared from the city.[26]

The rejection of Chinese workers in manufacturing by the American labor unions was also responsible for the decline in status of Chinese industrial workers. The Knights of Labor opposed the use of the Chinese, accusing them of lowering the wages of white workers by working as cheap laborers. The Workingmen's Party, led by the Irish seaman Dennis Kearney, also opposed the use of the Chinese.[27]

As a result of restrictive laws and the American workers' rejection of the Chinese participation in manufacturing, a major portion of New York's Chinese working population could be found in the service industry. By 1930, 83 percent of New York's Chinese working population was involved in small businesses, particularly restaurants and laundries.[28] According to one account, more than four thousand New York Chinese either worked in or owned restaurants.[29] One-third of the population of New York's Chinese community was connected to the laundry business as either workers or partners, or individual owners.[30] The largest concentration of laundry business was in New York with an estimate of 3,550 laundries when the Great Depression hit.[31] In many cases there was no distinction between an owner and labor as small businesses were run by self-employed individuals. Business owners worked alongside their employees in an extended business. The Depression made the situation for both workers and owners desperate because of the lack of customers in hard times. New York's Chinese laundry and restaurant population became vulnerable to bankruptcy and unemployment.

In order to combat the Depression, various kinds of small business and labor organizations emerged in the New York Chinese community. These organizations may not have conformed to the conventional conceptual definition of labor unions, which are generally thought to demand higher wages, shorter working hours, better working conditions, and increased benefits through collective bargaining and strikes. But the efforts of the Chinese poor, both workers and small businessmen, to organize to protect their economic interests and seek political recognition during the Depression, echoed the producer movement Sean Wilentz describes a century earlier in New York City.[32]

The Chinese Unemployed Council–Greater New York

The Chinese Unemployed Council–Greater New York (CUC) was one of the first Chinese immigrant labor organizations established in New York in the midst of the Depression that aimed to take care of the social welfare of the unemployed. Unlike the restaurant and laundry groups, which included both employees and employers, this organization was organized by a group of unemployed workers to survive the economic crisis on their own. The purpose of the formation of this organization was clearly stated in its declaration on January 4, 1933:

> the present economic crisis is getting worse,
> our hardship of being unemployed is also becoming
> more difficult to bear, so many around us have no
> food, clothing or shelter. Can we possibly sit
> here and do nothing waiting for death to come?
> No. . . . Therefore the only way out for us is to
> centralize all the strength of the unemployed to
> solve the hardships and the sufferings of the
> unemployed. . . . As a result we decide to go ahead
> with the formation of an unemployed organization.[33]

Stressing the shared experiences and sufferings of those who lost their jobs the Chinese Unemployed Council decided to enroll as many as possible of the unemployed and to provide mutual assistance among themselves. On January 13, 1933, ten days after the declaration, the Chinese Unemployed Council held its first membership meeting. At the meeting, the participants agreed that the council should become an organization that would "unite with all the forces of the unemployed" in the Chinese community, "regardless of their political leanings, or clan or village distinctions."[34]

The Chinese Unemployed Council was an independent organization of other community affiliations. Being new and small, its leaders perceived the importance of seeking support from labor organizations in the larger society in order to protect the interest of itself. The notion "to unite with American movements" so as to strengthen "Chinese-American unity" was clearly stated in the declaration of the council.[35] This suggested that, from the beginning, the organization was ready to move toward the integration of its activities with the American labor movement at large. Soon after its establishment, the CUC sent delegates to a national demonstration in Washington, D.C., as part of its commitment to participate in mainstream activities that sought federal and local public assistance to survive the economic crisis.[36]

To seek government financial assistance and support for Chinese immigrants was a bold action. Having been excluded for more than fifty years under the shadow of the exclusion laws, Chinese immigrants were haunted by the fear of getting into any trouble. Their experiences told them not to trust American government and they avoided any exposure of themselves in public. However, the devastating situation during the 1930s Depression pushed Chinese immigrants to reconsider their survival strategy. Encouraged by the demand of the CUC, they moved for a change. The CUC encouraged New York's Chinese to look for government assistance of any kind in order to survive. "To request assistance from federal and municipal sources," the

CUC insisted, was necessary to provide substantial aid to the Chinese immigrants to survive hard times during the Depression.[37]

Shih-shan Henry Tsai suggests that Chinese immigrants were too proud to apply for government assistance during the Depression. The Chinese immigrants, he contends, preferred starvation to the indignity of accepting government aid during hard times. They relied on self-help and community benevolence instead of turning to federal relief agencies for help.[38] Rather than following the "Chinese pride" theory, I believe that the fear that haunted the Chinese under the shadow of the exclusion laws hindered them from looking for government help. However, continuous hardship in the Depression turned the wave around.

Persistent racial discrimination had forced Chinese New Yorkers to look for some organizational and mutual assistance among themselves. However, the devastating situation during the Depression convinced them to also seek government support. By requesting such assistance, New York's Chinese increasingly demanded their equal right to attain help from the American government. According to the Federal Emergency Relief report, only 1.2 percent of the New York Chinese sought government relief before 1933. After 1933, when food tickets were distributed by the government relief agency, the *Chinese Nationalist Daily* reported more Chinese New Yorkers standing in the line.[39]

However, the government did not provide equal subsidies for the Chinese, and gave those who were on relief a food budget that reflected racial bias. The relief budget to the Chinese was 10 to 20 percent lower than that given to "whites" because the relief agencies believed that Asian Americans could subsist on a less expensive diet.[40]

For a half century since 1882, New York's Chinese had suffered humiliation from existing cultural bias and racial discrimination. They were forced to withdraw into their own community in order to protect themselves from unnecessary risks. The formation of the Chinese Unemployed Council during the Depression was a groundbreaking and bold experiment for the Chinese in New York. Its activities contributed to a growing demand that New York's Chinese be accepted by American society.

The emergence of the CUC challenged the authoritarian power of the CCBA. It signaled the beginning of the downfall of traditional social and political structure in the Chinese community, as it was organized without considering linkages of family or geographic origin. Previously, the CCBA had been the only body to deal with the outside world. The move of the Chinese unemployed workers to integrate their activities into the American labor movement demonstrated both growing self-consciousness and, as has been suggested, an increasing class consciousness.

More important, by joining mainstream activities to seek governmental assistance to survive the Depression, the Chinese unemployed workers' organization not only challenged the values of traditional charity organization, but in fact represented a new ideology. Instead of believing that relief work should be carried on independently and voluntarily by family and district organizations, the new ideology contended that the American government should take responsibility for the unemployed and the poor. The Depression was harsh. But the hard times also pushed New York Chinese to organize. The Chinese Unemployed Council was not the only labor organization to emerge in New York's Chinese community to take the matter in their own hands to combat the hardships during the Depression. Another example of such a labor organization was the Chinese Seamen's Union.

The New York Chinese Seamen's Union

The Chinese Seamen's Union, known as the Lein Yi Society, was an important labor organization established during the early 1930s. Because of the mobile nature of their jobs, Chinese seamen were not usually seen as members of New York's Chinese community. However, during hard times when many Chinese seamen lost their jobs on vessels, they stayed ashore and looked for jobs in New York City. Several district associations in the New York Chinese community had seamen members. Like other Chinese immigrants, Chinese seamen were subject to racial discrimination. They were often accused of being cheap laborers that robbed white seamen of jobs. The intensified job competition during the Depression made the situation worse. Established American labor unions opposed the use of Chinese seamen on American vessels. In January 1933, when a Dollar Shipping Company vessel, the S.S. *Lincoln*, reached New York harbor, an American labor union, the Seamen's International Union (SIU), protested its use of Chinese seamen. Claiming that "Chinese seamen charged low wages," thus "taking away jobs from Americans," the SIU demanded the immediate discharge of Chinese seamen from U.S. shipping companies.[41] The SIU also lobbied Congress to pass a bill barring all foreign seamen from working on U.S. ships. Soon its sentiment against Chinese seamen extended to all Chinese immigrants. Cooperating with the Immigration Office in raids to find illegal entrants in the Chinese immigrant community, the SIU facilitated the arrest of the Chinese. More than two hundred Chinese immigrants were ultimately deported after months of confinement on Ellis Island.[42]

This racially profiled attack aroused Chinese seamen. They decided to organize to combat the attack and protect their interests. In 1936, they established a Chinese seamen's union, the Lien Yi Society (LYS), in New York. More important, they looked for support from the mainstream unions that were sympathetic to their situation. Soon after its establishment, the LYS participated in a strike organized by the National Maritime Union (NMU).

The National Maritime Union was an important American maritime union. Claiming its independence from the SIU in 1935, it adhered to the principle of "no discrimination against any union members because of his race, color, political affiliation, creed, religion or national origin."[43] In 1936, the NMU called for a general strike demanding better treatment of its members. In order to make the strike successful, the NMU sought support from other labor unions, including the Chinese seamen's union. The Lien Yi Society decided to participate. Meanwhile, it asked the NMU to support its demand for an equal wage scale with other seamen hired by the Dollar Shipping Company and the legal right of Chinese seamen to shore leave.[44]

Representatives from both unions met in New York to work out an agreement. At the negotiation table, the NMU representatives of the Dollar Shipping Company urged the LYS to join their strike, but the LYS took a cautious attitude toward the issue. The shipping companies still held the $500 bonds of a number of Chinese seamen; therefore, if the strike failed, the jobs of these Chinese seamen would be in jeopardy. The negotiation lasted for days until the two unions finally reached an agreement.

With a promise that the NMU would support its demands for the equal treatment of the Chinese seamen, the LYS mobilized three thousand Chinese seamen to join in the NMU's strike. The strike was successful, as the ship company agreed to provide better food and adequate food supplies on vessels.[45]

The cooperation between the American and Chinese seamen's unions demonstrated a new trend in the American labor movement in the 1930s. During this decade, the American working class began to perceive the importance of a multiracial class consciousness to unify workers without consideration of race or national origin.

The shift of the American labor union from a conservative organization to a more open one provided an opportunity for the Chinese workers to reach out. Chinese laborers were accepted into the mainstream of the American labor movement for the first time in the past fifty years.

Although the favorable attitudes of American unions toward the Chinese provided inspiration, Chinese workers themselves played a key role in strengthening their labor movement in the 1930s. The active participation of many Chinese seamen in the National Maritime Union during the 1936 strike was a breakthrough for Chinese workers in forming alliances with the American working class. The LYS was considered one of the first Chinese labor unions to integrate with the mainstream of the American labor movement.[46]

On June 16, 1937, the Lien Yi Society, as an independent union, successfully organized a sitdown strike in New York to protest the Dollar Shipping Company's discriminatory treatment of Chinese seamen, and unfair layoffs in particular. The problem began in 1936 when Congress authorized federal subsidies to shipping companies carrying the U.S. mail. Congress insisted that for the sake of the security of the United States in wartime, those shipping companies that received government subsidies could hire no foreign seamen. This wartime legislation jeopardized the jobs of Chinese seamen hired by those shipping companies. Consequently, Chinese seamen were promptly laid off without any advance notice or warning.

Frustrated, the LYS called a sitdown strike to oppose the immediate layoffs. Chinese seamen working on the American vessels S.S. *President Taft* and S.S. *Polk* responded favorably. On June 26, 1937, they went on strike, demanding that the shipping companies offer six months' compensation pay for the layoffs, and that all seamen who had been laid off be guaranteed return passage to New York.

This protest won the backing of the National Maritime Union (NMU), which declared full support for the Chinese seamen's demands. Two days after the strike, the Dollar Shipping Company agreed to pay six months' compensation salary to those who were laid off.[47]

The success of the strike came as much from the external political events that affected unions as from New York's Chinese. The National Recovery Act's Section 7a (1933) and later the National Labor Relations Act (1935) allowed unions to organize aggressively, while the Depression made the need to organize more urgent. The success of the strike once again demonstrated an increasing class consciousness of American labor forces. As Charles Frankly described it, "There was apparently a slight shift from race consciousness to class consciousness [among unions]."[48] In the case of Chinese seamen, the NMU encouraged the fight for union collective action. Had the LYS not received such encouragement, the struggle would not have enjoyed as much success, as the LYS experience demonstrated.

The success of the strike also illustrated the ability of an independent Chinese labor union to protect its workers' interests. The formation of the LYS and its involvement in the American labor movement demonstrated the increasing class consciousness of New York's Chinese seamen. In their struggle for economic benefits, they also sought racial equality.

The Chinese Hand Laundry Alliance (CHLA)

Unlike the CUC and the LYS, the Chinese Hand Laundry Alliance (CHLA) was a new kind of trade union founded by a group of Chinese laundrymen in New York in 1933 in response to the Depression. In order to survive the Depression, they united to protect the interests of Chinese small businesses against discriminatory ordinance. Their activities reflected the desire of New York's Chinese to claim equal rights as a minority ethnic group. By allying with other American organizations to demand better working conditions and an improved quality of life, the CHLA moved into mainstream society.

According to one account, approximately thirty thousand Chinese lived in New York City in 1930. One-third of the working population in the Chinese community was involved in the laundry business in Manhattan and increasingly in Brooklyn, the Bronx, and Queens.[49] Most Chinese laundries were one-person, small hand laundries. Some laundrymen shared a business with one or two partners. During the Depression, the laundry business suffered great losses. As unemployment increased, fewer New Yorkers could afford to use laundries. Those who could afford it brought in fewer items. Many laundries went out of business for lack of customers; others had to cut prices and provide extra services in order to remain solvent.

When Chinese laundries offered free mending and free pick-up and delivery, the extra services became the subject of racist criticism. In April 1932, an article in one of the laundry trade journals, *Progressive Laundryman*, attacked the Chinese laundries' policy of regular pick-ups at their customers' homes. The article assumed that the regular pick-ups by the Chinese laundrymen took away business from non-Chinese laundries.[50]

At the same time, a newly formed white laundry trade organization launched a cartoon poster campaign showing Chinese laundrymen with queues and buckteeth using their spit to wet the clothing before ironing.[51] Attempting to squeeze Chinese laundries out, the laundry trade association further demanded that the Chinese laundries abide by their minimum prices.

To push their case, the laundry trade association went to the city authorities for support. In March 1933, the New York City Board of Aldermen, in support of the laundry association, proposed a city ordinance requiring a $25 annual registration fee for hand laundries. Most Chinese laundries were self-owned or one-person small businesses that could make a profit of only $400 annually. They could hardly raise the money to afford the required fees. In addition, this laundry ordinance required one-person laundries applying for licenses to post a $1,000 bond to cover the possible loss of customers' property.[52]

The attacks and restrictions were not new to those Chinese immigrants, who had suffered as scapegoats during economic recessions since the 1870s. As usual, Chinese laundrymen went to the CCBA for help, as it was considered a representative body of the Chinese community to protect the interests of Chinese immigrants in a hostile American environment. Yet, to the Chinese laundrymen's great disappointment, the CCBA did not show the appropriate concern over their suffering. Despite charging laundrymen money for looking into the matter, the CCBA did not take any substantial action.

Resentful of this example of the CCBA's corruption, the Chinese laundrymen bitterly criticized the CCBA for taking advantage of their grievances. All the "holy CCBA" tried to do, the Chinese laundrymen accused, was to use the laundry fee crisis to make more money for itself.[53] Despite its title as a benevolent association, the CCBA charged big money to look into the matter. The CCBA "exploited us in disguised names. It failed to protect our interests and, worse," Chinese laundrymen complained "it damaged our business."[54] Therefore, New York's Chinese laundrymen decided to form an independent organization to protect their interests.

On April 26, 1933, under the slogan "Laundry Alliance for the Laundrymen," the Chinese Hand Laundry Alliance (CHLA) was formally established in New York City. Headquartered on the top floor of a building at 196 Canal Street, its first mass meeting held in a Catholic church on Mott Street reportedly drew several thousand Chinese laundrymen.[55]

At the meeting, the CHLA issued a declaration calling for change that reflected the suffering of the Depression and the increase in institutional racism:

> Recently the New York City Council of Aldermen proposed a discriminatory ordinance against hand laundries. If the ordinance is unfortunately passed and becomes effective on July 1, tens of thousands of Chinese laundrymen would be stranded in this country. . . . That's why we have to fight against it with every effort. However, we Chinese laundrymen in New York City never had a formal organization of our own. . . . The CCBA and the organizations under its control cannot represent our case to the City government. They are but taking this chance selfishly to serve their interests.
>
> Based on these reasons, we set up the New York Chinese Hand Laundry Alliance. . . . With such an organization we can not only unite ourselves to fight the City government collectively so as to abolish the discriminatory ordinance, but also prevent such discrimination from occurring in the future.[56]

Immediately after its foundation, the CHLA proceeded to challenge the city ordinance. On May 23, the CHLA sent its two representatives, Lei Zhoufeng, the first president of the CHLA, and Zhu Xia along with William

M. Chadbourne, a lawyer, to appeal to the city government at a public hearing on the laundry ordinance held by the Public Welfare Committee of the Board of Aldermen.

At the hearing, Lei and Zhu insisted that the services provided by diligent Chinese laundrymen to their customers were welcomed by the residents of New York City, and that the proposed city ordinance was not in accordance with the principle of public judgment. Besides, most Chinese laundries were small businesses run by self-employed, often single individuals who could hardly raise the money to afford the required fees; therefore the ordinance discriminated against Chinese laundries pushing them to the verge of bankruptcy.

Moreover, Lei and Zhu argued that the proposed laundry code discriminated against all small businesses, as no small businesses, whether Chinese or non-Chinese, could afford the required fees. Therefore, the two representatives claimed, the CHLA was not simply seeking protection for the Chinese laundry business, but rather seeking justice for all small businesses.

After the hearing, the Public Welfare Committee passed the laundry ordinance with significant modifications. It reduced the registration fee from $25 to $10, and the security bond from $1,000 to $100.[57]

The CHLA considered the modification of the ordinance an encouraging victory that prevented the bankruptcy of hundreds of Chinese small businesses. Without the CHLA's effort, thousands of Chinese would have lost their jobs while the number of unemployed was increasing nationwide. Inspired by the victory, more Chinese laundries joined the CHLA. A few months after the modified ordinance was announced, the new organization claimed two thousand members.[58]

However, this triumph of the CHLA over the "bond ordinance" cannot be simply interpreted as a victory in business disputes between the Chinese and non-Chinese laundries. Chinese laundries acknowledged the importance of business stabilization. They intended to seek rules that would apply to all laundry businesses but they insisted on an equal base.

Chinese laundry workers initiated efforts to cooperate with other non-Chinese laundrymen to stabilize prices in the laundry business. On July 27, 1933, the Chinese laundry organization made a public announcement declaring that they and the non-Chinese laundrymen both intended and wanted to cooperate in business regulation.[59] In order to protect their business interests, the announcement stated that Chinese laundrymen were willing to charge twelve cents for washing a T-shirt, the same amount that the non-Chinese laundries charged.[60]

The victory of the CHLA over the registration fee and the laundry ordinance also demonstrated to the Chinese public the efficiency of an independent organization like the CHLA. Instead of the huge fees the CCBA charged for the ordinance case, the CHLA spent only a few hundred dollars in the court process.[61] The victory brought hope for those who were seeking independence from the CCBA.

Toward the end of 1934, another contentious issue disturbed the Chinese community. The controversy started when the License Department of New York issued an order requiring laundry owners to prove their legal status in this country before new licenses could be issued or old licenses renewed. The Chinese community believed that this new regulation was discriminatory toward the Chinese, as many of them could not submit a "proper" document to support their legal status in the United States since, under the existing naturalization laws, Chinese were restricted from both freely immigrating and gaining citizenship.

Besides, this new order would also jeopardize the livelihood of the Chinese in business in New York. By the end of 1934, there were eight thousand licenses issued by the city government to the Chinese laundries. About five hundred license holders were heads of families.[62] If their license could not be renewed, the lives of laundrymen's families would be severely affected. Furthermore, it would also worsen an already shaky job market.

Confronting the situation, the CHLA immediately took action to oppose this new ordinance. It demanded a public hearing which was granted by the License Department. In addition, the CHLA also began a campaign to win public support, circulating petitions for signatures from both New York's Chinese and Americans.[63]

The Chinese protest movement drew attention and sympathy from the American Friends of the Chinese People, an organization formed in January 1933 by a group of American intellectuals to seek a better understanding between Chinese and Americans. Its major concern focused on American foreign policy toward China. The proposed license renewal policy, discriminatory toward New York's Chinese, drew the attention of the American Friends of the Chinese People. Perceiving the crisis, the association convened an emergency conference, during which members formed a committee to support the Chinese community at the final hearings for the new license ordinance.[64]

Impressed by both the determination of the Chinese protesters and the positive support form the American association, the License Department withdrew the order in the first week of November. The cancellation of the proposed license ordinance can be counted as the second major victory for the CHLA since its establishment in 1933.

The alliance considered the victory their greatest achievement.[65] Moreover, the CHLA was conscious of the importance of the support of the

American organization in its victory. In its struggle against the unequal treatment of Chinese New Yorkers, members of the CHLA increasingly showed their desire to integrate and ally with other groups to improve their living standards. By participating in activities organized by other American associations, they showed a growing consciousness of the importance of cooperating with non-Chinese trade unions and groups. When the National Industrial Recovery Act was enacted in 1933, the Chinese laundry trade was quick to support it. On September 13, 1933, the CHLA mobilized more than five hundred of its members to participate in a citywide pro-NIRA march in New York City.[66]

In 1934, the CHLA sent a delegation to Carnegie Hall in New York City to attend a mass meeting of two thousand people representing sixteen service trades.[67] A representative of the Chinese Hand Laundry Alliance was chosen to speak on behalf of more than ten independent laundry organizations. While speaking for all laundry workers, Louis Wing, the representative, also expressed the desire of Chinese laundrymen to have equal access to a decent life. Mrs. Whitney, then deputy commissioner of licenses, strongly supported the laundrymen's goals as expressed by Wing:

> We Chinese laundrymen are just as desirous and just as anxious to obtain higher living standard as any man on the face of this earth. Unhealthy living conditions and hard labor are just as disagreeable to us as to anybody else. Our laundrymen will support whole heartedly any movement that has for its aim the bringing about of decent and human standard of life in industry and otherwise.[68]

Despite the exclusion laws that remained in effect until 1943, New York's Chinese during the Depression for the first time spoke publicly about their desire to get rid of unhealthy living conditions and hard labor. Their efforts to be accepted as part of the American society won recognition and support from American organizations.

As an independent organization, the CHLA increasingly perceived its responsibility to provide services and aid for the benefit of its members. The door of the CHLA was also open to those members who were in trouble. Four professional lawyers, who had been hired to deal with the State Labor Department and housing authorities, provided services to assist members in reporting blackmail and theft to the proper authorities. Negotiating with the landlords regarding tenement rent was also a part of the CHLA's job.[69] William M. Chadbourne was one of the lawyers who successfully assisted the CHLA in winning the laundry ordinance case.[70]

In addition to lawyers, the CHLA also employed four doctors to advise its members on health issues. Free medical treatment was provided to poor patients, who were also given the privilege of purchasing medicine in Chinatown pharmacies at a 50 percent discount.[71] In the event of a member's death, twenty-five cents was collected from each member as a compensation fund to help the immediate family of the deceased. A special fund was set aside by the association for laundry workers who were out of work.[72] By providing various assistances to its members, the CHLA increasingly became an important welfare agency for its members.

The CHLA was originally established as a hand laundry trade association to combat the Depression. Breaking away from the CCBA, it has been considered one of the first "leftist" groups that openly challenged the power structure of New York Chinatown.[73] As an independent trade organization, it successfully protested against unfair treatment from American trade unions and the city government. Its success over the annual registration fee and the security bond as well as over the license issue marked a victory in the demand for racial equality. In search of equal treatment, members of the CHLA also actively participated in mainstream events. Their engagement in the citywide pro-NIRA march in New York City and in the laundry business meeting demonstrated the desire of New York's Chinese to integrate into society.

The Chinese American Restaurant Association of Greater New York

The Chinese American Restaurant Association of Greater New York (CARA) was another important Chinese trade organization that emerged during the Depression. Chinese restaurants in New York employed a large number of Chinese immigrants. In the 1930s, more than four thousand workers[74] worked at approximately three hundred big and small establishments in the city.[75] During the Depression the Chinese restaurant business was among the first hit by the economic crisis. In the year 1930, more than 150 Chinese restaurants were forced to close. In Manhattan's Broadway district alone, the loss amounted to approximately $2,000,000.[76] Consequently, large numbers of restaurant workers found themselves jobless. Those restaurants that remained in business were threatened by intensified competition from others as well as from non-Chinese cafeterias.

Confronting the crisis, New York's Chinese in the restaurant business decided to organize to combat the Depression. As a consequence, they formed the Chinese American Restaurant Association of Greater New York (CARA) on May 9, 1932. Members of the association believed that by making a collective effort, they would survive the economic crisis. They also predicted that such joint effort would "bring about betterment for the industry" in the future.[77] The headquarters of the CARA were temporarily located in the Chin Lee restaurant at 1604 Broadway when it was first established. Later on, it moved to the Far Eastern Tea Garden at 10 Columbus Circle. Its membership extended to both restaurant owners and individual workers. One-sixth of the Chinese restaurants in New York area had joined the association by 1933.[78]

This structure represented a new type of trade organization in the Chinese community. Whereas membership in traditional guilds was only open to business owners or proprietors, the unpredictable hardship of the Depression united both restaurant owners and workers to combat difficulties. Individual workers took an active part in the association. By the end of 1933, with worker participation, membership of the CARA doubled.[79]

However, the leadership remained in the hand of prominent businessmen. They assured their commitment to the welfare of the association by contributing financially to the community. Lee Fu, an influential businessman, was the first president of the Board of Trustees, the decision maker. He also served the Committee of the General Affairs. Having owned the Far Eastern restaurant at 10 Columbus Circle,[80] he became more well known for his charitable contributions on behalf of the CARA. In the single year of 1935 during the hard times, he donated several times to welfare agencies, such as orphan asylums in the Chinese community.[81]

The CARA was a dynamic institution that provided tax services and served as an information center for job market and trading business. There were three major agencies in this restaurant association. The Accountant Agency played a key role in business transactions, reflecting the new attitude of New York's Chinese to comply with the U.S. government taxation laws. In order to make their cooperation convenient, the accountant agency provided tax instructions in Chinese and prepared and distributed tax forms to restaurants.[82]

This effort demonstrated the desire of New York's Chinese to be regarded as taxpayers—a new symbol of their engagement in American society. Perceiving the importance of following government laws, the CARA assisted the Chinese business community in understanding the revenue system by providing tax instructions in Chinese. It prepared tax forms to make it easier for small businesses to file taxes. In addition, the CARA also worked with the government to educate the Chinese. When the city authority of New York raised new taxes on cigars and liquor in 1935, the CARA advised the Chinese business community to abide by the American laws.[83]

The Accountant Agency also dealt with statistical analyses of the restaurant business and provided information periodically to owners on total gains or losses in the industry. The second business-oriented agency of the CARA was the Investigation Agency. It kept its members well informed about the contemporary business climate and provided updated information on the market price of various products.

While assisting in business matters, the CARA also demonstrated a sincere concern about the job market. Information on job openings became crucial for those who were desperately looking for opportunities. The tightened job market during the hard times made the situation worse. The Employment Bureau was the third agency of the CARA to provide aid and services particularly for restaurant workers. By posting employment opportunities, this agency committed itself to workers and the unemployed in particular.

The CARA served as an information center for both restaurant owners and workers. In addition to the major agencies, the CARA also published the *Convention Journal*, which carried news and information relating to the restaurant trade.[84]

The CARA was originally formed as a trade organization to combat the Depression. At the same time, it showed increasing interest in national economic policies. This growing political consciousness was demonstrated in its involvement in mainstream political activities, such as the one in August 1933, when it called a mass meeting to urge the active participation of Chinese restaurants in the NIRA program. The National Industrial Recovery Act (NIRA) was a result of concerns and impulses of the New Deal to cope with economic difficulties. Under the provisions of the legislature, the right of labors to organize and bargain collectively through unions was protected. The income of workers that would rise along with prices so that the purchase power would not lag behind was ensured. The NIRA also allowed public works spending designed to pump needed funds into the economy. Enthusiastic about the New Deal policy, the CARA organized a propaganda team to promote community support for the legislation. Copies of the act were printed in Chinese and distributed to the restaurants.[85] Furthermore, the CARA selected five of its members to cope with policies to ensure that the establishment and implementation of price and wage codes in the Chinese community accorded with the new legislation.

The commitment of CARA to the NIRA reflected its desire to integrate itself into the American labor union movement. It moved to participate in rallies organized by other associations. Along with members of CHLA, the CARA sent its fifty members to a citywide pro-NIRA rally held in New York on September 13, 1933.[86]

The NIRA later caused frustration among the nation's business communities and labor unions and was eventually declared unconstitutional by the

Supreme Court in 1935.[87] However, Chinese New Yorkers in 1933, like other Americans, joined in supporting New Deal efforts to combat the Depression.

The Depression gradually eroded the former isolation of the Chinese community in New York. The active participation of the CARA in mainstream events provided an access for its members and the community to contact the world outside. Because of the unfavorable racially exclusionary conditions from 1882 until 1943, Chinese New Yorkers seldom had a chance to go beyond their own community. Paul C. P. Siu sourly recalled his life as a laundry worker as monotonous and "isolated."[88] The Chinese laborers, he wrote, were treated like "a thing and a stereotype" by society. They felt they were a person only to be with their fellow Chinese within the social world where people "shared common interest and conventional understanding."[89] Because of the isolated environment, the social world of Chinese laborers was only "located between their quaint working places and their racial Chinatown." They had "no chance, no facilities" for leisure-time activities beyond their work.[90]

Realizing the problems, the CARA organized cultural activities to break down isolation and to encourage its members to understand that working-class culture encompassed more than just work. The idea of leisure rather than work in their spare time created a departure from traditional attitudes and values. In order to pursue the time and space for leisure-time entertainment, the CARA endorsed cultural clubs and supported basketball teams for workers. In its effort to inspire its members to join leisure activities, it also became a patron of such outings as trips to scenic spots to expose workers to another side of life than work.

The CARA believed that sightseeing and excursions would help to open its members' minds to an entirely new world.[91] It also created an opportunity for young workers to enjoy a healthy social life with workers from other organizations. On August 1, 1932, right after its formation, the CARA initiated a trip to Bear Mountain in New Jersey.[92] This plan received immediate support from other newly formed Chinese organizations New York. The Chinese Women's Association and the Chinese Young Women's Organization, for example, were delighted to join the trip; these two organizations were formed in 1931 for the purpose of improving conditions of Chinese women immigrants.[93] During the trip, participants enjoyed mountain climbing, rowing on the mountain lake, and swimming in the reservoir, as well as basketball games. A Chinese community newspaper, the *Chinese Nationalist Daily*, reported this trip as a "pioneer work in union history."[94]

Roy Rosenzweig suggests that the creation of American working-class leisure time and institutions is an expression of a value that challenged and, to some degree, rejected the moral order of America's upper and middle classes.[95] The leisure-time activities of New York's Chinese meant more. By participating in sports and sightseeing, they perceived the importance of their true personal value in contrast to the label of "cheap labor." The creation of leisure-time activities expressed the rejection of New York's Chinese against racial attitudes toward Chinese. Moreover, the concept of leisure rather than work in their spare time created a departure as New York's Chinese attitudes toward life and value changed. It enabled them to move away from isolation and integrate into the larger cultural society.

Conclusion

The Depression was a time of important changes in the Chinese community in New York City. It saw a vibrant organizational movement of Chinese laborers and Chinese small businesses. The CUC, LYS, CHLA, and CARA were among the first and the most active Chinese American organizations to emerge in response to the economic crisis. Although these organizations were originally formed as labor organizations and trade unions to deal with economic difficulties in the 1930s, their demand for equal treatment and legal protection by the American government effectively challenged the legacy of racist exclusion. Therefore, these organizations were also pioneer Chinese American civil rights organizations in New York City.

The successful conduct of the LYS in strikes and the victory over the issues of city ordinances and licenses by the CHLA, for example, provided evidence of Chinese New Yorkers' desire for change. The various activities of these newly established organizations played a vigorous role in making heard the voices of the weakest and most vulnerable people of society.

In their effort to survive the Depression, Chinese American organizations increasingly showed their interest in mainstream politics. Perceiving the importance of a collective effort for the benefit of New York's Chinese, they reached out to create alliances with other American organizations. Their effort to integrate into mainstream activities demonstrated the increasing self-consciousness of New York's Chinese to be part of American society.

More important, the formation of new organizations and their activities during the Depression constituted a strong trend that shook the roots of the Chinese community's traditional social and political structure. Because of existing cultural prejudices and exclusionary legislation, Chinese immigrants were driven to withdraw into their own community for protection. Within their traditional enclaves, the elites of the Chinese social and political hierarchy reinforced a restrictive atmosphere.

During the Depression, as various newly established organizations began to take over responsibilities for the interest of New York Chinese themselves, the CCBA was no longer the only authority to deal with the outside world, nor could it keep its autocratic control within the Chinese community. The role of district associations was also fading away as new organizations were formed without considering the ties of geographic origin or clan. A new social structure and order were taking shape with the increasing power of new organizations in the Chinese community.

Notes

1. There is voluminous literature on the Great Depression. John K. Galbraith, in *The Great Crash, 1929* (New York Houghton Mifflin, 1955) and Lester Chandler, in *America's Greatest Depression: 1929–1941* (New York: Harper and Row, 1970), discuss the events that caused the Depression. Charles Kindleberger, *The World in Depression* (Berkeley: University of California Press, 1973, 1986), discusses the Depression from the global perspective. Studs Terkel, *The Hard Times: An Oral History of the Great Depression* (New York: Pantheon Books, 1970), and Robert McElvaine, *The Great Depression: America, 1929–1941* (New York: Times Books, 1984), discuss the culture and values in the Depression Era. For a convenient reproduction of approximately 150 articles on all aspects of this topic, see Melvyn Dubofsky and Stephen Burnwood, ed., *The Great Depression and the New Deal* (New York: Garland Publishing, 1990).

2. George J. Lankevich, *New York City: A Short History* (New York: New York University Press, 2002), 162.

3. Frederick M. Binder and David M. Reimers, *All the Nations under Heaven* (New York: City University of New York Press, 1995), 178.

4. Selma Berrol, *The Empire City: New York and Its People, 1624–1996* (Westport, Conn.: Praeger Publishers, 2000), 111.

5. Frederick M. Binder and David M. Reimers, *All the Nations under Heaven* (New York: City University of New York Press, 1995), 178.

6. Among those Chinese living in the United States, there were 30,868 native-born Chinese Americans. U.S. Census; Betty L. Sung, *Mountain of Gold: The Story of the Chinese in America* (New York: The Macmillan Company, 1969), 269.

7. *New York Times*, Apr. 27, 1931; Hsuan Julia Chen, "The Chinese Community in New York: A Study in Their Cultural Adjustment 1920–1940" (Ph.D. dissertation, Washington D.C., American University, 1941), 60.

8. Huping Ling, *Chinese St. Louis: From Enclave to Cultural Community* (Philadelphia: Temple University Press, 2004), 116.

9. *Chinese Journal*, Dec. 12, 1930, 7; Hsuan Julia Chen, "The Chinese Community in New York: A Study in Their Cultural Adjustment 1920–1940" (Ph.D. dis-

sertation, Washington D.C., American University, 1941), 60; Thomas Chow, "Chinese Restaurants Association of Greater New York," Mar. 22, 1937, 1, Works Progress Administration (WPA): Federal Writers' Project, NYC Unit, Racial Groups in NY I, Roll 1 of 5, MN #21065, Roll #66 1936–40, Record Sub-series: Chinese in NY, Description: Organizations, Folder #48 (New York: New York Municipal Archives, 1936–1940), Microfilm.

The Federal Writers' Program under the Works Progress Administration (WPA) was part of the New Deal government subsidized relief work project during the Depression. One unexpected consequence of the project is documentation of the life of the New York Chinese community and its people in the 1930s. Chinese Americans participated in the writers' project.

10. Shih-shan Henry Tsai, *The Chinese Experiences in America* (Bloomington: Indiana University Press, 1986), 108.

11. Ira Rosenwaike, *Population History of New York City* (Syracuse, N.Y.: Syracuse University Press, 1972), 141.

12. Leong Gor Yun, *Chinatown Inside Out* (New York: B. Mussey, 1936), 133; Thomas Chow, "Chinese Population in New York," Jan. 11, 1937, 2, WPA Federal Writers' Project, NYC Unit, Racial Groups in NY I, Roll 1 of 5, MN #21065, Roll #66 1936–40 Record Sub-Series: Chinese in NY, Folder #50 (New York: New York Municipal Archives), Microfilm.

13. Bendiner, "Chinese, Japanese," in "Chinese in New York, Present Distribution in New York," Report of Federal Writer's Project, WPA, Box 1, Folder #50, 1936–1940 (New York: New York Municipal Archives), Microfilm. The author's full name was not given.

14. Theodora Chan Wang, *Condensed Report for the Years of 1932–1936 of the Chinese Women's Association*, 1936; Judy Yung, Gordon H. Chang, and Him Mark Lai, ed., *Chinese American Voices: From the Gold Rush to the Present* (Berkeley: University of California Press, 2006), 187.

15. Ira Rosenwaike, *Population History of New York City* (Syracuse, N.Y.: Syracuse University Press, 1972), 141.

16. Huping Ling recorded that many Chinese St. Louisans went to California and New York to seek better economic opportunities with their families during the Great Depression which caused the drop of Chinese population and the decline of the businesses, especially in hand laundries in St. Louis. *Chinese St Louis: From Enclave to Cultural Community* (Philadelphia: Temple University Press, 2004), 117.

17. *New York Times*, Aug. 7, 1931; Hsuan Julia Chen, "The Chinese Community in New York, 1920–1940" (Ph.D. Dissertation, Washington, D.C.: American University, 1941), 61. According to Chen, their request was granted by Justice Care.

18. Liu Pei-Chi, *Min Guo Hua Qiao Shi* [A History of the Chinese in the United States of America] (Taipei: Limin Wenhua Shiye Gonsi, 1976), 204; Renqiu Yu, *To Save China, to Save Ourselves: The Chinese Hand Laundry Alliance of New York* (Philadelphia: Temple University Press, 1992), 16; also see Chia-ling Kuo, *Social and*

Political Change in New York's Chinatown: The Role of Voluntary Associations (New York: Praeger Publisher, 1977).

19. Hsuan Julia Chen, "The Chinese Community in New York, 1920–1940" (Ph.D. Dissertation, Washington, D.C.: American University, 1941), 61.

20. Sharene Thomas, "Interview with Virginia M. Kee," *Tenement Times* 1, no. 2, (Spring 1990). Ms. Kee was the cofounder and president of the Chinese American Planning Council. She also sat on the board of the United Neighborhood Houses and on the Mayor's Advisory Board for Early Childhood Education in 1990. Virginia Kee recalled that during the Depression, kids sometimes brought their schoolmates home to share snacks in PS 1, which integrated all Chinese elementary school kids of PS 23 in the early 1930s.

21. A 1933 *Chinese Nationalist Daily* (*Ming Qi Ri Bao*) article reported that Mr. and Mrs. She decided to adopt an orphan boy in order to save his life. *Chinese Nationalist Daily*, July 7, 1933.

22. *Chinese Nationalist Daily*, Jan. 29, 1933, 3.

23. See chapter 1 for information on how the Chinese exclusion laws affected the lives and legal status of the Chinese in the United States.

24. John Higham, *Strangers in the Land: Patterns of American Nativism, 1860–1925* (New Brunswick, N.J.: Rutgers University Press, 1983), 72, 161, 162, 260; Xinyang Wang, "Economic Opportunity, Artisan Leadership, and Immigrant Workers' Labor Militancy: Italian and Chinese Immigrant Workers in New York City, 1890–1970," *Labor History* 37, no. 4 (Fall 1996): 496.

25. Laws of the State of New York, 1894, chapter 622, 1569; Labor Laws of the United States (Second Special Report of the Commissioners of Labor, Washington, D.C., 1896), 993; John Higham, *Strangers in the Land: Patterns of American Nativism, 1860–1925* (New Brunswick, N.J.: Rutgers University Press, 1983), 72.

26. *New York Tribune*, June 21, 1985; Xinyang Wang, "Economic Opportunity, Artisan Leadership, and Immigrant Workers' Labor Militancy: Italian and Chinese Immigrant Workers in New York City, 1890–1970," *Labor History* 37, no. 4 (Fall 1996): 481.

27. Chia-Ling Kuo, *Social and Political Change in New York's Chinatown: The Role of Voluntary Association* (New York: Praeger Publishers, 1977), 2.

28. *The Fifteenth Census, 1930, Population*, Vol. 5. General Report on Occupations, 95–97; Xinyang Wang, "Economic Opportunity, Artisan Leadership, and Immigrant Workers' Labor Militancy: Italian and Chinese Immigrant Workers in New York City, 1890–1970," *Labor History* 37, no. 4 (Fall 1996): 485.

29. Hsuan Julia Chen, "The Chinese Community in New York, 1920–1940" (Ph.D. Dissertation, Washington, D.C.: American University, 1941), 58

30. Bendiner, "Chinese, Japanese," in "Chinese in New York, Present Distribution in New York," Report of Federal Writer's Project, WPA, Box 1, Folder #50, (New York City: New York Municipal Archives, 1936–1940), Microfilm.

31. Judy Yung, Gordon H. Chang, and Him Mark Lai, ed., *Chinese American Voices: From the Gold Rush to the Present* (Berkeley: University of California Press, 2006), 138.

32. Sean Wilentz, *Chants Democratic: New York City and the Rise of the American Working Class: 1788–1850* (New York: Oxford University Pres, 1984); also see Roy Rosenzweig, *Eight Hours for What We Will: Workers and Leisure in an Industrial City, 1870–1920* (New York: Cambridge University Press, 1983).

33. *Chinese Nationalist Daily*, Jan. 11, 1933, 7; Peter Kwong, *Chinatown: New York Labor and Politics, 1930–1950* (New York: Monthly Review Press, 1979, 2001), 56; also see Peter Kwong and Dusanka Miscevia, *Chinese America: The Untold Story of America's Oldest Community* (New York: New Press, 2005), 182.

34. *Chinese Nationalist Daily*, June 17, 1933.

35. Ibid.

36. Sucheng Chan, *Asian Americans: An Interpretive History* (Boston: Twayne Publishers, 1991), 116.

37. *Chinese Nationalist Daily*, Jan. 17, 1933, 7.

38. Shih-shan Henry Tsai, *The Chinese Experiences in America* (Bloomington and Indianapolis: Indiana University Press, 1986), 109.

39. *Chinese Nationalist Daily*, Mar. 29, 1933.

40. Sucheng Chan, *Asian Americans: An Interpretive History* (Boston: Twayne Publishers, 1991), 115.

41. *Chinese Vanguard*, Feb. 1, 1933; Kwong Peter Kwong, *Chinatown: New York Labor and Politics, 1930–1950* (New York: Monthly Review Press, 1979, 2001), 119.

42. Peter Kwong, *Chinatown: New York Labor and Politics, 1930–1950* (New York: Monthly Review Press, 1979, 2001), 119.

43. Hugh Mulzac, *A Star to Steer By* (New York: International Publishers, 1963), 116. Mulzac was a cook-steward on the *Virmar*, a vessel operated by the Calmar SS Company during the strike. He recalled the principle as he told his experiences to Louis Burnham and Norval Welch, which became the book.

44. *Chinese Nationalist Daily*, Nov. 17, 1936, 3; Peter Kwong, *Chinatown: New York Labor and Politics, 1930–1950* (New York: Monthly Review Press, 1979, 2001), 121.

45. Hugh Mulzac, *A Star to Steer By* (New York: International Publishers, 1963), 109.

46. Peter Kwong, *Chinatown: New York Labor and Politics, 1930–1950* (New York: Monthly Review Press, 1979, 2001), 116.

47. *Chinese Vanguard*, June 26, 1937, 2; Peter Kwong, *Chinatown: New York Labor and Politics, 1930–1950* (New York: Monthly Review Press, 1979, 2001), 123.

48. Cited in Cheryl Lynn Greenberg, *"Or Does It Explode?": Black Harlem in the Great Depression* (New York: Oxford University Press, 1991), 112.

49. Bendiner, "Chinese, Japanese" in "Chinese in New York, Present Distribution in New York," Report: Federal Writers' Project, WPA, Box 1, Article 1-11, Folder #50, (1936–1940), Microfilm; Leong Gor Yun, *Chinatown Inside Out* (New York: B. Mussey, 1936), 96–97.

50. *Progressive Laundryman*, Apr., 1932, 19; Peter Kwong, *Chinatown: New York Labor and Politics, 1930–1950* (New York: Monthly Review Press, 1979, 2001), 63.

51. Leong Gor Yun, *Chinatown Inside Out* (New York: B. Mussey, 1936), 104.

52. Hsuan Julia Chen, "The Chinese Community in New York, 1920–1940" (Ph.D. Dissertation, Washington, D.C.: American University, 1941), 59.

53. *Chinese Nationalist Daily*, Apr., 1933, 19; Peter Kwong, *Chinatown: New York Labor and Politics, 1930–1950* (New York: Monthly Review Press, 1979, 2001), 65

54. *Chinese Nationalist Daily*, Apr. 24, 1933, 1; Renqiu Yu, *To Save China, to Save Ourselves: The Chinese Hand Laundry Alliance of New York* (Philadelphia: Temple University Press, 1991), 35.

55. Thomas Chow, "Chinese Laundry Association," Record Sub-series: "Chinese in NY," Federal Writers' Program, New York City, WPA Folder #48 Description: Organizations, New York City Municipal Archives, Microfilm, Feb. 8, 1937, 2; *The Chinese Nationalist Daily* reported that over one thousand Chinese laundrymen participated in the rally. *Chinese Nationalist Daily*, Apr. 25, 1933, 3; Leong reported an even smaller figure of more than six hundred Chinese attended. Leong Gor Yun, *Chinatown Inside Out* (New York: B. Mussey, 1936), 92.

56. *Chinese Nationalist Daily*, Apr. 24, 1933, 1; Renqiu Yu, *To Save China, to Save Ourselves: The Chinese Hand Laundry Alliance of New York* (Philadelphia: Temple University Press, 1992), 35; Judy Yung, Gordon H. Chang, and Him Mark Lai, ed., *Chinese American Voices: From the Gold Rush to the Present* (Berkeley: University of California Press, 2006), 184–85.

57. Thomas Chow, "Chinese Laundry Associations," Feb. 8, 1937, 2, Federal Writers' Project, WPA, Folder #48 (New York Municipal Archives, 1936–1940), Microfilm; Leong Gor Yun, *Chinatown Inside Out* (New York: B. Mussey, 1936), 88.

58. Thomas Chow, "Chinese Laundry Associations" Feb. 8, 1937, 2, Federal Writers' Project, WPA, Folder #48 (New York Municipal Archives, 1936–1940), Microfilm.

59. *Chinese Nationalist Daily*, July 6, 1933.

60. Ibid.

61. Renqiu Yu, *To Save China, to Save Ourselves: The Chinese Hand Laundry Alliance of New York* (Philadelphia: Temple University Press, 1992).

62. These figures were estimated by the president of the CCBA. Thomas Chow, "Chinese Population in New York," Jan. 11, 1937, 2, Federal Writers' Project, WPA, Folder #48 (New York Municipal Archives, 1936–1940), Microfilm.

63. Thomas Chow, "Chinese Laundry Association," in "Chinese in New York," Feb. 8. 1937, 3, Federal Writers' Project, WPA, Folder #48 (New York Municipal Archives, 1936–1940), Microfilm.

64. Thomas Chow, "American Friends of the Chinese People," Oct. 28, 1936, Record Sub-series: Chinese in New York, Description: Organizations, Federal Writers' Program, WPA, Folder# 48, Microfilm.

65. Thomas Chow, "Chinese Laundry Association," in "Chinese in New York," Feb. 8. 1937, 3, Federal Writers' Project, WPA, Folder #48 (New York Municipal Archives, 1936–1940), Microfilm.

66. Peter Kwong, *Chinatown: New York Labor and Politics, 1930–1950* (New York: Monthly Review Press, 1979, 2001), 87.

67. Leong Gor Yun, *Chinatown Inside Out* (New York: B. Mussey, 1936), 104.

68. Ibid., 105.

69. Hsuan Julia Chen, "The Chinese Community in New York, 1920–1940" (Ph.D. Dissertation, Washington, D.C.: American University, 1941), 58.

70. For a brief biographical sketch of William M. Chadbourne, see John W. Leonard, *Who's Who in Jurisprudence: A Biographical Dictionary of Contemporary Lawyers and Jurists* (New York: J. W. Leonard, 1925), 249.

71. Hsuan Julia Chen, "The Chinese Community in New York, 1920–1940" (Ph.D. Dissertation, Washington, D.C.: American University, 1941), 58.

72. Ibid.

73. Judy Yung, Gordon H. Chang, and Him Mark Lai, ed., *Chinese American Voices: From the Gold Rush to the Present* (Berkeley: University of California Press, 2006), 183.

74. Hsuan Julia Chen, "The Chinese Community in New York, 1920–1940" (Ph.D. Dissertation, Washington, D.C.: American University, 1941), 54.

75. Thomas Chow, "Chinese Restaurants Association of Greater New York," in "Chinese in New York," Record Sub-series, Description: Organizations, Mar. 22, 1937, 1, Federal Writers' Program, WPA Folder #48, Microfilm.

76. *Chinese Nationalist Daily*, July 1932

77. Hsuan Julia Chen, "The Chinese Community in New York, 1920–1940" (Ph.D. Dissertation, Washington, D.C.: American University, 1941), 55

78. Thomas Chow, "Chinese Restaurants Association of Greater New York," in "Chinese in New York," Record Sub-series, Description: Organizations, Mar. 22, 1937, 2, Federal Writers' Program, WPA Folder #48, Microfilm.

79. Hsuan Julia Chen, "The Chinese Community in New York, 1920–1940" (Ph.D. Dissertation, Washington, D.C.: American University, 1941), 55.

80. Thomas Chow, "Chinese Restaurants Association of Greater New York," in "Chinese in New York," Record Sub-series, Description: Organizations, Mar. 22, 1937, 3, Federal Writers' Program, WPA Folder #48, Microfilm.

81. *Chinese Nationalist Daily*, June 3, 1935.

82. Hsuan Julia Chen, "The Chinese Community in New York, 1920–1940" (Ph.D. Dissertation, Washington, D.C.: American University, 1941), 56.

83. Ibid.

84. Ibid., 58.

85. Ibid., 58.

86. Peter Kwong, *Chinatown: New York Labor and Politics, 1930–1950* (New York: Monthly Review Press, 1979, 2001), 87.

87. The new program of NIRA appeared to work well at first. At its center was a new federal agency, the National Recovery Administration (NRA), which was later declared unconstitutional as the Supreme Court ruled that Congress had unconstitutionally delegated legislative power to the president to draft the NRA codes.

88. Paul C. P. Siu, *The Chinese Laundryman: A Study of Social Isolation* (New York: New York University Press, 1987), 137.

89. Ibid.

90. Ibid.

91. *Chinese Nationalist Daily*, Aug. 1, 1932.

92. *Chinese Nationalist Daily*, Aug. 1, 1932.

93. These two organizations also played an important role in supporting the anti-Japanese war in China. See chapter 5 for more information.

94. *Chinese Nationalist Daily*, Aug. 1, 1932.

95. Roy Rosenzweig, *Eight Hours for What We Will: Workers, Leisure in an Industrial City, 1870–1920* (New York: Cambridge University Press, 1983).

CHAPTER THREE

The Great Depression and Cultural Organizations

The Depression was a time of important changes in the Chinese community in New York City. In addition to a vibrant organizational movement of Chinese laborers and small businesses, the Depression also witnessed the rise of Chinese American cultural clubs and associations. In their effort to survive the Depression, New York's Chinese Americans involved themselves in society culturally as a means of both personal improvement and social integration.

Discrimination and restrictions against the Chinese in the United States alienated them from the larger American society. Challenging the existing racial prejudice, American-born Chinese proclaimed that they "should be given a better opportunity in social life in America."[1] More significantly, they began to engage in language learning, music and art performances, and sports activities as a way to assert themselves as American citizens. This chapter explores this involvement with a focus on their organized cultural and educational activities which not only helped reinforce a Chinese identity but also promoted a growing consciousness of an American one.

Educated Young Chinese New Yorkers in the 1930s

Both across the nation and in New York, American-born Chinese were major participants in cultural activities. College students figured importantly in this regard. Scholars, such as Chih Meng and Betty Lee Sung, suggest that educated young Chinese Americans distanced themselves from Chinatown Chinese because they considered themselves the elite and did not want to mingle with "low-class" Chinatown Chinese.[2] They stayed within their own student communities as racial discrimination also alienated them from society.

The educated young Chinese American population was constituted by diverse groups of high school students, college graduates, and young professionals. They were from various geographic origins. Many were born in China. They crossed the Pacific Ocean to the United States to seek higher education in the American eastern coastal cities at the turn of the century. Others were American-born Chinese. The 1920s saw the coming of age of second-generation American sons and daughters of Chinese descent of divergent social classes. By the 1930s many members of this youth group enrolled in colleges. The 1937 *Directory of Chinese Students in America* recorded 1,414 Chinese registered in 262 American colleges and universities in the 1935–1936 academic year, 1,733 in the next academic year. In New York, 280 Chinese were studying in twenty-seven colleges and universities in 1937. Although many were American-born and others were from China, they were both simply recorded as "Chinese" in registration records.[3]

The educated youths, especially the American-born second-generation Chinese immigrants, were resentful as they were excluded and not seen as Americans. Pardee Lowe, an American-born of Chinese descent, recalled that he, like other Chinese Americans, made every effort to be as American as possible. This effort was "manifested in every conceivable manner possible—in dress, speech, slang, ideas, sports, entertainment, and reading matters." However, the American society refused to accept them as Americans and he had no feelings of belonging.[4] "People were always surprised to see me reading American books and magazines and exclaimed 'oh! Do you read English too?'" another Chinese American complained. "It gets my goat!" when people showed their surprise as if she should not speak, read, or write in English.[5] This confusion, antagonism, and frustration were common feelings among second-generation Chinese immigrants as their dreams and efforts of personal improvement through education were shattered.

The 1930s saw changes in the attitude of young Chinese American college students. They turned their frustration and confusion into a positive action and began to redefine themselves as Chinese Americans. Not being "ashamed of the old culture," as some scholars suggested,[6] they engaged themselves in their ethnic community with trained skills as a way to improve themselves. They also turned their attention to the welfare of their community. They worked hard to overcome the isolation and exclusionary atmosphere of New York's Chinese community by bringing in programs such as English-language classes and educational and entertaining clubs. The desire and perspective of integrating the ethnic community into society was clearly stated in the *Chinese Christian Student*, a popular newsletter circulating among Chinese American college students:

> [I]t is the vigor and understandability of the second generation of the thoughtful youth, which can eventually be depended upon to change the present social level of hard labor and limited enterprise in emerging and penetrating into other services in general within Chinatown. The younger generation of Chinese immigrants in New York had an inevitable obligation to construct their community into a new center of community as a partnership . . . of the "melting pot" civilization of America.[7]

The assimilation was a product of the Progressive Movement at the turn of twentieth century. Aiming at assisting new immigrants from southern and eastern European countries in particular to adjust them to the social and economic environment in the new world, middle-class men and women initiated several campaigns such as settlement house projects, English-language classes for adults, educational training programs for working mothers, and playgrounds for children in big cities like Chicago and New York. With the premise of American political thought and the idea of the "melting pot," new immigrants also believed that they would advance in American society by adopting the values and accepting the rules of the world to which they had moved. Yet, caught in between the old and the new, immigrants, particularly the second generation of immigrants, found it difficult to assimilate. Like Sara Smolinsky, the immigrant heroine of Anzia Yezierska's novel *Bread Givers*, who battled her father for independence, they only came to discover that "I can't live in the old world and I am yet too green for the new. I don't belong to those who gave me birth or to those with whom I was educated."[8]

The ideas and practice of "melting pot" and the practice of assimilation were under attack when the efforts of blacks, Hispanics, Indians, Asians, and others to forge a clearer ethnic group identity started in the 1960s. They were less willing to accept the standards of the larger society and more likely to demand recognition of their own ethnic identity. Challenging the idea of assimilation, they advocated instead a cultural pluralistic society in which racial and ethnic groups would preserve a sense of their own heritage and their own social and cultural traditions.[9]

Scholars debate on the nature of the Progressive Movement with its emphasis on assimilation or "Americanization." Some, like Robert Wiebe, suggest that the widespread disorder and unrest as a result of the economic and social change contributed to the rise of groups of middle-class men and women, organizations, and institutions to stabilize and enhance their position in society. Others, such as J. Joseph Huthmacher, believe that much of the force behind progressivism came from members of the working class, especially immigrants, to improve their life. Eric Rauchway argues that American Progressives, apart from the prevalence of liberal prejudices, tended to address the importance of immigration and women and their desire to search for their social and political identity.[10] The concept and practice of assimilation had an impact on Chinese immigrants. Influenced by the revival of religious gospel movement in the Progressive Era, Christian churches were established in Chinese communities throughout the United States. Christian missionaries served as a pushing force to improve the life of Chinatown residents. As a result, the first Chinese Presbyterian Church was established in New York City. The Rev. Huie Kin became the first minister of this church. As a Chinese progressive reformer, Mr. Kin, and his wife, Mrs. Kin, a New Yorker of Dutch descent, reached out to Chinese immigrants. With their assistance, the first Chinese kindergarten was established in New York's Chinatown in 1903.[11] The *New York Times* reported a social excursion organized by Mrs. Kin and other Christian women activists when some twenty Chinese immigrant wives "reveled with their children in the sunshine and shade of Westerly, Staten Island."[12] Yet the hostility of society toward Chinese persisted. Chinese New Yorkers were seen as aliens and heathens. Chinatown was not considered part of the social entity of the country. Instead, it was seen as an exotic enclave. Progressive activists never targeted ethnic Chinese community seriously in their agenda.

The assimilation had a new meaning in the 1930s when Chinese immigrants associated it with their goal to integrate them into society as part of their effort to be recognized as American citizens. It took on even greater significance when they advocated for racial equality that set up an example for the future generations to follow. Assimilation also had a special meaning for educated young college students and graduates who took the responsibility for a change, rather than relying on reformers from outside, moved into their own ethnic community, and redefined themselves. Unlike their precedents, whose endeavor focused on "Americanization," college students and graduates pioneered the dual identity of Chinese Americans.

Women college students and graduates played an important part in the move. Mabel Penghua Lee and Theodora Chan Wang, for instance, became active participants in various Chinese community activities associated with their endeavor to improve the social and educational conditions of the Chinese American community in New York. Mabel Penghua Lee was a daughter of a Chinese Baptist minister. After her graduation from Columbia University, she worked as a social worker in New York's Chinatown.[13] Theodora Chan Wang was a college graduate of the University of California, Berkeley.

She then went to New York and received a master's degree from Columbia University. She also became a social worker helping Chinese immigrants in Chinatown.[14]

Motivated by the desire to promote the common interests of college students and to "uplift" the Chinese American working class, many college students went to Chinatown and volunteered to teach Chinese immigrants Mandarin, English, and mathematics in the Chinese School. Among them was Huang Zhenhua, daughter of one of the leaders of the 1911 revolution in China. She volunteered to teach Mandarin, the official Chinese language, to the residents of Chinatown; most of them spoke Cantonese, a local dialect. English classes and other educational programs, such as lectures and movie presentations on women and children's hygiene, were also established to elevate the literacy and domestic skills of Chinatown residents.[15]

Representing the desires of the students to redefine both themselves and their relationship to the Chinese community, college graduates also involved themselves in sports activities to promote spirit in competition and courage. Lung Chin and Calvin S. Chin, among others, became coaches of Chinatown sports teams to promote out-of-school activities to involve young Chinatown residents in mainstream recreation.[16]

The endeavor of the educated youths to improve the social and educational conditions of the Chinese American community in New York also resulted in organized activities. The Chinese Students' Alliance of Eastern States of the United States, for instance, established the Social Welfare Committee. Under the leadership of Hu Pingsa, a student at Wellesley, committee members volunteered to teach classes in the Chinese School in Chinatown. They also organized a benefit bazaar, selling Chinese handicrafts to raise money for initiating the Chinese Boy Scouts of New York. With their enthusiasm, the first Chinese American Boy Scouts of the United States was founded in New York City.[17]

The Chinese Women's Association was another important organization that effectively served the need of Chinatown women residents. Created by a group of educated Chinese New Yorkers in 1931, the association elected Theodora Chan Wang, a graduate of Columbia University, to be its first president. By 1936, membership of this association reached to over 350.[18] The total Chinese population, according to one account, was about ten thousand in New York in the early 1930s.[19] But due to the U.S. immigration restrictions, the male and female ratio among the Chinese was out of proportion. Out of the total population, there were only about 250 Chinese families with an average of about four children in each family.[20] Even though some historical records revealed that as early as 1900 some Chinese immigrant women started to earn a living and others worked to support their family, and a few became store owners, the majority remained at home due to the tradition and the circumstances in society.[21] Standing at the forefront to provide services such children nursing classes, reading clubs that involved high school girl students to help their mothers in literacy improvements, and trips to museums and art centers, the Chinese Women's Association became a vital force to push the civic and cultural involvement of women residents of Chinese community in society.

The purposes and activities of young educated Chinese Americans in their involvement in the ethnic Chinese community spoke to the increasing consciousness of second-generation Chinese immigrants about themselves and their changing attitude and social responsibilities toward society.

In search of a new identity, young educated Chinese Americans participated in various educational and cultural activities. However, they pursued two different approaches. Some participated in activities to reinforce their Chinese cultural heritage defined to be "China pride." Others advocated what was called "American pride." In the effort for a new self-definition, those who emphasized Chinese heritage pioneered the concept of "China pride" as a way to "rediscover the fine heritage of Chinese ancient civilization" and to make "China pride" a contribution to the "great fabric of American life."[22] Others who advocated "American pride" endeavored to seek place and identity in society. This approach emphasized equal access for Chinese Americans to the mainstream.

In their effort to involve themselves in society, young Chinese Americans also moved toward organized participation. More than twenty new organizations sprang up during this time, representing different groups of Chinese Americans that cut across gender, class, and generation. These organizations, large and small, along with their activities, encouraged informal and formal networks. They created a new agenda specifically geared to the participation of a people previously isolated. More resilient and effective than individuals, these united forces bound New York's Chinese community together to pursue cultural involvement in society.

The Chinese American Cultural Clubs

In search of their self-definition as Chinese Americans during the 1930s, second-generation Chinese immigrants created various kinds of cultural clubs. Among them were the Ging Hawk Club, the Chinese Cultural Club, the Chinese Art Club, the Chinese Musicians Association, and the Chinese Athletic Club. These organizations offered some of the pioneering activities that ranged from English-language learning and writing contests that focused on Chinese American identity, to sports games that involved the young with other ethnic groups. These activities offered New York's Chinese Americans opportunities to express themselves in ways that built self-confidence for their future in the United States.

The Ging Hawk Club

The Ging Hawk Club was active as a Chinese American youth club. Situated at 32 Mott Street in the center of New York's Chinatown and founded as a girls' organization in the 1930s, it was affiliated with the Young Women's Christian Association in New York.[23] The Ging Hawk Club had a membership of twenty-two girls at the beginning.[24] Over the next couple of years, it became one of the most active organizations among second-generation Chinese immigrants. By 1936, its membership extended to both girls and boys who were American-born Chinese high school and college students. The age of the club members ranged from seventeen to twenty-five years.[25]

"Ging Hawk Club" literally meant "the club for the inspiration of the Chinese." Frustrated by the rejection of society, sons and daughters of Chinese descent turned to their ancestral land. Their passion for Chinese culture and heritage was demonstrated in organized activities such as gatherings and Chinese New Year's celebrations. They were encouraged by China's achievements in contemporary times and they often brought them to the attention of the larger community. The 1934 October Forum organized by members of the Ging Hawk Club at Columbia University to celebrate the twenty-fourth anniversary of the establishment of the Chinese Republic was an example of such activities.[26]

Both American and Chinese college students and professors participated in the event. Important government officials of both the United States and China were invited to the celebration. Among the distinguished professors present at the celebration, William H. Kipatrick, professor of Columbia University Teachers' College, gave the keynote address. Dr. C. J. Lin, president of Fujing Christian University, Dr. Francis C. M. Wei, president of Hua Chung College, and Julean Arnold, American Commercial Attache to China, also spoke at the forum. In their speeches, both Chinese and American scholars spoke highly of China's achievements in awakening national consciousness to fight against foreign intrusions. Advocating a unified republic in China, speakers also paid tribute to New York's Chinese immigrants for their contributions to the building of their home country.[27]

Despite its endorsement of "China pride," the Ging Hawk Club was concerned about the future of young Chinese Americans in the United

States. Realizing that racial antagonism and cultural clashes were major obstacles to the advancement of the young generation of Chinese immigrants, it organized activities to encourage the young to build self-confidence and establish themselves in American society. Arranging essay contests became one of such activities. Through discussions among the young, this club focused on their "American pride." Its first essay contest, titled "Where Does Our Future Lie?" turned out to be successful. The subject made young Chinese consider the issues that all immigrants, particularly the Chinese, faced. More important, the contest also emphasized what it meant to be responsible American citizens.

Open to all Chinese American boys and girls in the United States between seventeen and twenty-five years of age, the contest requested an essay of one thousand to fifteen hundred words in length. It also offered a $10 award for the first two winners. To make the contest professional, the club invited Dr. Mabel Penghua Lee, a Columbia University alumna, and Professor Harry Rathbone of the Department of Journalism at New York University to serve as judges. Dr. Tsue Chuyu and Anna Lee, the president of the club, were also among the judges.[28] In the third week of June 1936, the club announced the prizewinners of the contest. The *Chinese Christian Student*, a major Chinese American newsletter in New York, published the first-prize essay.[29]

Robert Dunn, a MIT college graduate, won first prize. What Dunn said reflected the growing consciousness of American-born Chinese to be Americans. Convincing his readers of the principles of liberty and equality that had protected him and allowed him the chance for education in the United States, Dunn wrote of "owing much pride and gratitude to America" and looked forward to paying the debt he owed to the country.[30] He held that the future of Chinese Americans lay in the land where they were born. Confident in the protection of the principle of democracy in the United States, he called on Chinese Americans to "clear up misunderstanding among ethnic groups, and to move towards individual freedom and racial equality." Appealing to Chinese Americans to break away from self-imposed isolation and develop "a good impression of the Chinese among Americans . . . through personal contact" as a means of integrating themselves into society, Dunn voiced the growing consciousness of Chinese Americans' dual identity and their demand for liberty and justice.[31]

In its effort to endorse both "China pride" and "American pride" in constructing Chinese American identity, the Ging Hawk Club also organized social activities to introduce the younger generation to American cultures and values. The Thanksgiving and Christmas seasons were the busiest times for the club to organize such gatherings. Parties and ballroom dancing attracted the young. Of its dance parties, the Thanksgiving Barn Dance at the Y.W.C.A. at 341 East 17th Street in 1933 was of particular interest.[32]

Dressed as farmers' daughters, members of the club greeted their guests at the door of the building. No traditional turkey dinner was served at the party. Instead, "a fifteen pound live turkey was kept in full view" at the Thanksgiving Day party. A Chinese American newsletter humorously commented that this turkey "was probably the only turkey in New York City which lived through Thanksgiving Day." Students from China and young Chinese Americans were invited to the dance party. Professor Henry Schilling of the history department at Hunter College and his wife were among the guests.[33] A Chinese newsletter reported that "it was a grand time" for young Chinese Americans to get "acquainted with each other."[34] The warm atmosphere of friendship impressed the participants most. Students from China also enjoyed the party, which gave them an opportunity to make friends with the American-born Chinese in attendance.[35]

Social gatherings, it was felt, promoted mutual understanding among Chinese Americans. In June 1936, the Ging Hawk Club endorsed a farewell meeting at the International House to congratulate students graduating from colleges in the New York City area.[36] Hong Dong, vice chairman of the New York Unit of the Chinese Students Christian Association, was invited to preside over the meeting. More than sixty students and their friends participated in the event.[37]

The Ging Hawk Club developed rapidly through the 1930s, extending its activities to include forums on China issues, writing contests concerning the future of American-born Chinese, and social parties to introduce American culture. Started as a girls' organization, the club and its activities involved both American-born and Chinese students. The club also provided opportunities to promote mutual understanding among young Chinese Americans, and, more significantly, it encouraged young Chinese Americans to become more aware of their Chinese heritage while assisting them to build up their self-confidence reinforcing the value of being Chinese Americans in the 1930s.

The Chinese Cultural Club

The Chinese Cultural Club was another important Chinese American cultural organization. Like the Ging Hawk Club, this club committed itself to the improvement of the Chinese American community. Founded by a group of second-generation Chinese immigrants in 1933, the Chinese Cultural Club's membership reached around one hundred by 1937.[38] Emphasizing the bilateral allegiance of second-generation Chinese immigrants, it set up an agenda to educate the young to understand both Chinese and American cultural heritage. With the obligations to "develop Chinese culture among the Chinese in New York" and to adopt the culture of the United States,[39] it also focused its activities particularly on language learning both in Chinese and English.

Most Chinese immigrants in New York City spoke Cantonese, a southern dialect in China. They kept their tradition at home and in the ethnic community, which had strong influence on the second-generation Chinese immigrants as they needed to learn it to communicate. Furthermore, illiteracy was high among the old generation. According to a statement by the Chinese National Association of the Mass Education Movement, the percentage of illiterates was over 85 percent in the 1930s. For this and various other reasons, the Chinese were somewhat forced to live and rely upon themselves knowing very little about American life and culture. Even though they were in the United Sates, they seemed to live in a village back in China, as one community activist described.[40] The restrictive Chinese exclusion legislations made it difficult for Chinese immigrants to engage in mainstream activities. Isolation had been a serious problem for members of the ethnic Chinese community. Both Chinese- and English-language learning became crucial for them to get out of the isolation and to reach out to society. Learning Mandarin, the Chinese official language, would reduce the illiteracy and it opened an access for Chinese immigrants to broaden views in connection with a larger society in China. English-language learning would assist Chinese immigrants to break the isolation and enable them to engage in mainstream activities.

Members of the club devoted themselves to the improvement of the institution. They regularly met once a month to discuss various programs. They had managed free language-learning programs since its establishment. Both Chinese and English classes were held once a week, and members as well as other young people were welcome to participate.[41] In addition to the language classes, the club also maintained a library, and members of the club made substantial efforts to collect books on Chinese civilization and culture. The library also kept books on American literature. Open every night to the general public, the library provided room and space for Chinese New Yorkers to come and spend their spare time.[42]

The club also arranged forums and lectures on topics about contemporary China. Editors of the local Chinese press and prominent Chinese visitors from abroad were invited to speak to the public so as to keep the Chinese community in New York informed about the development in China. For instance, in 1936, Tao Xingzhi, a famous educator and writer from China, was invited to give a lecture on Chinese educational reforms.[43] Club members were very much concerned about the war against the Japanese invasion in China in the 1930s. As Chinese descendents, the war spurred club members' enthusiastic support for their home country.[44]

Again, the Chinese Cultural Club, as did the Ging Hawk Club, also concentrated on American cultural awakening of second-generation Chinese immigrants. Aiming at helping Chinese Americans gain access to the mainstream and establish themselves in society, activities of this organization often placed emphasis on understanding of the cultural heritage of their adopted land. In addition to the English classes and books available on English and American literature, the club organized activities to engage the youth in government assisted programs. It invited WPA workers to teach in their programs and encourage the youth to write about their experiences in the United States.[45]

The Chinese Cultural Club also arranged social activities. Aiming to help Chinese American youth become less isolated and "to tighten the bond of friendship between Americans and Chinese," members of this club initiated social nights. Again like the Ging Hawk Club, it held dance parties in the club and members were encouraged to bring friends.[46]

The activities organized by the Chinese Cultural Club provided opportunities for young Chinese Americans to develop their interests in cultural and social involvement. These efforts offered yet another instance in the larger pattern shaped by those organizations claiming acknowledgment for the Chinese as respected members of the larger community.

The Ging Hawk Club and the Chinese Cultural Club were important organizations involving Chinese Americans in activities to promote the understanding of both their Chinese heritage and their American consciousness. At the same time, other cultural groups arose in the 1930s. Like these two organizations, they had a specific agenda to involve Chinese Americans in special activities such as in art, music, and sports. They were equally important in assisting Chinese Americans in their search of both self-definition and social integration.

The Chinese Art Club

The Chinese Art Club was one such organization whose specific agenda was to engage Chinese Americans in advancing Chinese American arts. Ancient Chinese art of different periods had been displayed in the Metropolitan Museum of Art, the Brooklyn Museum, and other art museums in New York City before the 1930s. However, modern Chinese American art had been seldom exhibited in public before this period. The establishment of the Chinese Art Club reflected the growing consciousness of Chinese Americans who were searching for self-definition in the 1930s.

Formed at the beginning of 1936, the Chinese Art Club used gallery exhibition as an organizing tool to provide Chinese Americans with opportunities to express themselves. Located at 10 Pell Street in New York's Chinatown, its activities also gained support from the larger society.[47]

Its first art show of 1936 immediately drew public attention. The *Chinese Christian Student* reported it as a successful event as "no such show was ever seen in Chinatown" before. It was considered the first art gallery exhibition of Chinese American artists even though three of the exhibitors had their works shown uptown and were accredited by some known art groups.[48] In 1937, one year after its opening show, the Chinese Art Club opened its second annual art exhibition in its newly founded gallery at 175 Canal Street. Larger, brighter, and more spacious, the gallery attracted more visitors. Two art critics reportedly attended the opening reception of the show, and the function was documented in the art column in a local newsletter.[49]

The annual art shows exhibited both Chinese and American themes and art styles, reflecting the vast range of interests of the artists. The combination of Chinese art techniques and American scenery combined in artworks of the artists demonstrated an awareness of their advanced Chinese culture and their passion for the United States.

The gallery activities achieved more when fifty artworks of fifteen Chinese American association members and nine American artists were presented in its third annual exhibition in March 1938. The themes of the works in the exhibition ranged from the ancient world to the present. In addition to traditional Chinese ink paintings, oil paintings, and watercolor paintings, sculptures and woodcuts were also displayed. K. L. Eng's work, *Refugee*, was the center of attention in the 1938 art exhibition. It presented the anger and sorrow of a group of Chinese women and children who were leaving their home to escape Japanese air bombing, looting, and killing.[50]

Other paintings depicting the beauty of American landscapes also caught visitors' interest. Mowee Tiant, a watercolorist, painted the tranquility of rural New York. Viewers to the exhibition spoke highly about this work, with one Chinese commentator writing that Mowee's "light and delightful landscape of rural New York" added color to the art show. By visually transferring his passion for the beauty of the land where he was born, Chen Suichang's impressive landscape of Lower Manhattan, a view seen from his Mott Street studio, also captured the public attention.[51]

Works by other American artists were presented in the gallery as a way of integrating the show into mainstream cultural events. Oronzio Maldareli's *Dancer*, Genoi Pettit and Arthur Schweider's *Life*, and Ronnie Elliot's drawing were among the most admired. Guy MacCoy's painting of a Missouri scene drew a lot of attention from visitors. It was considered by many artists a successful example of applying Chinese painting techniques to the American scene. An art critic commented that MacCoy's skillful utilization of the old Chinese line and perspective produced a "completely Chinese mood on a Missouri theme." A Chinese local newsletter reported that the 1938 Chinese Art Club's show demonstrated "considerable advance in quality over previous exhibit[s]."[52]

In addition to art exhibitions, members of the Chinese Art Club also sponsored lectures on art. Some popular Chinese American artists were invited to give lectures on art to young Chinese Americans. On March 16, 1938, Chu H. Jor, a well-known artist, was invited to give a special lecture that traced the history of Chinese art.[53]

The Chinese Art Club was the first professional organization of Chinese American artists to organize annual gallery exhibitions to provide space and opportunities for Chinese American artists to express themselves through their artworks. Giving them a forum to air their feelings, views, and ideas about both China and the United States, the Chinese Art Club and its organized art exhibitions aided young Chinese American artists in rediscovering themselves.

The Chinese Musicians Club and the Cantonians

The Great Depression witnessed the flourish of music and performance as a tool of inspiration particularly in big cities such as Chicago and New York. The Chinese Musicians Club and the Cantonians were Chinese American musicians' associations. Also founded in the 1930s, and located in New York's Chinatown, musical performances of these organizations not only inspired Chinese New Yorkers in the hard times when so many lost their jobs but also nurtured the spirit of young Chinese Americans.

Music, an important part of the life of Chinese immigrants, derived from a long-shared heritage that cut across boundaries of region, dialect, and class. Music served as an instrument for people to express ideas, passions, and understanding that cut across the boundaries of nations, languages, and cultures. Before the 1930s, amateur musicians' groups performed traditional Chinese music. Many American-born Chinese New Yorkers cherished this cultural inheritance. Some were trained to be professional musicians. However, born and educated in the United States, American music also had a powerful influence on Chinese New Yorkers. The establishment of the Chinese Musicians Club and the Cantonians in the 1930s, for instance, marked the beginning of Chinese American musical organizations that were dedicated to both Chinese and American music and performances that transformed music and the way musicians looked at themselves.

The Chinese Musicians Club had its club room situated in Chinatown at 57 Mott Street. It attracted young Chinese New Yorkers to its choir. Many second-generation Chinese immigrants went to the club after school. They practiced both Chinese and American songs. Jazz songs were often translated into Chinese to express musicians' feelings more accurately. Not being confined within their own circle, members of the club also held musical activities open to the public. It was reported Chinese audiences enjoyed their performances.[54]

The club also had a Chinese orchestra that focused on Chinese music performances. Musicians played with traditional instruments such as drums, chimes, flutes, bells, and shengs that not only attracted Chinatown residents but also drew the interest of other ethnic groups.[55] Like the choirs, young musicians often held musical evenings open to the larger population in a musical hall at 55 Mott Street as many Americans joined the crowd.[56]

The Cantonians was another Chinese American musicians' association. Organized in 1932, membership of this association was diverse. Volunteer members from the Chinese community were largely experienced amateur musicians. Others were former Columbia University student band musicians. The association formed an orchestra soon after it was established. Foo Y. Lee became the orchestra's first director.[57] This was one of the first musical organizations consisting of both Chinatown residents and college students. The cooperation between the two reflected a new trend and desire of the ethnic Chinese New Yorkers to work together to enhance the life of Chinatown residents. No longer standing aloof from the ethnic Chinese community, college students were involved in the activities organized in Chinatown.

Committing themselves to the improvement of the life of Chinatown, young Chinese American college graduates introduced Western band music to their ethnic Chinese community. Bass horn, trumpet, clarinet, and Western drums were new to their audience but they showed great interest in the performances. College student musicians also innovated a new way to perform. They played Cantonese local music with Western band instruments to attract more audiences. It reported that New York's Chinatown residents had developed an interest in new music performance, and they attended the Cantonians' performances quite often.[58]

The endeavors of young Chinese American musicians to introduce Chinese music played with Western instruments found new audiences in a larger society. Young Chinese American members of the Cantonians did not play solely in their own ethnic community. Instead, they reached out and sought access to introduce themselves. According to a historical record, the association managed "several engagements on Broadway" in an attempt to "expand its influence" into society at large.[59] Meanwhile, young Chinese American musicians also played American music with Chinese musical instruments.

Music has been a powerful instrument that connected people with notes and sounds that languages cannot convey. During the 1930s, young Chinese New Yorkers found music an alternative way to express themselves. They also found it a channel through which they reached out and involved themselves in the American society culturally. Music performances became so important that they transformed performers that reflected transnational characteristics of both Chinese and American cultural identities of young Chinese New Yorkers.

The Chinese Dramatic and Benevolent Association of New York (CDBA)

The Chinese Dramatic and Benevolent Association of New York (CDBA) took its title to stress its commitment to the support of China. Established in New York in 1926, the CDBA was situated at 165 Bowery Street in New York's Chinatown. Early members of this association were mainly Chinese-born and educated. It then extended its membership to American-born Chinese. Chinese American college graduates began to join it in the early 1930s. Dedicated to the development of China, members of this association composed and performed to raise money among New York Chinese to endorse campaigns and movements to reform China. Their performances, likewise, benefited Chinatown residents. By introducing Chinese modern art and performances, the activities of this organization not only kept the Chinese in New York close to China but also invigorated the cultural life of New York's Chinese community.

New York's Chinese, like other ethnic groups of people, had a strong feeling for their ancestral county. They were very much concerned about the development of China. The drama association implemented its goals to serve the need of its community. The performances with themes on China served as a channel to link New York Chinese to their homeland. China had undergone tremendous changes since the early twentieth century. The 1911 revolution ended thousands of years of dynastic rules of emperors, and the 1925 unification military campaigns weakened the powers of regional and local warlords, thus strengthening the government of the newly established republic. The May Fourth Movement of the late 1910s through the early 1920s and the New Life Movement of the 1930s aroused the Chinese national spirit with emphasis on cultural and educational improvement. The concept of modernization shaped the national policies.

Educated in China and then moved to the United States, members of the drama association joined by Chinese American college graduates cooperated with the situation in China in arranging stage performances and sponsoring playwrights to stimulate Chinese nationalism and patriotism. From 1927 to 1936, the association created and staged five major multiepisode plays: *The National Enmity*, *Cai Er*, *The Bloody Cloud*, *Heroic Sons and Daughters*, and *Cai Tingkai* to dramatize political issues in China and emphasize the importance of changes.[60]

Influenced by China's new cultural movements which advocated the use of the vernacular style in Chinese literary and writing and pushed modern themes in dramatic arts, the CDBA also introduced Chinatown residents to modern Chinese plays.[61] In order to uplift literacy of the people, scholars in China initiated a movement to push the change in classic writing style to make it easier for mass education. Instead of old and classic literature style, they advocated the usage of daily spoken language in writing and book printing. Furthermore, contemporary national heroes and heroines who devoted their lives to their country replaced ancient kings and royal families in literature and on the stage. Cooperating with the change, the drama association improvised the story of Cai Er and Cai Tingkai, for example, who contributed to the defense of China, and made them the major characters on the stages.

The seven-scene drama titled *Cai Tingkai* was particularly successful. General Cai Tingkai was a well-known Chinese national hero. As a military commander, his troop, the 19th Route Army, launched a military campaign to defend Shanghai against Japanese occupation in 1931.[62] The drama to eulogize the heroic deeds of both General Cai and his soldiers was so successful that, according to a report, when General Cai came to New York for fundraising in 1934, three thousand Chinese New Yorkers greeted him. Calling him "Savior of Shanghai," a "constant stream of American reporters" followed him and he "reviewed a Chinese parade" of his supporters in Chinatown on August 28.[63] Approximately $30,000 was raised to support the war and help the refuges.[64]

The CDBA provided opportunity for college students to show their artistic and musical talents. Female students played a vigorous role in composition and performance. Yu Jung Chang, for instance, wrote and directed a Chinese drama. In a six-scene dramatic show reflecting the transition of Chinese female students from traditional Chinese to modern American, she and other college graduates such as the Huie sisters, Mabel Lee, and Florence Thom had their separate roles.[65] The funds they raised through the performance constituted one-fourth of the proceeds gathered by the Columbia Chinese Students' Famine Committee.[66]

Active in its support of China, the CDBA also cooperated with other Chinese American organizations. When the Chinese American Aviation Association in New York sought assistance for fundraising for its training programs to support Chinese military resistance to Japanese occupation, the CDBA arranged drama performances to sponsor this effort.[67] On many other occasions, the CDBA helped raise money for war victims in China. Benefit shows to collect money from Chinese New Yorkers to set up a hospital in China exemplified the CDBA's efforts to support China through performance art.[68]

Members of the CDBA were conscious about the advantage of art techniques in drama playwriting and shows. They often sought to artistically improve their performances by attending lectures on the subject of the art of theater. Occasionally, the club invited artists to come to the club room to demonstrate. On March 16, 1936, the association invited George Kin Leung, a Chinese dramatist, to give a lecture on Chinese theater to its members. After the lecture, they had a technical discussion on the tradition and demonstration of Chinese art.[69]

The CDBA provided young Chinese New Yorkers with a powerful forum to express themselves. Not confining themselves within their own students' entity, college students managed to reach out to the larger ethnic Chinese community with their shows and performances. The performances and other organized activities aiming at fundraising for the support of China kept New York Chinese attached to China culturally and politically. At the same time New York Chinese were also aroused to participate in supportive activities. What the CDBAs did in the 1930s demonstrated that the involvement of college students in Chinatown vitalized the life of the Chinese community.

The Chinese Athletic Club

In addition to art, music, and drama clubs, the sports teams organized in this era were perhaps the most significant of the efforts of Chinese Americans to move into the mainstream of American culture. The Chinese Athletic Club of the 1930s became the leading athletes' association in New York to supervise teams in basketball, swimming, and boxing.

Sports differed from other cultural activities in requiring participants to be more aggressive. The courage and self-confidence needed in games and competitions assisted young Chinatown residents in building pride and strength as they stepped out of their ethnic community. "We always celebrate Christmas at our little house," Anna May Wong recalled in her interview about her childhood. However, as a second-generation American-born Chinese, she felt so frustrated and miserable when "American boys used to chase me around at recess, called me a Chink and pulled my little pigtail."[70] Racial discrimination in the guise of American orientalism and the stereotyped image of "yellow face" haunted Chinese Americans. The 1930s witnessed the increasing protest of Chinese Americans against prejudice, exemplified in Anna's counterattack at a truck driver who called Anna "Chink" when he yelled to her and demanded her to get out of the way. That was the turning of a corner for her when she "blazed back a remark equally insulting at him and he wilted."[71]

The Chinese Athletic Club was originally formed in 1911, when a group of young Chinese Americans sought access to the sports facilities of the Church of All Nations.[72] During World War I, as many club members left to serve in the American army, the Chinese Athletic Club ceased to exist as an ethnic sports team under the Church of All Nations. Remaining members joined other integrated teams.[73] It was not until the early 1930s that the Chinese Athletic Club revived.

Independent of any affiliation, the club created more sports attractions, and more young Chinese Americans participated in its organized sports activities. In the 1930s, as before, its membership continued to be composed largely of American-born Chinese.[74] The different athletic teams such as the basketball team, the swimming squad, and the boxing team were subdivided according to different age groups. Chinese American athletes in junior teams were between ten and fifteen years of age. The senior teams usually consisted of athletes who were under twenty years of age.[75]

Both Chinese American and other ethnic professional athletes were invited to coach to make their teams competitive. Former team members were also invited to be coaches. Lung Chin, who was on the first Chinese basketball team in 1920, became a basketball coach in 1930 while he was coaching the Police Athletic League of New York.[76] Calvin S. Chin became the coach of the swimming squad in 1934.[77]

In addition to former team members, popular sports stars were also invited by the Chinese Athletic Club to coach young Chinese American athletes in an effort to professionalize its sports teams and get them ready for games and competitions with other ethnic groups. Bill McCullogh, a former basketball star at St. John's University and a sportswriter for the *Brooklyn Times Union*, was invited as a basketball team coach in 1934. Stanley Guest became a coach of the boxing team in 1932, and stayed until 1935.[78]

Under these coaches' guidance, Chinese American youth sports teams trained vigorously and improved their standing in competitions. In 1934, teams began to participate in games and competitions outside their own Chinese community. On January 7, 1935, a Chinese local newspaper reported that the Chinese Athletic Club would send its teams to compete against other ethnic sports teams at a sports event to be held on the Prospect Hall Court in Brooklyn.[79] Its basketball team played the "Templers," a team from Brooklyn, on a Brooklyn court around the same time. A local newsletter reported that the Chinese Five beat the team.[80]

The Chinese American sports teams were even more successful in 1935. When McCullogh coached the basketball team, it played eleven games and beat several teams from other ethnic communities, including the Bank Team and the Original Celtics from the Brooklyn district.[81]

In addition to their successes in basketball games, Chinese athletes also excelled at boxing. Boxing was not popular among Chinese Americans. However, under Stanley Guest's guidance, several Chinese athletes became successful at this sport. A Chinese American boxer nicknamed "Stan" held a record of fifty victories out of fifty-nine bouts as bantam weight in the professional ring. Leo Gum reached the finals in the 1935 boxing tournament at Textile High School. Pinky Chan entered the professional ring and won his first bout in the same year.[82]

The Chinese Athletic Club involved New York Chinatown's young residents in mainstream cultural activities through sports that helped to release the frustration of racism. Their athletic achievements were encouraging to the team players. Tommy Chu, a former Chinese team player, once told an interviewer that he felt racial discrimination "everywhere in New York City."[83] "You needed living quarters, and you saw an apartment for rent in the newspaper," he said. "You could go to those people at 9 o'clock in the morning and knock on their door, ring the bell, and they'll tell you that they had just rented it." Frustrated and helpless, Chu told his interviewer that he did not feel the same way when he played games. "At least in sports," Tommy Chu said, "there was the potential of defending your pride by defeating the opponent."[84]

Chinese American athletes found sports a powerful institution that enabled them to express themselves as proud American citizens. They were encouraged to win when they went to play, as winning was considered an important way for young Chinese Americans to gain self-confidence.[85] Contrasted against the traditional Chinese philosophy of tolerance and not to struggle but to flow along with the tide, the philosophy of "play to win" demonstrated the shift in attitude and practice of Chinese Americans toward society.

The Girl Boxing Team was formed around the same time in New York. Different from Western boxing sports, members of this team practiced Chinese martial arts that stressed arts of defense.[86] According to an annual report, the Girl Boxing Team was "frequently called upon by other clubs to give sword and shadow boxing exhibition."[87] By introducing Chinese sports, team members fostered self-confidence in inherited culture. Their performances were well received and the audience enjoyed them very much.

However, the importance of sports was not simply a matter of achievement and self-definition. Team sports provided a mode of contact between Chinese American youth and other ethnic groups. "In our free time, we used to stay right in Chinatown," Hong Wu, a former team member recalled,[88] because "the Italian kids would taunt us."[89] They often scorned that "Chinese were afraid to cross Canal Street."[90] Sports activities engaged young Chinese Americans in confronting outsiders directly. Through sports, a new relationship between young Chinese Americans and players from other ethnic groups was established. The newly established relations were well described in a memoir of a team leader who recalled that while playing against each other, Chinese and Italian boys started to get to know each other. After several games, the Italian kids became friendly toward Chinese boys.[91]

Sports, like other cultural activities, aided both the physical and the psychological welfare of the participants. Aiming to integrate themselves into mainstream society, the Chinese Athletic Club and its organized sports activities and games helped New York Chinatown's young residents to step out of their ethnic community. By providing an opportunity for Chinese Americans to confront and cope directly with outsiders, sporting activities also inspired the young generation of Chinese immigrants to be self-confident and self-reliant. Participation in team sports thus helped young Chinese Americans to develop a sense of community, unity, and strength.

Conclusion

The shadow cast by the exclusion era's legacy shaped the nature of the Chinese American identity. Commenting on Chinese American cultural identity, Frank Chin, a Chinese American playwright, once said that as members of the second generation of Chinese immigrants have been separated by geography, culture, and history from China, they have evolved cultures and sensibilities distinctly not Chinese. Instead, the power of mainstream values of the United States helped shape the Chinese American identity.[92] However, racism that is deeply rooted in American cultures and was historically institutionalized has also effectively affected Chinese Americans. It is the racist admonition "that all Chinese are alike, because of skin color" that sets them to work together for some form of white acceptance.[93] Nevertheless,

Chin suggests, Chinese American culture is distinctly not white American either.[94] Instead, it has its own traits.

Similar to Chin, Joan Faung Jean Lee suggests that the second generation of Chinese immigrants have developed values inherently American. Partially it is because of their strong desire to do well in American society. The vocabulary of success is defined in American terms: from language to cultural symbols. Chinese Americans may retain some of their parents' values, but by virtue of having grown up in the United States, their overriding identity and experiences are shaped by the living environment in America. Holding that Chinese American values are the product of society at large, Lee also realizes the desire of American-born Chinese to have more knowledge of China and a greater understanding of their roots.[95]

Furthermore, in the debate of whether the United States of America has been a melting pot or multicultural mosaic in the 1990s, historians have contended that various ethnic groups contributed to the American cultures by both maintaining their cultural traditions and creating new ones. The combination and the interweaving of the old and the new constituted the pluralistic culture of America.

Discussions on Chinese American culture and identity by Chinese American scholars provide a variety of visions of aspects of American cultures in a special way. Telling the stories and experiences of Chinese Americans, particularly those of American-born, they underscore the ethnic character of American cultures and the marginalized position of Chinese Americans in society. Although resenting being measured by the ethnicity standards of the immigrant generation, as Gloria Heyung Chun reveals, Chinese Americans also refused to succumb to American mainstreaming. Acting as political representatives, translators, ethnographers, cultural advance guards, and entertainers staging Chinese American culture and identity for the broader public, Chun says, they are "poised to safeguard their parental ethnic community as well as to carve out new opportunities for themselves in America."[96]

Cultural identity is an ongoing process as immigration continues. Scholarly discussions on the formation of Chinese American culture and identity also have some implications of differences between generations. As the evidence of this chapter reveals, racism created and perpetuated isolation for New York's Chinese. Excluded by society and living in their own ethnic community, they kept close ties with China and maintained their cultural heritage as a way to express their concerns.

However, members of the second generation of Chinese immigrants in the 1930s were the pioneers in search of Chinese American identity. Advocating social reform and civic improvement in the ethnic Chinese community, they participated in cultural activities in larger society as a way to claim themselves as Chinese Americans. Sports teams, art and musical clubs, and cultural associations, along with their organized activities, were grassroots attempts by Chinese Americans to integrate themselves into American society. Although different in program and agenda, these organizations and their activities formed a strong trend towards crossing the cultural barriers in the United States. The social world of Chinese immigrants no longer remained, as Paul Siu once described, "their quaint working places and their racial Chinatown."[97]

Chinese American cultural identity has been inextricably linked by confusion, adaptation, refusal, and creation. Yet Chinese Americans endeavored to forge a meaningful place for themselves in the United States.

Notes

1. Kit King Louis, "Problems of Second Generation Chinese," *Sociology and Social Research* 16 (Sept. 1931–Aug. 1932): 454.

2. Chih Meng, *Chinese American Understanding: A Sixty-Year Search by Chih Men* (New York: China Institute in America, 1981); Betty Lee Sung, *The Story of the Chinese in America: Their Struggle for Survival, Acceptance, and Full Participation in American Life from the Gold Rush Days to the Present* (New York: Collier Books, 1967); Shih-shan Henry Tsai, *China and the Overseas Chinese in the United States 1868–1911* (Fayetteville: University of Arkansas Press, 1983) and *The Chinese Experience in America* (Bloomington: Indiana University Press, 1986).

3. *Directory of Chinese Students in America* (1937); *Chinese Christian Student*, Feb. 1937, no. 4. For more information on Chinese students, see Willi Ye, "Crossing the Cultures: The Experience of Chinese Students in the U.S.A. 1900–1925" (Ph.D. dissertation, New Haven, Conn.: Yale University, 1989); Y. G. Wang, *Chinese Intellectuals and the West, 1872–1949*, (Chapel Hill: University of North Carolina Press, 1966); W. Reginald Wheeler, Henry King, and Alexander B. Davidson, ed., *The Foreign Student in America: A Study by the Commission on Survey of Foreign Students in the United States of America under the Auspices of the Friendly Relations Committees of the Young Men's Christian Association and the Young Women's Christian Association* (New York: Association Press, 1925).

4. Pardee Lowe, "Second-Generation Dilemmas," in *Chinese American Voices: From the Gold Rush to the Present*, ed. Judy Yung, Gordon H. Chang, and Him Mark Lai (Berkeley: University of California Press, 2006), 168.

5. Ibid., 169.

6. See Chih Meng, *Chinese American Understanding: A Sixty-Year Search by Chih Men* (New York: China Institute in America, 1981); Betty Lee Sung, *The Story of the Chinese in America: Their Struggle for Survival, Acceptance, and Full Participation in American Life from the Gold Rush Days to the Present* (New York: Collier Books, 1967).

7. H. Y. H., "Our Second Generation Youth," *Chinese Christian Student*, June 1939, 5.

8. James West Davidson, *Nation of Nations: A Narrative History of the American Republic* (New York: McGraw-Hill, 1994), 706.

9. Scholarly discussions on progressivism and the Progressive Movement are well presented in books and articles as Richard Hofstadter, *The Age of Reform* (1955); Gabriel Kolko, *The Triumph of Conservatism* (1963); Robert Wiebe, *The Search for Order, 1877–1920* (1967); Daniel Rodgers, *In Search of Progressivism* (1982); and Eric Rauchway, *The Refuge of Affections: Family and American Reform Politics* (2001).

10. Robert Wiebe, *The Search for Order, 1877–1920* (1967); Eric Rauchway, *The Refuge of Affections: Family and American Reform Politics* (New York: Columbia University Press, 2001)

11. Huie Kin, *Reminiscences* (Peiping, China, 1932), 72–73.

12. *New York Times*, July 10, 1901.

13. *Chinese Christian Student* Nov. 10, 1936.

14. *Chinese Nationalist Daily*, Apr. 13 1932; *New York Times*, Apr. 11, 1937.

15. Hua Liang, "Fighting for a New Life: Social and Patriotic Activism of Chinese American Women in New York City," *Journal of American Ethnic History* 17, no. 2 (Winter 1998).

16. *Chinese Athletic Club Excursion Journal*, 1935, Chinatown History Project, archives, Museum of Chinese in America.

17. "The Report of the General Welfare School in New York by Resolution of the Columbia Club," *Chinese Students' Monthly* 6 (1910): 199, 289; 7 (Jan. 1912): 253–59; Hua Liang, "Fighting for a New Life: Social and Patriotic Activism of Chinese American Women in New York City," *Journal of American Ethnic History* 17, no. 2 (Winter 1998): 15.

18. Theodora Chan Wang, *Chinese Women's Association Condensed Report for the Years of 1932–1936*; Judy Yung, Gordon H. Chang, and Him Mark Lai, ed., *Chinese American Voices: From the Gold Rush to the Present* (Berkeley: University of California Press, 2006), 186.

19. Ibid.

20. Ibid.

21. The U.S. Bureau of Census revealed that a single married woman and the elder daughter of a Chinese merchant, for instance, toiled in 1900 as seamstresses to support themselves and help increase familial income. A sixteen-year-old Chinese girl worked in 1910 as a saleswoman. Another twenty-eight-year-old Chinese American widow was reported by the census of 1900 to be a dry-goods store owner and head of the family. By 1920 over two-thirds of the second-generation Chinese American daughters of New York's Chinatown were attending schools, and 10 percent of them took odd jobs after class. They worked as tearoom waitresses, typists, theater usherettes, and saleswomen, earning money for their own education. U.S.

Bureau of Census, *Fourteenth Census of the United States, 1920, Population Schedules, New York*; Hua Liang, "Fighting for a New Life: Social and Patriotic Activism of Chinese American Women in New York City," *Journal of American Ethnic History* 17, no. 2 (Winter 1998): 2.

22. Alice Fong, "A Challenge to the Chinese-Americans," *The Western Student*, an occasional supplement to the *Chinese Christian Student*, November 1932, 2.

23. The Chinese Young Women's Christian Association was the first Chinese American women's social and educational organization in New York City. Thirty-nine Chinese women, "all born" and educated in the United States, signed a petition in 1918 to form an organization of their own. Officially established in 1920, it became active in the subsequent twenty years. Therodora Chan Wang (Mrs. Chen Zhongfang) served as its general secretary for ten years before she became the president of the Chinese Women's Association in 1932. Under her leadership, the Chinese Young Women's Christian Association devoted most of its effort to the "cultivation and enhancement of Chinese women's civic characters." As soon as the association was formed it set out classes to teach English to Chinese women. In the 1920s and early 1930s, the association continued its English class and offered other educational programs, such as lectures and movie presentations on women and children's hygiene. The association also conducted fundraising campaigns to raise money for the Chinese School in the neighborhood and for Chinese sufferers of war and famine.

24. Theodora Chan was its appointed leader at that time. Evelyn Lee and Anna Lee became president and vice president of the club in 1933. *Chinese Christian Student*, Nov.–Dec. 1933. Chan later married William Wong, who became a president of a Chinese students association in the mid-1930s. Both of them remained active in students' activities.

25. *Chinese Christian Student* 26, no. 1–2, 1936, 8. Louise Chin was the secretary of the organization when Anna Lee became the president. *Chinese Christian Student* 26, June 1936, 2.

26. It cooperated with eleven other cultural associations in this event. "October 10 Celebration in New York," *Chinese Christian Student* 25, Oct. 1934.

27. To support China in its effort for modernization, New York's Chinese invested in the building of railways, schools and parks in their hometown. Ibid.

28. *Chinese Christian Student* 26, no. 1–2, 1935, 8.

29. *Chinese Christian Student* 26, no. 7, June 1936.

30. Robert Dunn, "Where Does Our Future Lie?" *Chinese Christian Student* 26, no. 1–2, 1935.

31. Ibid.

32. It was held on Nov. 30, 1933. *Chinese Christian Student*, Nov.–Dec. 1933.

33. Ibid.

34. Ibid.

35. Ibid.

36. "New York Unit in Farewell Meeting for Graduating Students," *Chinese Christian Student*, June 1936

37. Ibid.

38. This club was located on the top floor of the building at 144 Second Avenue. S. Michelson, "Chinese Cultural Club," "Chinese in New York," WPA Federal Writers' Project, NYC Unit: Racial Groups in New York, 1936–1940, Folder #48 (New York City: New York Municipal Archives), Microfilm.

39. "The Chinese In NYC," a report compiled by the WPA Writer's Project, 1938, achieves, Museum of Chinese in America.

40. Theodora Chan Wang, *Chinese Women's Association Condensed Report for the Years 1932–1936*; Judy Yung, Gordon H. Chang, and Him Mark Lai, ed., *Chinese American Voices: From the Gold Rush to the Present* (Berkeley: University of California Press, 2006), 187.

41. "The Chinese In NYC," a report compiled by the WPA Writer's Project, 1938, achieves, Museum of Chinese in America.

42. "Chinese in NY," WPA Writers' Project, 1934.

43. *Chinese Nationalist Daily*, Oct. 9, 1936.

44. See their activities in chapter 5.

45. "Chinese in NYC," archives, Museum of Chinese in America.

46. Ibid.

47. Nathan Austubel, "Chinese Organizations," WPA Writers' Project, Folder #48, Microfilm.

48. *Chinese Christian Student*, Mar.–Apr. 1938.

49. Ibid.

50. Ibid.

51. Ibid.

52. Ibid.

53. Chu's painting, *still-life*, had been shown in Grand Central and other uptown galleries. Ibid.

54. Ibid.

55. "The Chinese in NYC," a report compiled by the WPA Writer's Project, 1938, 22, archives, Museum of Chinese in America.

56. Ibid.

57. Archives, Museum of Chinese in America.

58. Ibid.

59. Ibid.

60. *The Chinese Dramatic and Benevolent Association (Mei Guo New York Meing Zhi Bai Hua Ju Shi), Tenth Anniversary*, Oct. 12, 1936; archives, Museum of Chinese in America. This association performed in support of the Northern Expedition, a military campaign for a unified China. The Northern Expedition was an anti-warlords military campaign for the unification of China. It was launched by the Republic government in China in 1924. The Chinese Communist Party effectively cooperated

with the campaign. *The National Enmity* presented Chinese warlords as felonies to the unification of China. *Cai Er*, an eight-episode play, dramatized Cai Er, a Chinese general who was devoted his life to the establishment of a constitutional republic in China. Both *The Bloody Cloud* and *Heroic Sons and Daughters* were two four-scene dramas that paid high tribute to the Chinese soldiers and civilians who were fighting against the Japanese occupation of China.

61. *Chinese Dramatic and Benevolent Association, Tenth Anniversary*, Oct. 12, 1936, 15. The Chinese Dramatic and Benevolent Association of New York advocated the use of the vernacular style in its performances to promote democratic ideas. Yaoron Wu, chief organizer of New York's Chinese Dramatic Association and playwright, wrote in 1936 that the application of vernacular to dramas and plays was vital to the reform movement to modernize drama.

62. *Chinese Dramatic and Benevolent Association, Tenth Anniversary*, Oct. 12, 1936.

63. Shih-shan Henry Tsai, *The Chinese Experience in America* (Bloomington: Indiana University Press, 1986), 111.

64. T. C. Wang, *Chinese Women's Association Condensed Report for the Years 1932–1936*; Judy Yung, Gordon H. Chang, and Him Mark Lai, ed., *Chinese American Voices: From the Gold Rush to the Present* (Berkeley: University of California Press, 2006), 187.

65. Miss Yu Jung Chang, grand-niece of the famous Chinese diplomat Li Hongzhang, was studying at the Secretarial Training School of the Young Women's Christian Association in New York in around 1910. She created the Chinese Women's Club for Mutual Encouragement in New York. The Huie sisters were the daughters of Rev. Huie Kin, who became the first minister of the Chinese Presbyterian Church in New York City. Also see Hua Liang, "Fighting for a New Life: Social and Patriotic Activism of Chinese American Women in New York City," *Journal of American Ethnic History* 17, no. 2 (Winter 1998): 2.

66. Ibid.

67. The Chinese American Aviation Association was established for the purpose of training young Chinese Americans to be ready to fight side by side with the Chinese in China in support of the anti-Japanese war effort.

68. *Chinese Dramatic and Benevolent Association, Tenth Anniversary*, Oct. 12, 1936.

69. *Chinese Christian Student*, Mar.–Apr. 1938, 7.

70. Both of Anna May Wong's parents were born in California, as she was herself. She made over sixty films in an acting career that spanned two world wars. Anna May Wong, "I Am Growing More Chinese Each Passing Year," 1934, interviewed by Harry Carr; Judy Yung, Gordon H. Chang, and Him Mark Lai, ed., *Chinese American Voices: From the Gold Rush to the Present* (Berkeley: University of California Press, 2006), 178.

71. Ibid.

72. The Church of All Nations welcomed different groups of ethnic youth in the Lower East Side of Manhattan to come together to join its secular programs. As requested, the Chinese Athletic Club was formed in 1911 in order to use the

church's athletic facilities. "Youth Sports League," 17, archives, Museum of Chinese in America.

73. Interview with Lung Chin, "Oral History," 21, Chinatown Historical Museum archives, Museum of Chinese in America.

74. Ausubel, "Chinese Athletic Club," archives, Museum of Chinese in America.

75. "Chinese Athletic Club," archives, Museum of Chinese in America.

76. Ibid.

77. *Chinese Athletic Club Excursion Journal*, 1935, 21, Chinatown History Project, archives, Museum of Chinese in America.

78. Ibid.

79. Archives, Museum of Chinese in America.

80. The *Brooklyn Times Union* reported the event. Archives, Museum of Chinese in America.

81. *Chinese Athletic Club Excursion Journal*, 1935, 22, archives, Museum of Chinese in America.

82. Ibid.

83. Tommy Chu, "Oral History," 21, archives, Museum of Chinese in America.

84. Ibid.

85. "When you go out there, you play to win" was one of the major principles of the Chinese Athletic Club. Lung Chin, "Oral History," 19, archives, Museum of Chinese in America.

86. The Girl Boxing Team was endorsed by the Chinese Women's Association. T. C. Wang, *Chinese Women's Association Condensed Report for the Years 1932–1936*; Judy Yung, Gordon H. Chang, and Him Mark Lai, ed., *Chinese American Voices: From the Gold Rush to the Present* (Berkeley: University of California Press, 2006), 191.

87. Ibid.

88. "A Preliminary Discussion," *Youth Sports League*, 1910–1950, 15; Chinatown History Project, Chinatown Historical Museum archives, Museum of Chinese in America.

89. Tommy Chu, "Oral History," 19, archives, Museum of Chinese in America.

90. Ibid.

91. Ibid.

92. Frank Chin is a Chinese American playwright. His play *The Chickencoop Chinaman* was produced at the American Place Theater in New York in 1972 and became the first Chinese American play in New York state history.

93. "Who's Afraid of Frank Chin? Or Is It Ching?" *Bridge: The Asian-American Magazine* 2, no. 2 (Dec. 1972): 30; Gloria Heyung Chun, *Of Orphans and Warriors: Inventing Chinese American Culture and Identity* (New Brunswick. N.J.: Rutgers University Press, 2001), 116.

94. Frank Chin, Jeffery Paul Chan, Lawson Fusao Inada, and Shawn Hsu Wong, ed., *Aiiieeeee! An Anthology of Asian American Writers* (Washington, D.C.: Howard University Press, 1974, 1983), preface, xi.

95. Joann Faung Jean Lee, *Asian Americans: Oral History of First to Fourth Generation Americans from China, the Philippines, Japan, India, the Pacific Islands Vietnam and Cambodia* (New York: The New Press, 1992).

96. Gloria Heyung Chun, *Of Orphans and Warriors: Inventing Chinese American Culture and Identity* (New Brunswick, N.J.: Rutgers University Press, 2001).

97. Paul Siu, *The Chinese Laundryman: A Study of Social Isolation* (New York: New York University Press, 1953, 1987), 138.

CHAPTER FOUR

The Great Depression and Political Organizations

The period between 1930 and 1945 saw the emergence of a politically mature young generation of American-born Chinese. Just as the workers in their labor organizations and the young in their cultural organizations tried to break down the barriers of exclusion, Chinese New Yorkers adopted a new political strategy and participated in mainstream political activities as a means of surviving the Depression. This chapter will present evidence that demonstrates the political consciousness of New York's Chinese Americans.

Traditionally, Chinese immigrants were depicted as a group who stayed away from any possible entanglements with the world outside their community, because of racial discrimination. Scholars suggest that because of racial segregation, the Chinese in the United States usually turned their political zeal to what was happening in their homeland rather than becoming involved in American politics.[1] These explanations are true in many ways. However, born and raised in the United States, Chinese Americans, especially Chinese Americans in New York, became politically conscious in the 1930s. Involvement rather than disengagement in American politics was a major shift in attitude and practice to claim themselves as Chinese Americans.

The Depression and Chinese Americans

The Great Depression was the most severe economic crisis in American history. It caused unemployment, bankruptcy, and starvation. Job shortages during the Depression reinforced racial antagonism. Whites in many southern cities demanded that all blacks be dismissed from their jobs. In 1930, the Black Shirts, a political organization in Atlanta, launched a campaign with the slogan "No Jobs for Niggers until Every White Man Has a Job!"[2]

As the Depression deepened, African Americans suffered from greater unemployment than they had in the past. Although many blacks migrated to the cities in the North searching for work, the situation in the North was no better than in the South. In New York, black unemployment was nearly 50 percent.[3] The unemployment rate was even higher in other northern cities. Many blacks became homeless.

Hispanic Americans were subject to similar patterns of harsh experience during the Depression. Many Hispanics, particularly Mexicans, were forced to leave the country by officials who arbitrarily removed them from relief rolls or simply rounded them up and transported them across the border. Half a million Chicanos left the United States for Mexico in the first years of the Depression.[4]

The Depression also worsened the situation for Chinese in the United States. Politically and socially segregated, Chinese immigrants had withdrawn into their own community. However, disengagement did not save Chinese immigrants from what they wished to avoid. Instead, they were frequently victimized whenever there was political and economic turmoil. The Depression reinforced longstanding patterns of discrimination. The majority of Chinese Americans in New York City, like in other Chinatowns throughout the United States, continued to work in Chinese-owned laundries and restaurants. They could hope for no job opportunities outside the world of Chinatown. Although a few had odd jobs outside the Chinese community, they were threatened with the loss of them, as a young man, who had worked as an "elevator boy" in a Jewish hospital, described, since all Chinese employees were being discharged in a compliance with the demands of other workers that their jobs be given to "white" people.[5]

Chinese American college graduates found it more difficult to move into mainstream professions during the Depression. They suffered from increasing competition for even low-paying jobs such as stockgirls and salesmen, though they had college degrees. Chinese immigrants had suffered racial discrimination since the enactment of the exclusion laws. Many Chinese immigrants hoped that education could bring improvement for their children. They took advantage of the American free public education system and worked hard to seek possibilities for their children's future.[6] The Depression destroyed the expectations of many Chinese immigrants.

The reinforcement of racial discrimination during the Depression also jeopardized the desire of young generation Chinese immigrants to build up their careers in the United States. They were born in the United States, went to American schools, and were educated in colleges. Many of them made "every effort to be as American as possible." Some gave up Chinese schools against their parents' will in an attempt to fit in society. Yet the cruel reality made them desperate. They ended up working as truck drivers, potato sorters, or busboys. Lily, a law major at Barnard College who did not give her full name during an interview, said that she was looking for a job in American law firms after her graduation. After an unsuccessful search in her profession, she was prepared to accept any kind of job. However, she could not find a position, even as a salesgirl in a Manhattan department store: at the job interview, she had been informed that she could not be hired because she was "Chinese." She told the interviewer that she was born in the United States, but treated like a foreigner.[7]

As the job competition intensified, racial barriers escalated for Chinese American college graduates in their search for careers in society. They were not trusted even by a government agency. Y., a college graduate who specialized in engineering, was told by his job interviewer from the New York State government that he could not get the job he applied for because it would be too tough for him to handle American workers.[8]

Second-generation Chinese immigrants were upset about racial discrimination. Commenting on the racially exclusionary trend in the job market during the Depression, Flora Belle Jan, a Chinese American college graduate, wrote scornfully in 1931 that "with thousands of fair-haired, blue-eyed collegians . . . looking for a job," there was apparently "little chance for Chinese American youth" to squeeze in.[9]

The reinforced racial discrimination made it difficult for American-born Chinese college graduates to receive a position in the tightened job market. With few or no job prospects in the society at large, Chinese American college graduates had no choice but to look for opportunities within the Chinese community. For example, Thomas Low, a college graduate, received "a clerkship in a Chinese shop" after he failed to get a professional job outside his own ethnic community. Low was described as a brilliant and hardworking student. His professors and schoolmates predicted "a wonderful future" for him when he was a junior college student. He himself was confident that he would get a position "in an American firm" after graduating from college. However, he eventually ended up working in a Chinese store in New York's Chinatown.[10]

Others participated in family businesses directly after graduating from college as a way to survive. They followed the occupations of their fathers in storekeeping, or in the restaurant and laundry business. Peter Lee became involved in his family's tea trading business in New York's Chinatown after he graduated from Columbia University.[11] A 1932 Massachusetts Institute of Technology graduate returned to New York only to find himself working in a meat-packing company, taking orders from Chinese restaurants and stores.[12]

There were various other responses to the desperate situation. Some became disillusioned. Others decided to leave the country to which they once pledged. Frustrated with the situation in which they were trapped and disillusioned by the lack of job prospects in the society at large, a few Chinese American college graduates became cynical. Some, like Fred Wong, with a master's degree in commerce, took to gambling. They were seen as "always playing *Ma Jiang* in a corner bazaar in Chinatown" after being repeatedly rejected for jobs.[13] Others left the United States. "Going West . . . further west . . . across the Pacific to China" became an outcry of angry Chinese American youth as they felt the American dream of freedom and prosperity was not available to them.[14] A Chinese American college graduate told a reporter after he decided to go to China that, after having "absorbed a bitter diet of racial prejudice," he could not be happy living in the United States anymore. He decided to leave the United States after his career advancement had been limited by racial intolerance in the job market.[15] An American-born college student was engaged to a native-born Chinese college student and decided to go with him back to China after their graduation as she felt that China was the "only place for American born college graduates to live." In China, she said, "we can be somebody. We can even walk the streets without being stared at." There they had a feeling of "belonging" that was "absent in American."[16] An estimated 20 percent of the American-born Chinese went to China in the 1930s.[17]

Depending on education as a solution to their problems failed. Realizing that their isolation compounded the problem during the Depression and education alone could not rescue them from racial discrimination, second-generation Chinese immigrants increasingly turned to political participation as a means of protecting themselves. This growing political consciousness was demonstrated by their involvement in American politics in the 1930s. At the same time, new Chinese American political organizations emerged during this period to engage more of New York's Chinese in American mainstream activities.

Chinese American Political Organizations

The economic depression in the 1930s, combined with years of racist prejudice and denial of rights, shaped the existing political conscience. The growing political consciousness of New York's Chinese to participate in American politics was demonstrated by such organizations as the Chinese American Citizens Alliance, the New York Chinese American Voting League, and the New York Chinese American Committee of the National Democratic Party. Participating in New York local political campaigns and in both the 1932 and the 1936 presidential elections, these groups brought eligible voters from New York's Chinatown into electoral politics.

New York Chinese performed their American civic duties particularly by casting their votes in political elections. They did it not only to justify their citizenship, but also to impress on society that they were worthy of this privilege. Furthermore, they used the opportunity to protect their own interests as well. Political activists and their organizations involved Chinese immigrants in American mainstream politics to break down the political silence of New York's Chinese community. No longer confined within their own ethnic community as a means of protection, New York Chinese began to reach out and to involve themselves in American society.

The ardent participation of these organizations in American mainstream politics reflected the expanding political consciousness of New York's Chinese Americans. By participating in general American activities, they not only challenged the traditional ways in which Chinese immigrants had dealt with a hostile society, but also claimed the political rights of American citizenship denied by the exclusion policies.

The Chinese American Citizens Alliance (CACA)

The Chinese American Citizens Alliance was one of the first Chinese American political organizations determined to exercise the political rights of ethnic Chinese who were American citizens. Originally formed in 1916 as an independent organization by a group of American-born Chinese in New York and situated at 6 Mott Street, in the center of Chinatown, this organization took the lead in exercising the political rights of Chinese Americans.[18] Its wartime efforts to support American military recruitment and to endorse the purchase of war bonds during the Great War, as well as its peacetime efforts to participate in New York local political campaigns right after the war, demonstrated the early emergence of the political consciousness of Chinese Americans for civil rights.

They continued their political efforts during the economic depression in the 1930s. Struggling to survive the Depression, the CACA pursued a new political strategy. More ambitious than before, it involved New York's Chinatown residents in the two major national presidential elections. In the meantime it also endeavored to mobilize the people to support the New Deal programs. By 1936, the Chinese American Citizens Alliance had a new leader, Liu Xuechao.[19]

Background

To look at the legacy of its political practices in the 1930s, we need to go back to World War I to see how the CACA began its involvement in American politics. The assassination of the Archduke Franz Ferdinand, heir to the throne of the Austro-Hungarian Empire, in 1914 sparked the war and it quickly spread over the European continent, engaging the armies of almost all major European nations. Most Americans looked on with horror and kept their distance from it until 1917, when the government of the United States formally entered the war in support of the Allies against the Central Powers. Both sides were exhausted by the end of war. It was a painful, even traumatic experience for the American people. They were disillusioned as the "war to end wars," and the war "to make the world safe for democracy," became neither. Instead, it led to the years of international instability that ultimately generated another world war.

Yet Chinese Americans' support of the war should not be justified by justification of the war itself. Despite years of denial of their rights and obligations as citizens, they participated in the war propaganda and went to the war front to protect against racial discrimination. They were motivated by American patriotism and ready to serve the country they pledged to. More important, they exercised their duty to actively participate in war affairs to demonstrate they were loyal American citizens.

New York Chinese Americans cooperated with the government war agenda. Early in 1916, when the United States was waging war against the Central Powers, the CACA was actively involved in U.S. government war propaganda. Members of the CACA put up advertisements along streets and organized rallies in Chinatown in support of American war engagement.[20] When the United States entered the war, the alliance urged young Chinese Americans to join the American army to claim the rights of citizenship by serving their country. Consequently, many of New York's Chinese Americans signed up to join the army. According to the *Chinese Reform News*, approximately 10 percent of soldiers who were recruited from New York were Chinese Americans.[21]

To make the Chinese American recruitment an important community event, the CACA organized rallies to attract and mobilize Chinatown residents to join in the national event. It cosponsored a big parade in New York's Chinatown on September 29, 1917, to honor the new recruits. Fifty newly recruited soldiers were in the front marching in the street.[22] Joining the

American army was also an important family event. Recruits had their pictures taken and there were parties to honor them as well.[23]

In addition to encouraging young Chinese Americans to exercise their right as citizens to join the army to serve the United States, the CACA also organized activities to inspire Chinese New Yorkers to purchase war bonds. Its war bond purchase drive on October 10, 1917, was a particular success. More than ten young Chinese Americans with the leader of the campaign, Lee Shuhen, went on the street to persuade Chinese New Yorkers to fulfill their "duty and obligation" as American citizens and to make contributions for the country. As a result, $2,000 worth of war bonds were bought on that day by New York's Chinatown residents.[24]

Scholars try to understand the goal of Chinese Americans in the participation. Commenting on duties and rights of Chinese Americans, some suggest that because of being excluded by society, Chinese Americans focused more on rights rather than duties in their struggle to be received as citizens by society. They "fought for their rights—the right to be in the United States, the right to vote, and the right to own property."[25] Yet New York Chinese Americans did not separate rights from duties. They exercised duties to claim their rights as American citizens.

Members of the CACA took the right to vote seriously. Everyone born in the United States and everyone naturalized was automatically a citizen and entitled to equal protection of the laws by both state and national government. It was constitutionally protected and part of citizenship requirements. Avoiding the right to vote meant the self-denial of citizens. It was crucial to exercise their rights to vote to claim their citizenship.

The CACA committed itself to political activities especially in elections. It engaged itself in the first postwar local political elections. The years 1917–1918 marked an election year for both the state and the city government of New York. Republicans and Democrats were competing at both levels. New York Chinese responded differently accordingly. Some presented their favorite for the Republicans. Others showed their sympathy to the Democrats. The CACA gave its support to the two Democratic and Tammany candidates, Alfred E. Smith and John F. Hylan, in their campaigns for New York governor and mayor of New York City, respectively.

The CACA tried to use their votes to influence politicians to improve conditions in Chinatown. They supported Alfred E. Smith because he was a popular man due to his enthusiastic support of progressive reform. His commitment to the improvement of working conditions and the adoption of workmen's compensation appealed to New York's Chinese community. They supported John F. Hylan, the Democratic nominee for New York City mayor, because he not only demonstrated his concern about the overcrowding of classrooms in public schools, but also showed his sympathy to underrepresented minorities.[26]

In order to encourage all eligible Chinese American voters to participate in elections as a means of protecting their political rights, the CACA suggested the two reliable nominees by putting up big posters along Chinatown streets, urging the Chinese community to give its support to the Democratic candidates.[27] In addition, it also organized mass meetings to publicize the elections. On October 31, 1917, the CACA held a mass meeting to engage New York's Chinese American voters in the local government elections. Reminding them that "every Chinese who was born in the United States has the right to vote," the CACA advocated for the casting of votes by Chinese Americans.[28]

For more than three decades following the Exclusion Law of 1882, racism frustrated Chinese Americans' efforts to become involved in American mainstream politics. Staying away from possible entanglement with the world outside the Chinese community became part of the protective measures of Chinese immigrants. Moreover, eligible voters in New York's Chinatown were hesitant to use their vote, feeling that racism and their small numbers made the vote an empty privilege. By contrast, the CACA encouraged all eligible Chinese Americans to participate in the election and promised that New York's Chinese community would enjoy "happiness and prosperity" and the "Chinese Americans would benefit" if Smith and Hylan won.[29]

For the first time in history, the CACA linked the welfare of the Chinese community to that of society at large. Convincing Chinese American voters that good politicians would benefit the Chinese community, the CACA mobilized Chinese Americans to participate in the local elections. Similarly, by engaging this constituency in mainstream politics, the CACA also challenged the self-imposed isolation of New York's Chinatown residents. Both its wartime and peacetime efforts demonstrated the growing political energy of the second-generation Chinese immigrants to identify themselves as American citizens.

CACA in the 1930s

As a spearhead of the integration movement, the CACA committed itself to awakening Chinese Americans to be responsible citizens of the United States. During the two decades following its establishment, the CACA remained an active and independent political organization in New York's Chinatown. When the country was hit by economic catastrophe in the 1930s, the CACA reorganized in order to adjust itself to the political climate.

In the midst of the economic crises, the CACA's new political agenda was to endorse New Deal legislation and its programs such as the National Industrial Recovery Act. The challenge of rescuing the industrial economy from the spiraling deflation of the early 1930s was important to the new Roosevelt administration. Accepting the consensus among economic experts, the Roosevelt administration took steps allowing trade associations to cooperate in stabilizing prices within their industries. It also ensured a major program of public works spending designed to pump needed funds into the economy. The CACA saw the NIRA as a crusade designed to restore employment. Committing itself to the support of the New Deal program, the CACA extended its effort to get involved in the National Recovery Administration's organized activities. It sent its members to participate in mainstream mass parades and rallies and to display the Blue Eagle emblem signs of the NRA to catch public attention.[30]

The NRA leadership appreciated the involvement of the CACA in the NRA programs. On October 5, 1933, the New York City NRA authority sent a letter to the CACA, complimenting the association on its contributions to NRA efforts to bring about economic recovery. In this letter, other Chinese organizations, such as the Chinese Laundromat Association and the Chinese American Aviation Association, were also praised for their commitment to the NIRA.[31]

The reorganized CACA became an even stronger political association in the 1930s, continuously committing itself to inspiring Chinese Americans to use their votes as a way of integrating into society. It kept its legacy to commit itself to local politics. The year 1933 was an election year for New York City government. During the election campaign, a Republican, Fiorello H. La Guardia, emerged as a strong political figure. Committed to fighting corruption and to reorganizing city government, La Guardia received major support from his rival party, the Democratic Party.[32] The CACA had been pro-Democratic. Considering the campaign program prominent to the Chinese community, the CACA, among other Democratic organizations, gave its support to La Guardia, the Republic-fusion candidate in his mayoral campaign, hoping he would contribute to the benefit of Chinese Americans.[33]

The outcome of the election pleased Chinese New Yorkers. Drawing upon voters who saw the urgency for reform, Fiorello H. La Guardia won. The CACA hailed the victory of La Guardia with a high expectation. Chen Changsong, the English secretary, sent La Guardia a telegraph congratulating him on behalf of the CACA.[34] Although greatly exaggerating their importance to his victory as La Guardia won major votes from Italian and Jewish communities, the CACA expressed its expectations for the future of the New York's Chinese community under La Guardia's new administration:

> During the local election, the Chinese American Citizens Alliance committed itself to the support of Mr. Fiorello H. La Guardia. As a consequence, Mr. La Guardia won this election. We hope Mr. La Guardia, as a new New York mayor, will contribute to the welfare of Chinese Americans.[35]

The Republican Party received the commitment of the CACA and its support of La Guardia. Right after the election early in November 1933, the CACA received a letter from Mr. Maylon, one of the campaign managers for La Guardia. In his letter, Mr. Maylon expressed his appreciation for Chinese American efforts on behalf of La Guardia.[36] In particular, Mr. Maylon praised Ni Zhoupin, a Chinese American political advocate, for his commitment to the successful political campaign:

> Mr. Ni Zhoupin was one of the first Chinese Americans who ardently participated in the election. His effort tremendously helped in the political campaign movement. . . . I could not find a better way to express my personal appreciation for the great effort that Mr. Ni Zhoupin made to bring the championship for Mr. La Guardia.[37]

Ni was honored and invited to the campaign headquarters to celebrate the event on November 8, 1933.

More important, however, the CACA was involved in both the 1932 and the 1936 national presidential elections. The involvement of Chinese New Yorkers in national politics demonstrated their insistence on political democracy and their intention to be included in the mainstream political system. Cooperating with the New York Chinese American Voting League, the CACA played an important role in securing Chinese American votes for the Democratic candidate, Franklin D. Roosevelt, in his 1932 campaign. Again, in 1936, joining the New York Chinese American Committee of the National Democratic Party in an effort to support Roosevelt in his second-term election, the CACA helped secure more Chinese American votes. With the assistance of these Chinese American political organizations, Roosevelt successfully polled a huge majority in New York's Chinese community for his reelection, approximately three out of every four eligible Chinese voters.[38]

The actual involvement of Chinese Americans represented by the CACA in both local and national politics demonstrated an attitude toward American mainstream politics changing from disengagement to involvement. Claiming their rights as American citizens by adopting participation as a tactic, the CACA extended its political activities in the 1930s and engaged more of New York's Chinese residents in integrating into society. Following the CACA's lead, more Chinese American political organizations emerged during this period. One such organization was the New York Chinese American Voting League.

The New York Chinese American Voting League (NYCAVL)

The ferment of the Great Depression generated political activists and their organizations in New York's Chinese community. There were about eight thousand documented Chinese Americans in New York in 1930 and many more undocumented Chinese whose children would eventually have the right to vote.[39] Perceiving a potential political constituency among this population, both the Republican and the Democratic parties began to move to the Chinese community looking for possible votes. They cooperated with Chinese American political advocates just as the new organizations advocated political involvement in American society. The New York Chinese American Voting League (NYCAVL) was one of these leading political organizations.[40]

The NYCAVL was formed in 1932. Like the CACA, it was determined to assist Chinese New Yorkers in claiming their rights as American citizens by participating in the national election campaigns. Like general Americans, Chinatown residents were divided between the Republicans and Democrats. As with the Americans, the same motives impelled each of the groups. The wealthier Chinese Americans believed that the Republican Party would preserve their status, while those who wanted changes hoped the Democrats would win so they could get better positions. As the 1932 presidential election approached, political advocates felt the urgency to organize.

Like the CACA, the NYCAVL gave its support to the Democratic Party and its candidate, Franklin Delano Roosevelt. Franklin Roosevelt had already been a well-known figure in the party for years. He initiated positive programs of government when he served as the governor of New York. Emphasizing the economic grievances that most Democrats shared enabled him to win his party's nomination. In the course of his campaign against Herbert Hoover, he challenged the Republican Party by portraying the economic crisis as a domestic problem and argued that the most important solutions could be found at home. He pledged and convinced the Americans with a new deal to the economic problems. In the first three years of the Great Depression, the New York Chinese community suffered tremendous losses. Not content with the Republican policies that insisted the Depression was international in origin and that any attempt to combat it must be international, the NYCAVL believed Franklin D. Roosevelt's campaign policies would be more helpful to its community than the policies of Hoover's administration.

In its support of the Democratic Party, the NYCAVL wasted no time to campaign for the election right after its establishment. Members of the league put up big posters to draw the attention of the public and to get out the votes for Roosevelt. It organized mass meetings to encourage eligible Chinese Americans to vote.

The league also cooperated with the Democratic Party during the presidential campaign, inviting Democratic politicians to speak at its conventions. Affiliating itself with the Democratic Party, the New York Chinese American Voting League represented a new way for Chinese New Yorkers to assert their civil rights as Americans. As the Election Day was approaching, the NYCAVL intensified its efforts. On October 31, 1932, the NYCAVL held a big convention for the Chinese Americans on the East Coast to come to New York's Chinatown in support of Roosevelt.

The convention proved to be a success. More than three hundred people attended.[41] Representatives of the Democratic Party and important pro-Democratic community leaders made presentations at the gathering. In order to highlight the political alliance with the Democrats, a way of political integration, the league invited party representatives to speak at the convention.[42] Ma Kangming, a Chinese community leader, also gave an impressive speech. Unlike other speakers, who emphasized Roosevelt's New Deal domestic policies, Ma's speech focused on Roosevelt's foreign policy toward China. Like other immigrant groups who supported American candidates with policies sympathetic to their homeland, his description of Roosevelt's support for the territorial integrity and political sovereignty of China aroused Chinese immigrants.

Nationalism aroused New York Chinese over China's Shandong territory and gathered support for Roosevelt. Chinese New Yorkers related themselves to their homeland in China. The nationalist feelings for China among the American Chinese increased when the news came that the Paris Peace Conference had agreed to transfer Germany's concessions in China's Shandong province to Japan as an agreement to end World War I. The Chinese on both sides of the Pacific were outraged. They protested against the treaty. They went on demonstrations to respond to the "Shandong decision," demanding the return of the territory back to China to maintain the integrity of the country. As a partial consequence of the protests, the United States initiated a negotiation among big powers in Washington to pledge an integrated China and the continuation of its open door policy in China.[43] Roosevelt's promise to carry on the Nine Nation's Treaty of the Washington Conference, which advocated pressing Japan to return Chinese territory to China, gained a lot of support from the Chinese American community.[44]

The NYCAVL made another great effort to ensure Chinese American votes for Roosevelt. On November 7, the NYCAVL organized a rally in New York's Chinatown, urging "every Chinese American" to cast his vote for the Democratic Party candidate, Franklin D. Roosevelt. According to the *Chinese Nationalist Daily*, participants were inspired and they pledged their support for the Democratic Party.[45]

During the 1932 political campaigns, the NYCAVL received enthusiastic support from the *Chinese Nationalist Daily* in its endorsement of the Democratic Party. The *Daily* was a local Chinese newspaper. Published in Chinese, it carried news related to the New York Chinese community and the Chinese communities in other cities in the United States. Business activities, political events, and cultural performances were the major topics covered by the newspaper. In addition, it also provided information about the political and economic situation in China, as New York Chinese were very much concerned about their home country.

By the early 1930s, the paper shifted its coverage from the local and overseas to what was happening in the United States, directing the attention of New York's Chinese to events in the larger society. In 1932, it increased its effort to involve Chinese New Yorkers in the national election through publishing more articles and editorials concerning such social issues as Prohibition and unemployment. On August 1, 1932, the *Chinese Nationalist Daily* reported a political debate on social issues, indicating that the New Deal proposal was more applicable than the policies of Hoover's administration to the current situation.[46] On August 27, it published an article favorably analyzing Roosevelt's proposal to end Prohibition.

The *Daily* cooperated with the NYCAVL to intensify its efforts to bring more votes for FDR in the following months. On November 2, 1932, it published a long editorial on the differences between Franklin Roosevelt and Herbert Hoover. Indicating that Roosevelt's solutions to the current devastating economic situation would open more opportunities to the jobless and benefit the Chinese community, it encouraged Chinese Americans to vote for Roosevelt.[47]

To the surprise of no one, Roosevelt won a big victory. The result was overwhelming, with most states for him except a few northeastern states in the Electoral College. Democrats also won majorities in both houses of Congress. On November 10, the *Chinese Nationalist Daily* released the results of the election, hailing the Democratic Party's landslide. According to the news report, Franklin D. Roosevelt, the newly elected president of the United

States, gained 14,217,414 votes, which was 57.4 percent of the popular vote to Hoover's 37 percent.[48] At the same time, the *Daily* also hailed those Chinese American voters who cast their votes for Franklin Roosevelt.[49]

The big victory for Franklin D. Roosevelt demonstrated the popularity of his political and economic policies as persuasive solutions to the economic crisis. It also indicated the desire of the devastated Americans, including Chinese Americans, for radical change.

The Chinese American Voting League played an important role in bringing in Chinese American voters for Franklin D. Roosevelt. Even though there was no figure to document the actual votes of Chinese New Yorkers in this election, the positive commitment and efforts of the organization in the 1932 presidential election demonstrated a tremendous change in the political behavior of Chinese Americans. No longer driven by fear, New York's Chinese Americans stepped out of isolation to seek the political recognition of society through active involvement in American mainstream politics. This new political trend continued, and in 1936, when the nation was preparing for another presidential election, Chinese New Yorkers again participated.

The New York Chinese American Committee of the National Democratic Party (NYCAC)

The year 1936 marked another national presidential election year. The Republicans nominated Governor Alfred M. Landon of Kansas; the Democrats, meanwhile, renominated Franklin D. Roosevelt. In order to cooperate with the Democrats' campaign to reelect President Roosevelt, pro-Democratic Chinese American activists rallied once more. As a consequence, the New York Chinese American Committee of the National Democratic Party (NYCAC) came into being.[50] Like the CACA and the NYCAVL, the NYCAC also stressed the empowerment of Chinese Americans through participation. More significantly, Chinese Americans once again linked their political activities with mainstream events. The claim of the affiliation of the NYCAC with the Democratic Party reflected the desire of Chinese American political activists to integrate with the larger society.

President Roosevelt and his New Deal programs enjoyed popularity. The administration's attack on the injustice of big business companies and the tax reforms that targeted the rich received support of many Americans. The Wagner Act that provided workers with more federal protection and the Social Security Act that ensured federally sponsored social insurance for the elderly and the unemployed appealed to many Americans as well. Like general Americans, Chinese New Yorkers saw hope in the Roosevelt administration.

Second-generation Chinese immigrants experienced certain improvement during Roosevelt's first term. The establishment of the WPA Writers' Project and the Civil Works Administration (CWA) provided Chinese Americans with job opportunities. Chinese New Yorkers, like other Chinese American youth across the country, served in the programs. A member of CWA recalled the joyfulness of his position in the program, saying that as "one of the many Chinese who joined up the program," he found the pay good and he was happy to be treated "like a white man."[51] Chinese American youth were involved in the WPA Writers' Project. They received chances to interview and write the experiences of Chinatown residents. Thomas Chow, for example, interviewed young Chinese American college graduates in New York City in 1934.[52] The records of interviews have become valuable historical documents written by Chinese Americans themselves.

There have been debates on the legacy of Roosevelt's first administration. Some criticized the unwillingness of the Roosevelt administration to provide substantial assistance to minorities, especially the African Americans, to improve race relations because of his consideration of the support of southern Democrats. They were convinced that New Deal relief agencies did not challenge, and in many case reinforced, existing patterns of discrimination. The Civilian Conservation Corps established separate black camps. The WPA routinely relegated black, Hispanic, and Asian workers to the least-skilled and lowest-paying jobs. When funding ebbed, they were the first to be dismissed. However, the administration did much to help them advance. The president himself appointed a number of African Americans to significant second-level positions to create a network of officeholders for political consultations known as the "Black Cabinet." Eleanor Roosevelt spoke openly on behalf racial justice and put continuous pressure on the government to ease discrimination against minorities, especially blacks and women.

Many Chinese Americans saw the progress in the Roosevelt administration and expected improvement for the Chinese community. They decided to give their support to Roosevelt to run for the second term. The establishment of the NYCAC reflected the desire of those Chinese Americans. Situated at 47 Mott Street in Chinatown, the NYCAC immediately set to work for Roosevelt's reelection. Members of the party initiated such activities as putting up portraits of Franklin D. Roosevelt along the streets of New York's Chinatown to draw Chinatown residents' attention to the election. They also put up big signs that read "Vote for a Gallant Leader President Franklin D. Roosevelt" in the Chinese community.[53]

In order to involve as many Chinese American voters as possible in the campaign, the NYCAC emphasized the right of Chinese Americans to vote and urged New York's Chinese to vote for Roosevelt:

> It is the time for Chinese Americans to register for the election. Eligible voters should not abandon your right to participate. Exercise your franchise! Come on and hurry up! Let us work together to bring about the reelection of President Roosevelt.[54]

This message sent a strong signal to the whole community. Committed to political participation, the NYCAC hoped its effort would persuade New York Chinatown residents to join them. The NYCAC also organized campaign rallies to urge Chinese Americans to take part in the political process. The one on October 17, 1936, was an example of such activities.

The *Chinese Nationalist Daily* reported this event. According to the newspaper, this rally was another cooperative effort of the NYCAC and Democrats. To make the rally a big event so as to draw potential Chinese American voters to the Democratic Party, the NYCAC invited both community activists and politicians from the Democratic Party to join them at the rally. Important Chinese community leaders such as Li Gongxing and Li Shengtse presented at the rally.[55] Delegates from the Democratic Party were invited to speak to the public in the New York Chinese community to consolidate the cooperation of Chinese New Yorkers and Democrats in the election.[56]

To advance the integration into mainstream politics, the NYCAC also extended its campaign activities to the larger society. When Democrats organized activities to support their party candidate, the NYCAC urged New York Chinese to participate. In one such event on October 20, it mobilized New York's Chinese Americans to participate in a citywide pro-Democratic parade. A local Chinese newspaper reported that approximately twenty thousand "working class New Yorkers" joined the rally in support of Roosevelt. Among them were Chinese Americans.[57]

During the 1936 presidential election, the *Chinese Nationalist Daily* once again played an important role in politically involving Chinatown residents in American society. It rallied with the New York Chinese American Committee of the National Democratic Party to support the Democratic reelection. Columns of the newspaper were devoted to portraying the achievements of the Roosevelt administration and the significance of the New Deal measures.

Media influenced and, in many cases, played an important role in shaping the public opinions. Pardee Lowe, a Chinese American in the 1930s, believed that it was not only the newspapers in Chinese in Chinese communities across the United States that provided information and analyses of the current political events, but the newspapers in mainstream also played a crucial part in bringing news to Chinese American families, especially those who were professionals. Reliance "mainly based upon the reading of the American daily newspapers for outside news" became a custom for them.[58] K. Scott Wong also suggested that as those born and educated in the United States, second-generation Chinese immigrants were most comfortable speaking English. They usually turned to the English-language presses for resources as they were consciously reflective on the social and political changes they were experiencing.[59] However, the majority of New York Chinatown residents relied on the local Chinese newspaper as a major source that assisted them to understand events in mainstream politics. Understanding the vital role of newspapers, the *Chinese Nationalist Daily* continued its coverage on the political events in the larger society, especially during the 1930s national elections.

On September 17, 1936, George Chinton, a pro-Democratic Chinese American activist, contributed a lengthy article to the *Chinese Nationalist Daily* reviewing Roosevelt's domestic policies benefiting New York's Chinese community:

> Only three years have passed since President Roosevelt has taken over the government. Within such a short time, due to his painstaking effort, all kinds of business have entered a state of recovery. . . . Our Chinese business, for instance, is doing much better than before.[60]

Chinton's newspaper article also caught the attention of the readers who were concerned about the foreign policy of Roosevelt administration and the future relations between the United States and China. Ensuring the better relationship between the two countries under Roosevelt leadership, Chinton called on Chinese Americans to support President Roosevelt for his second-term reelection. He concluded:

> The time for presidential election is near. When November 7 comes, let all Chinese Americans vote for him. I sincerely believe that our welfare will be enhanced, and relations between China and the United States will become closer.[61]

To inspire eligible New York Chinese to vote, more newspaper articles and editorials concerning various social and economic issues followed. On October 9, the *Chinese Nationalist Daily* hailed Roosevelt's promise not to increase taxes.[62] On October 24, the local Chinese newspaper reported the advantages of the bank deposit policy.[63] On October 30, it published a poll on popular opinion on the Republican and Democratic presidential nominees, which indicated the public's favorable view of Roosevelt.[64] The day before Election Day, the *Chinese Nationalist Daily* made a final drive to involve more Chinese New Yorkers in the election. It published an editorial crediting Roosevelt with the New Deal's program to assist unemployed workers and farmers.[65]

The local Chinese newspaper's constant reports and coverage of various mainstream issues reflected shifting interests and attitudes of New York's Chinatown residents to political events in the larger society. The commitment of the *Chinese Nationalist Daily* and its endorsement of the New York Chinese American Committee of the National Democratic Party contributed to the shift. Their effort to support the Democratic reelection was received with much appreciation by the Democratic Party. To recognize the endeavor of the Chinese American organization, the New York Democrats held a special party for Li Wen on October 29, 1936, honoring this pro-Democratic Chinese community leader for his ardent commitment to Franklin D. Roosevelt's reelection.[66]

The outcome of the 1936 presidential election was another landslide for President Roosevelt. He won almost twenty-eight million popular votes to Landon's sixteen and a half million. The victory once more demonstrated the popularity of Roosevelt and his New Deal. About one thousand Chinese Americans in New York cast their votes for President Roosevelt.[67] It was the genuine effort of the New York Chinese American Committee of the National Democratic Party that brought in so many Chinese American votes for Roosevelt.

A historian has estimated that of those New York Chinese Americans who voted, nearly 75 percent cast their ballots in favor of Franklin D. Roosevelt's second-term presidency.[68] Other Chinese New Yorkers endorsed the Republican Party in the 1936 national presidential election. Like pro-Democratic New York's Chinese, pro-Republican advocates also organized to encourage Chinatown residents to participate in mainstream politics. They assured eligible voters that there was no need for them to take an English test to register, and encouraged those who had lived in New York since 1921 and were thirty-five years of age to do so.[69] As a result, "a lot of Chinese Americans registered as Republicans" during the election.[70]

As the election was drawing closer, a pro-Republican organization put an advertisement in the *Chinese Nationalist Daily*, urging Chinese Americans to cast their votes for the Republican candidate.[71] There is no record of how many of New York's Chinese voted for the Republican Party in the 1936 national election. But the evidence shows the growing political consciousness of New York's Chinese Americans, both pro-Democratic and pro-Republican in their participation in the election.

Conclusion

The Depression in the 1930s was a severe shock to New York Chinese Americans. It induced despair and frustration as the Depression reinforced racial discrimination. Educated young Chinese Americans found it more difficult for them to integrate into society. However, the hard times also mobilized them to search for solutions.

Understanding that fear and panic would not prepare them for their future life in the United States, New York's Chinese Americans became increasingly interested in American mainstream politics rather than remaining concerned with the politics of their own ethnic community. This growing political interest was demonstrated in their enthusiasm to organize political associations and engage in mainstream political activities.

The burgeoning of such organizations as the Chinese American Citizens Alliance, the New York Chinese American Voting League, and the New York Chinese American Committee of the National Democratic Party was a manifestation of the growing self-consciousness of New York Chinese as Americans. In their effort to gain the recognition of society at large, these organizations actively participated in important American political campaigns of the 1930s.

The involvement of Chinese Americans in American mainstream politics constituted a movement that moved them toward integration into society. The profound changes in the political behavior of Chinese Americans from disengagement to participation characterized their political consciousness in the 1930s.

Notes

1. L. Eve Armentrout Ma, *Revolutionaries, Monarchists and Chinatowns: Chinese Politics in the Americas and the 1911 Revolution* (Honolulu: Hawaii University Press, 1990); Him Mark Lai, *The Chinese of America 1785–1980* (San Francisco: Chinese Culture Foundation, 1980); Gloria H. Chun, "'Go West . . . To China': Chinese American Identity in the 1930's," in *Claiming America: Constructing Chinese American Identities during the Exclusion Era*, ed. K. Scott Wong and Sucheng Chan (Philadelphia: Temple University Press, 1998), 174

2. John Dollard, *Caste and Class in a Southern Town*, second ed. (Madison: University of Wisconsin Press, 1957); Cheryl Lynn Greenberg, *"Or Does It Explode?": Black Harlem in the Great Depression* (New York: Oxford University Press, 1991).

3. Cheryl Lynn Greenberg, *"Or Does It Explode?": Black Harlem in the Great Depressing* (New York: Oxford University Press, 1991).

4. Abraham Hoffman, *Unwanted Mexican Americans in the Great Depression* (Tucson: University of Arizona Press, 1974).

5. Pardee Lowe, "Second-Generation Dilemma, 1930's," in *Chinese American Voices: From Gold Rush to the Present*, ed. Judy Yung, Gordon H. Chang, and Him Mark Lai (Berkeley: University of California Press, 2006), 167.

6. After finishing grammar school, the majority of the younger generation of Chinese immigrants was forced to drop out of school and to join the workforce to help their families. However, some managed to continue their education. Approximately two thousand registered in American public schools and colleges in the early 1930s. Flora Belle Jan, "An American-Born Looks at Young Chinatown," *Chinese Christian Student*, Jan. 1931, 1.

7. Thomas Chow, "Interview with Young Chinese American College Graduates in 1934," Chinese in NYC, WPA Writers' Project, Folder #48 (New York City: New York Municipal Archives), Microfilm.

8. Hsuan Julia Chen, "The Chinese Community in New York, 1920–1940" (Ph.D. Dissertation, Washington, D.C.: American University, 1941), 91. A few young Chinese American college students received job offers. They immediately found that they were unable to continue to work because of harassment.

An Armour Institute of Technology student secured a job in a radio company only to find the company bankrupt a few months after he was hired. See Flora Belle Jan, "An American-Born Looks at Young Chinatown," *Chinese Christian Student*, Jan. 1931, 7.

9. Ibid., 7.

10. Ibid.

11. Chinatown Historical Museum Archives, Museum of Chinese in America.

12. Hsuan Julia Chen, "The Chinese Community in New York, 1920–1940" (Ph.D. Dissertation, Washington, D.C.: American University, 1941), 91.

13. Flora Belle Jan, "An American-Born Looks at Young Chinatown," *Chinese Christian Student*, Jan. 1931, 7.

The *Chinese Christian Student* was published monthly from 1927 to 1947 by the Chinese Students' Christian Association in North America, founded in 1909. It was located at 347 Madison Avenue, New York City. Vungyuin Ting was the president of the organization in 1936. Rockwood Chin was the treasurer. Wen Hsien Chen was the secretary. Y. E. Hsiao was the general secretary. Arthur A. Young was the editor of the newsletter.

14. Gloria Heyung Chun, *Of Orphans and Warriors: Inventing Chinese American Culture and Identity* (New Brunswick, N.J.: Rutgers University Press, 2000), 15.

15. Sucheng Chan, *Asian Americans: An Interpretive History* (Boston: Twayne Publishers, 1991), 115.

16. Pardee Lowe, "Second-Generation Dilemma, 1930's," in *Chinese American Voices: From the Gold Rush to the Present*, ed. Judy Yung, Gordon H. Chang, and Him Mark Lai (Berkeley: University of California Press, 2006), 169.

17. Gloria H. Chun, "'Go West . . . To China': Chinese American Identity in the 1930's," in *Claiming America: Constructing Chinese American Identities during the Exclusion Era*, ed. K. Scott Wong and Sucheng Chan (Philadelphia: Temple University Press, 1998), 174.

18. Earlier in 1895, the Chinese American Citizens Alliance in San Francisco was established to improve the sociopolitical status of the American-born Chinese. As political organizations, both advocated for the rights of Chinese Americans.

19. *Chinese Nationalist Daily*, Nov. 20, 1936.

20. *Chinese Reform News* (*Zhong Guo Wei Xin Bao*), June 4, 1919.

21. *Chinese Reform News*, Sept. 26, 1917.

22. *Chinese Reform News*, Sept. 29, 1917.

23. Ibid. According to the *Chinese Reform News*, those who were recruited by the army were proud to have an opportunity to serve the country as Americans.

24. *Chinese Reform News*, Oct. 24, 1917.

25. Sucheng Chan, *Asian Americans: An Interpretive History* (Boston: Twayne Publishers, 1991); Shehong Chen, *Being Chinese, Becoming Chinese Americans* (Champaign: Illinois University Press, 2002), 123.

26. There was no historical evidence to document his contact with Chinese Americans. However, John F. Hylan became the first New York chief executive to hold conferences with blacks. Frederick M. Binder and David M. Reimers, *All the Nations under Heaven: An Ethnic and Racial History of New York City* (New York: Columbia University Press, 1995), 168.

27. Ibid.

28. *Chinese Reform News*, Oct. 31, 1917.

29. Ibid.

30. *Chinese Nationalist Daily*, Oct. 5, 1933.

31. Ibid.

32. Thomas Kessner, *Fiorello H. La Guardia and the Making of Modern New York* (New York: McGraw-Hill Publishing Company, 1989); Chris Mcnickle, *To Be Mayor of New York* (New York: Columbia University Press, 1992).

33. *Chinese Nationalist Daily*, Nov. 8, 1933.

34. Ibid.

35. Ibid.

36. Ibid. This is the translation of the Chinese newspaper in Chinese. The full name of Maylon was not given.

37. Ibid.

38. Hsuan Julia Chen, "The Chinese Community in New York, 1920–1940" (Ph.D. Dissertation, Washington, D.C.: American University, 1941), 98–99.

39. According to U.S. Bureau of the Census data, there were 1,926 American-born Chinese and 6,488 foreign-born Chinese Americans living in New York. Ira Rosenwaike, *Population History of New York City* (Syracuse, N.Y.: Syracuse University Press, 1972), 141.

40. *Chinese Nationalist Daily*, Nov. 7, 1932.

41. *Chinese Nationalist Daily*, Oct. 31, 1932.

42. Ibid.

43. The Washington Conference of 1921 was an attempt of the United States to prevent future wars while building safeguards that would not hamper American freedom of action in the world. The Washington Conference also produced two other related treaties: the Nine-Power Pact to keep an open door policy in China, and the Four-Power Pact by which the United States, Britain, France, and Japan promised to respect one another's Pacific territories and cooperate to prevent aggression.

44. *Chinese Nationalist Daily*, Oct. 31, 1932.

45. *Chinese Nationalist Daily*, Nov. 7, 1932.

46. *Chinese Nationalist Daily*, Aug. 1, 1932.

47. *Chinese Nationalist Daily*, Nov. 2, 1932.

48. *Chinese Nationalist Daily*, Nov. 10, 1932. This figure is quite different from the figures provided by official announcement. Robert Underhill cites 22,815,539 popular votes for FDR, and 15,759,930 popular votes for Herbert Hoover. *FDR and Harry: Unparalleled Lives* (Westport, Conn.: Praeger, 1996), 56.

49. *Chinese Nationalist Daily*, Nov. 10, 1932.

50. *Chinese Nationalist Daily*, Oct. 8, 1936.

51. Pardee Lowe, "Second-Generation Dilemma, 1930's," in *Chinese American Voices: From the Gold Rush to the Present*, ed. Judy Yung, Gordon H. Chang, and Him Mark Lai (Berkeley: University of California Press, 2006), 167.

52. "Chinese in NYC," WPA Writers' Project, Folder #48 (New York City: New York Municipal Archives), Microfilm.

53. *Chinese Nationalist Daily*, Oct. 8, 1936.

54. Ibid.

55. *Chinese Nationalist Daily*, Oct. 17, 1936.

56. Ibid. At the end of the convention, representatives of both the Chinese community and the Democratic Party exchanged a Chinese national flag and an American flag to confirm their cooperation in support of Roosevelt's reelection.

57. *Chinese National Daily*, Oct. 25, 1936.

58. Pardee Lowe, "Second-Generation Dilemma, 1930's," in *Chinese American Voices, from the Gold Rush to the Present*, ed. Judy Yung, Gordon H. Chang, and Him Mark Lai (Berkeley: University of California Press, 2006), 175.

59. K. Scott Wong, *Americans First: Chinese Americans and the Second World War* (Cambridge, Mass.: Harvard University Press, 2005), 4.

60. *Chinese Nationalist Daily*, Sept. 17, 1936.

61. To impress Chinese Americans, Chinton also spoke of the Roosevelt administration's foreign policy. Chinton confirmed to those who were concerned about China that President Roosevelt had kept his promise to continue his policy of respect for China's sovereignty and territorial integrity. Meanwhile, Chinton also stressed

the continuation of the Roosevelt administration's policy to enforce Sino-American economic cooperation, which was vital for the Chinese American business community. *Chinese Nationalist Daily*, Sept, 17, 1936, 4; Hsuan Julia Chen, "The Chinese Community in New York, 1920–1940" (Ph.D. Dissertation, Washington, D.C.: American University, 1941), 99.

62. *Chinese Nationalist Daily*, Oct. 9, 1936.

63. *Chinese Nationalist Daily*, Oct. 24, 1936.

64. *Chinese Nationalist Daily*, Oct. 30, 1936.

65. *Chinese Nationalist Daily*, Nov. 7, 1936.

66. The party was held when FDR was visiting New York City. *Chinese Nationalist Daily*, Oct. 29, 1936.

67. *The Chinese Republic News*, Sept. 26 and Nov. 4, 1936.

68. Hsuan Julia Chen, "The Chinese Community in New York, 1920–1940" (Ph.D. Dissertation, Washington, D.C.: American University, 1941), 99.

69. *The Chinese Nationalist Daily*, Oct. 9, 1936.

70. Ibid.

71. Ibid.

CHAPTER FIVE

War and New York's Chinese Community

During the Depression, New York Chinese became self-assured in their identity as Chinese Americans. This paralleled international events of the 1930s when Japan, Germany, and Italy extended warfare to nations in Asia, Europe, and Africa. In the Depression, New York Chinese organized in many different ways to combat predominant traditional means and attitudes, and established themselves as Americans while reinforcing their identity as Chinese. The war in China contributed to the newfound sense of Chinese American dual identity. When Japan invaded China, New York Chinese identified strongly with their homeland and supported the Chinese military defense system and civilian relief efforts. At the same time they appealed to the American government to denounce Japanese violation of Chinese sovereignty as Americans. This chapter discusses the experiences of the Chinese in New York in the war era before Pearl Harbor.

In his studies on the Chinese American search for identity, Him Mark Lai maintains that pervasive racism and discrimination alienated the Chinese in the United States, thus reinforcing their identification with China. The enthusiastic involvement of Chinese Americans in support of the Chinese war effort reflected this close relationship.[1] Similar to Lai, other scholars, such as Gloria H. Chun and L. Eve Armentrout Ma, suggest that it was Chinese nationalist zeal that kindled the Chinese Americans' enthusiasm for the war effort. The violation of China's sovereignty by European powers and Japan from the turn of the century up to World War II, they believe, continually fueled nationalistic feelings and contributed to the war effort among the Chinese in America.[2]

However, a different, more inclusive perspective is needed to explain the complexity of Chinese Americans in their search for identity. After two and three generations, the Chinese in the United States had developed strong patriotic feelings for the land where they lived and worked. The notion to defend China as a means of preserving freedom, justice, and humanity for all nations in the world also motivated Chinese Americans. Their endorsement of China's defense for justice and freedom extended to other nations such as Poland and Czechoslovakia. They defined their commitment to the "cause of international justice and peace" to be in "the name of human justice."[3]

Furthermore, Chinese New Yorkers' support of China also demonstrated their desire to change their own social status in American society. Feeling that their humiliating status in American society was a result of their weak national background in the international arena and understanding that as long as China remained subjugated, prejudice would continue to depress their social and economic standing, the Chinese in the United States committed themselves to a China that would be strong enough to support its people overseas.

Historians in the West generally agree that the invasion of Poland by Germany sparked the global warfare in 1939, while scholars in China maintain that the invasion of China by Japan in 1937 started World War II. The war in China and Europe aroused New York's Chinese. During the war, they participated in various activities to support resistance to imperialist military expansion, particularly Japan's invasion of China. Popular organizations crossing lines of gender, class, and profession were formed in addition to mass protests. These organizations provided financial assistance for civilian relief and military personnel training. The formation of various organizations and their activities to support China, particularly women's and students' coalitions, fostered the cohesion of New York's Chinese community.

Chinese New Yorkers' Response to the Japanese Invasion of China

First, we need to examine both the historical background of relations between China and Japan since the mid-nineteenth century and how the Chinese in the United States related them to their homeland. The Japanese military government had pursued territorial expansion in its foreign policy since the Meiji Restoration. Its victory over China in seizing Taiwan and replacing Chinese imperial control over the Korean Peninsula in 1895 encouraged Japan to wage a successful war against Russia in 1905. As a result, Russia ceded its occupied Chinese territories to Japan. The Versailles Treaty of 1917 allowed Japan to take more Chinese territory as a consequence of World War I.

New York's Chinese felt humiliated at China's hopelessness and defenselessness in confronting the violation of its sovereignty and territorial integrity. They believed that their poor treatment in this country was a reflection of China's weakness in international affairs. Greatly concerned about China's political future and their social status in the United States, New York's Chinese had offered political and financial support to revitalize and transform China into a modern nation since the late nineteenth century.

This support accelerated when Japan launched a large-scale war and occupied a vast area of Chinese territory in the early 1930s. More Chinese New Yorkers joined the demonstrations against the ruthlessness of the Japanese. They rallied in front of government buildings to make their demonstrations more visible to catch the attention of New Yorkers at large. A big demonstration in 1933 reflected this increasing popular support. According to a report, two thousand Chinese New Yorkers, including women and children, participated in this demonstration on October 10.[4]

It was the first heroic attempt of the Chinese New Yorkers to bring their concern about the war to the American society at large while most American citizens remained apathetic. The extension of popular protests to the city streets demonstrated the change of the consciousness among Chinese in New York as well. An observer noticed that half of the participants in the October demonstration claimed to be American citizens. They marched to the City Hall of New York City singing the song "America" to appeal for American support of China.[5]

Popular organizations were formed in support of China at the same time. The Anti-Japanese Association of Chinese Residents of New York, the All American Anti-Imperialist League, the Chinese Women's Relief Association, the Young Peoples League, the Chinese Student Patriotic Association of Greater New York, the American Bureau for Medical Aid to China, and the Save-China Aviation Association were among the most vigorous organizations. Their activities ranged from fundraising through cultural performances and donation collections to military personnel trainings. Collective efforts to support China not only strengthened the effort to support China but also helped to build a growing sense of the community's strength.

Organizations for Chinese Military Defense

The Anti-Japanese Association of Chinese Residents of New York and the All American Anti-Imperialist League were the two early popular alliances established particularly for the purpose of China's military defense. Founded in May 1928, the Anti-Japanese Association formed a coalition of fifty-six Chinatown organizations in New York.[6] Denouncing the Japanese occupation of China, both the association and the league committed themselves to radical changes in the defense strategy against the nonresistance policies of the Chinese government. They organized mass demonstrations advocating military actions against the Japanese.[7] In addition, they were also active in arranging speeches and forums on war in China. News on the encroachment of Japanese troops upon China's territories aroused Chinese New Yorkers.[8]

Support for China stimulated the Chinese in New York, particularly after the "Shanghai Incident." On January 28, 1932, Japanese troops attacked Shanghai, a major industrial city in China, after their successful occupation over the vast territory in the northeast. Commanded by General Jiang Guangding and Tsia Tingkai, local troops of the 5th and the 19th Route Army immediately launched a defensive war against the Japanese military attack. At the crucial moment of national calamity, the Chinese central government continued its nonresistance policy and refused to provide any military support when Shanghai people decided to fight back. As a consequence, the local troops were forced to withdraw from Shanghai after thirty-three days of bloody struggling on March 3 because of military supply shortage. Many soldiers died in the fight.[9] In May, the Chinese government signed an armistice with the Japanese government, permitting the legal station of Japanese troops in Shanghai.

New York's Chinese residents felt indignant at the news. They sharply criticized the nonresistance policy of the Chinese central government to hand over China's territories without any fight. Holding that China "should not seek an armistice by giving away her territory," Chinese New Yorkers advocated for military defense. China "should be militarily well-prepared and use the military force as powerful backing on the peace negotiation table," they maintained, and they urged an immediate military involvement of the Chinese conventional troops against the Japanese occupation.[10]

During the Shanghai defense war, Chinese New Yorkers voluntarily contributed to the war effort to raise funds in support of military campaigns against the Japanese. According to the *Chinese Nationalist Daily*, they donated fifty thousand helmets to the 19th Route Army at one time. The generous contributions of New York Chinese received the acknowledgment of the local troops. On August 30, General Jiang Guangding and Tsia Tingkai, commanders of the 19th Route Army, sent a telegraph to express their gratitude for the support of the Chinese in New York.[11]

To advocate China's military resistance against the Japanese invasions, other organizations were also established among New York's Chinese. The Chinese Patriotic Association in New York (CPA), the Save-China Aviation Association (SCAA), and the Anti-Japanese Association of Overseas Chinese (AJAOC) were some of the important organizations. Members of these organizations varied. Some of them were native Chinese who came to the United States for better opportunities. Some were American-born Chinese descendents. Many received education in New York. Others were common residents of Chinatown. The formation of these organizations demonstrated the increasing anti-Japanese sentiments among Chinese New Yorkers and a growing consciousness of the unification of Chinese Americans in support of China.

The support activities of these organizations also focused on military campaigns. Members of the organizations made all possible efforts to raise funds to meet the imminent needs of China in the air fight. China did not have an effective air force to combat Japanese in the early 1930s. As the war developed, the air for the most part was controlled by Japanese air force, which bombed and strafed Chinese troops and other targets, killing hundreds and thousands of civilians. Understanding China's urgent need of a strong air power, Chinese New Yorkers initiated programs to train pilots ready to fight against the Japanese. In August 1932, the CPA in New York announced that it would raise $200,000 to train pilots and ground crew from among the Chinese in the United States. The AJAOC declared that it would sponsor a military training institution, the Overseas Chinese Aviation School, to work on military training drills. With thirty military veterans as members, the SCAA decided to focus its training program on badly needed aviation personnel and technicians in China.[12]

The SCAA was a powerful coalition of several Chinese American organizations including the New York Chinese American Aviation Volunteers and the East Coast General Committee of Overseas Chinese Aviators. With its headquarters in the Chinese School in New York's Chinatown, these organizations made a joint effort to support China's defense. On August 18, 1932, the SCAA held its founding ceremony. According to the *Chinese Nationalist Daily*, Chinese and American flags were hung on each side of the conference hall to demonstrate the solidarity of Chinese Americans in support of Chinese war. Chen Kueiwu, the president of the association, delivered an opening speech. Stressing that "the most crucial task" for China was to drive the

Japanese out of the country and to regain Chinese territories, Chen announced the determination of the Chinese American coalition to support China's cause.[13]

The SCAA opposed Chiang Kai-shek (Jiang Jieshi), the president of the Chinese government, for his nonresistance policy to the Japanese invasion. A resolution reached at the end of the ceremony criticized President Chiang for a weak China, "not a country of sovereignty," where the people were "suffering from the plundering wars among imperialist nations."[14]

China had suffered great pain since the Opium Wars in the middle of the nineteenth century. The division of its territories into concessions controlled by various imperial powers and the ceding of Hong Kong to Great Britain as a result of the Nanjing Treaty demonstrated the corruption and the weakness of the previous Qing government. The occupation of vast land of China by Japan due to the chaos of power struggles among warlords and the weakness of the Nationalist government with its nonresistance policy aroused the Chinese on both sides of the Pacific. Committing to the defense of China against any forms of occupation, the SCAA was willing to take any possible way to provide assistance to China. It called for a joint action of Chinese Americans to urge military resistance in its support for a strong China:

> It is the time for the Chinese people to combat against imperialist plundering. All unequal treaties must be abolished. All imperialist nations must be driven out. . . .
>
> [As Chinese descendants] we are aware of the need of China. We decide to take the responsibility to help in all ways we can since Chiang Kaishek (Jiang Jieshi) held non-resistance policy.[15]

To emphasize the principle of its military support of China, a weapon display was held at the SCAA's opening ceremony. A local Chinese newspaper reported the exiting event.[16] Chinese New Yorkers presented at the exhibition hall. With "high patriotic spirit," many expressed their willingness to join the military training programs. Others wished that they had a chance to go to China to combat the Japanese directly.[17]

The SCAA also ran an information center. It issued a newsletter to keep the public informed about the war in China and the activities organized by the SCAA.[18] A few days after the founding ceremony, the association formally publicized its announcement for recruits.

To make the aviation training institution professional, the SCAA vigorously coordinated with experienced veterans and looked for funds to purchase equipment necessary for training. Soon after its formation, on August

22, a special committee was assigned to raise funds for the purchase of an aircraft for field training.[19] The training program became so successful that when General Tsai Tingkai of the 19th Route Army of Shanghai came to New York for fundraising in September, three cadet pilots of the Chinese Aviation Association flew over his ship to demonstrate their fighting spirit and military capacity.[20]

In the years of supporting Chinese military defense, the SCAA constantly dispatched aviation personnel to China to help the country in its effort to build up an air force and to meet the needs of the pilot training. Huang Jinci was one of the first military mission representatives sent to Lo Yang Chinese Aviation School in central China to set up an aviation training program in 1935. Holding an American pilot's license, Huang was considered an excellent and experienced pilot with a good command of both "piloting and engineering" by his colleagues on both sides of the Pacific.[21] Xie Zuguang, Kong Mingguong, and Situ Yiping were among those who graduated from the aviation training program and were sent to China. These young Chinese Americans were New York University graduates. Committed to the cause of Chinese defense, they decided to go to China to fight the Japanese, leaving their professional expectations behind.[22]

The SCAA also stressed the importance of a unified China to mount a strong defense. The political situation in China had been complicated by wars among various factions. It had suffered warlords' wars since the downturn of the Qing dynasty at the turn of the twentieth century. The military conflicts to compete for territories and sphere of influence among regional warlords were intensified since the establishment of the Republic in 1911. The impotent new government was unable to contain the warlords' wars. Power struggles within the government made the chaotic situation worse. Although the Nationalist Party eventually seized power and a strong central government was on its way to be built, the fear of the growing Chinese Communist Party resulted in its military campaigns to destruct the rival party in the late 1920s and early 1930s.

The vulnerable situation created by the internal conflicts made it possible for foreign intrusions. Historical evidence proved the tragedy. Japanese encroachment upon Chinese territories starting from the turn of the twentieth century up to the 1930s was a good example of such tragedy. Being aware of the vulnerability, the SCAA openly condemned the warlords' wars for a divided China and denounced sheer partisanship for the weakened country. Calling for the ceasefire of warlords' wars and the truce of civil wars among political parties in China, it appealed for preserving a unified China to protect the country from foreign intrusion.[23]

The Chinese in the United States felt as furious as their Chinese compatriots at the defeat of China, especially when Japan militarily invaded China in 1931 killing and forcing millions of Chinese off the occupied land. In China, literary and music works reflected the sorrow, frustration, and fury of those who lost their land and home. In the United States, Chinese Americans set September 18, the day when the Japanese launched a war to occupy the territories in the northeast, as "Humiliation Day," to commemorate those who had lost their homeland and those who had been killed in the war. In New York, the Chinese held an annual mass rally every year to commemorate "Humiliation Day." Continuously committed to a unified China against Japanese occupation, the SCAA participated in the annual event. Chen Kueiwu, president of the SCAA, made a speech to a rally on the 1932 "Humiliation Day." Calling for a unified China "to fight off invasion," he urged the cooperation among different parties and factions to engage in the defensive war: "We should share the common goal of fighting together with the masses to raise the morale of all military personnel and regain the lost Chinese territories," he maintained.[24]

The wars in China aroused Chinese New Yorkers. Advocating for military defense, they organized and provided substantial assistance to the defensive war in China. At the same time, the 1930s witnessed the rise of women and students organizations to support China's defense. Focusing on civilian relief in China, their effort mobilized New York's Chinese. Joint activities also brought New Yorkers at large together.

Women's Organizations for Chinese Civilian Relief

During the years when China was being plundered by the Japanese occupants, New York's Chinese women, in particular, organized. They contributed to relief work for Chinese civilians, assuming a role that was unusual for them in public activities.

Traditionally, Chinese women stayed at home cooking, cleaning, and taking care of their children. Historical research reveals the change of Chinese women in New York as early as in 1900. A few of them began to play a role in family-operated businesses, such as laundries and grocery stores, laboring alongside their husbands to support their families. A Chinese widow was found to be a store owner managing a business by herself on Mott Street.[25] The 1920s saw the rise of the second-generation Chinese women immigrants who moved out of their homes. Some found jobs in public facilities working as tearoom waitresses, typists, theater usherettes, and saleswomen, earning money. Others worked for their own education. However, most Chinese women New Yorkers were generally confined within the Chinese community. Besides, they did not have an equal right in business decisions in a male-dominated society. Household responsibilities kept women occupied.

The isolation of the Chinese community also limited Chinese women in dealing with the outside world. New York's Chinese had been forced to withdraw into their own community to protect themselves from unnecessary risk of racial entanglements since the enforcement of the Chinese exclusion laws, which were responsible for racial segregation as well as for the scarcity of women in the Chinese community. The laws made it even more difficult for women to come to the United States. The sex ratio of the Chinese population in this country was disparately high. In 1890 there was one Chinese female to every twenty-seven Chinese males in the United States.[26] The 1900 U.S. Census recorded 2,353 Chinese females living in the country.

Historic records on early Chinese women in New York City are scarce except for Louis Beck's brief depiction of a few Chinese prostitutes.[27] Not until 1900 did the United States census report fifty-eight Chinese women residents in Chinatown on the Lower East Side of Manhattan, including thirty-two adults and twenty-six daughters. By 1920 the figure reached 303, of which 144 were adults and 159 were minors.[28] These women found their lives isolated.[29] In addition to avoiding any unnecessary racial entanglement, heavy housework and responsibilities kept them retained at home.

The war in China in the 1930s aroused Chinese American women New Yorkers. Extending their humanitarian concern and sympathy to the people in China, they stepped out of their isolation. The war also transformed New York's Chinese women. They participated in mass demonstrations to make their voices heard publicly for the first time in history. They initiated activities such as benefit parties and auctions to raise money to support Chinese relief. More importantly, they formed their own organizations, another way of expressing their consciousness and strength. The Chinese Women's Association (CWA), the Chinese Young Women's Patriotic League (CYWPL), and the Chinese Women's Relief Association (CWRA) were such women's organizations. To engage Chinese New Yorkers in an effort to support the war against the Japanese, New York's Chinese women extended themselves from economic activities to political campaigns. Their reactions demonstrated shifting attitudes toward their places both at home and in society. Their activities in the war marked a turning point from isolation to involvement.

The CWA was one of the earliest and most effective women organizations across the United States, as historians such as Judy Yung contend.[30] The Japanese invasion of China drew women from all walks of life into the public arena to contribute to the war effort. Chinese women in other major cities of

San Francisco, Chicago, Seattle, and Portland organized and participated in fundraising, propaganda, and Red Cross–organized activities. Situated in the Annex Building of the Chinese Public School in the center of New York's Chinatown, the CWA declared its formation in 1931.[31] Theodora Chan Wang became the first president of this organization. Membership steadily increased to 350.[32]

The records of the CWA demonstrated the effectiveness of the effort in its commitment to the Chinese defensive war. As early as October 14, 1931, it lashed out at the non-interference rhetoric of a newspaper editor who called for America to stay out of the war. Calling this stance "immoral" and "cowardly," the CWA urged the United States to uphold its pledge to help settle international disputes to keep global peace.[33] When General Tsai Tingkai of the 19th Route Army of Shanghai came to New York for fundraising, the CWA held a welcome fundraiser dinner party at Port Arthur Restaurant at 7 Mott Street to show its support on September 1, 1932. More than two hundred Chinese community women residents participated. The CWA was so successful in mobilizing New York Chinese women that by the end of 1932 it raised $30,000 for the war relief effort in China. These funds were exchanged to Chinese local currency and immediately transferred by telegraph to the Shanghai Consolidated Benevolent Association and Shanghai Emergency Hospital for the imminent relief of the wounded soldiers and war refugees.[34]

The CWA organized fundraiser activities in various bold and creative ways. Dragon parades and street dances attracted many New York residents, both Chinese and other ethnic groups. A sum of $7,694.46 was raised in a single day of February 28, 1932. According to the residents' annual report, thanks to the spontaneous and generous response of both Chinese community residents and "American sympathizers," this organization became the leading women's organization in China's war relief effort.

Other women's organizations such as the CWRA and the CYWPL also committed to the war relief effort. Established in 1932, according to a newsletter, the CWRA provided financial aid for Chinese civilian relief during the Shanghai defense war.[35] In February 1932, the CYWPL organized its first fundraising parade. With a Chinese national flag held by four girls at each corner in the lead to show their support of China, women demonstrators marched through New York's Chinatown. Sympathetic spectators along the streets quietly donated coins and dollar bills, some wrapped in red paper, to support the women's effort to help the refugees of Shanghai. Appealing for public support of China, New York's Chinese women also called on Chinese Americans to boycott Japanese goods.[36]

The Chinese American women's effort to support Chinese relief work received ardent support from the Chinese community at large in New York. In March 1932, when the CYWPL held an auction bazaar to raise funds for the relief work, the Chinese School in Chinatown provided the room and space. Merchants donated precious Ming vases and old brocades to assist the fundraising. During the eight-day auction bazaar, the CYWPL, according to Bonner, raised a large amount of money for Shanghai by selling the items donated by the Chinese community.[37] The CYWPL received even more support in the following year. On one occasion, as many as six hundred Chinese New Yorkers contributed at its fundraising benefit party.[38]

The women's effort to support China continued when Japan accelerated its war in 1937. They participated more in mass demonstrations and organized more fundraising activities. On July 7, 1937, Japanese military forces secretly attacked Beijing, marking the onset of wholesale Sino-Japanese war. The war spread quickly. Japanese troops moved southward after the fall of Beijing, occupying, within a few months, the large cities of Tianjin, Shanghai, and Nanjing, spreading terror with a policy of "burn all, kill all, loot all." In October 1937, Pearl S. Buck, an American journalist, reported from China that in the wake of the Japanese invasion,

> Thousands of innocent people [were] dead, peaceful villages [were] destroyed, women and children [were] killed . . . cities of the world [were] ruined . . . prisoners [were] tortured.[39]

"This . . . war in China," she wrote, was one of "utter disregard for individual human life," a "mechanical means of death . . . the ultimate of terror."[40]

Reports of Japanese cruelty shocked the world as well as the people of the United States. Most importantly, they focused the hatred of overseas Chinese against the Japanese while strengthening the sympathies of the Chinese to their homeland. "People were talking mostly about China's war with Japan at the dinner table after a long day of work," Paul Siu recalled.[41] When friends got together in restaurants in Chinatown on Sundays, they also talked about the war.[42]

The CYWPL accelerated its support for China. Joined by other community members, its activities spread across lines of gender, class, and age. In October 1937, the CYWPL members led a mass parade in New York's Chinese community protesting against the Japanese invasion of China. A month later, in another mass demonstration, two thousand Chinese American women and men marched through New York's Chinatown. Carrying a banner of dollar bills sewn into the Chinese characters for their slogan of "Fight against Japan to the Bitter End to Save China," they called for more financial contributions while expressing their determination to support the Chinese to the end of war. The CYWPL also continued its activities raising money for Chinese war victims and refugees. Its one-week fundraising drive held in the Chinese School in New York's Chinatown included amateur opera productions as well as a week-long bazaar.[43]

The Chinese Women's Relief Association (CWRA) also contributed greatly to the support of China. While the CYWPL was a Chinatown-based woman's organization, with most of its members American-born and living in New York's Chinatown, the CWRA was an upper-class women's organization. Many of its members were former Chinese students sent by the Chinese government to the United States to study. Situated at 5 East 57th Street, the CWRA was established in late September 1937 to raise money especially for Chinese war relief. Within a few months, it became a moderately large relief work institution with over fifty members and raised "a good amount of money" among upper-class Chinese Americans.[44]

Its symposium on Chinese issues held at the Colony Club in November 1937 and its benefit reception at the Park Lane Hotel on December 5, according to a local Chinese American newsletter, were "very successful financially."[45] In less than five months since September 1937, the association raised a sum of 60,000 Chinese dollars for Chinese relief.[46] Shortly after the transfer of the money to China, an installment of $30,000 in Chinese currency was collected and reported to be "almost ready for transmission" within a few months.[47]

The anti-Japanese war in the 1930s created the momentum for New York's Chinese women to take on public responsibilities. For the first time in history, they formed their own organizations to translate their humanitarian impulses into action. Their efforts to participate in the public gatherings, bazaars, and benefit parties for donations heightened their feelings of initiative. These activities also gave them a sense of purpose and achievement. Supported by other members of the Chinese community, New York's Chinese women and their organizations contributed greatly to Chinese relief work. In less than six months after Japan launched a wholesale war against China, a total of $1,800,000 was collected in New York alone in 1937 through individual donations, business and community associations, and organized fundraising.[48]

Identified themselves as Chinese women, they acted as Americans in fundraising that was not Chinese.

Students' Organizations in Support of China

The Japanese invasion of China also united Chinese students in New York, who joined New York's Chinese in opposition activities. While they had once considered themselves as elites, these activities helped Chinese students change their consciousness and attitude toward other Chinese. Their involvement in support of China also received the recognition of those in China.

Chinese students in New York were small in numbers. There were only 280 Chinese students studying in twenty-seven colleges in 1937.[49] American college registrar records included both American-born Chinese students and students from China in the "Chinese" category.[50] In practice, the two groups of students had their separate organizations on campus which served their respective purposes. American-born Chinese were more concerned about their civil rights as American citizens, while students from China expected to go back. They focused more on the contributions they were able to make to China as a result of their training.

The Japanese invasion of China, however, brought both groups together. Various coalitions for the defense of China were established on and off campus among Chinese students regardless of place of birth or national identity. These student organizations committed themselves to the preservation of an independent China with its sovereignty and territorial integrity. Strongly opposing the nonresistance policy of the Chinese government, they announced that if the Chinese government "ignore[d] the will of the Chinese people," the Chinese students in the United States would "not recognize the government as representative of the nation." They promised resistance:

> We, the Chinese students in New York . . . do solemnly pledge ourselves to exert our united strength for the resistance . . . for the preservation of the independence, sovereignty and territorial integrity of China.[51]

Their early joint action to form a picket line in front of the Japanese Consulate demonstrated the unity of Chinese students. In September 1937, one hundred Chinese students, organized by the Chinese Student Patriotic Association of Greater New York (CSPA), formed a picket line in front of the Japanese Consulate on Fifth Avenue and 42nd Street in New York to protest the Japanese military attack on China. Waving placards emblazoned with slogans of "Stop the Killings" and "Down with the Japanese Imperialism," the students demanded immediate withdrawal of Japanese troops from China.[52]

The CSPA was an important Chinese student organization to support China. Other organizations such as the Chinese Students League of Greater

New York (CSL) and the Chinese Student Christian Association (CSCA) also played an active role. In addition to demonstrations, they organized cultural activities and street collections to raise money needed in China.

Street collection was not a social convention of Chinese students. Culturally, Chinese students considered themselves elites. Standing and collecting money in the streets would embarrass them as they saw it similar to street begging. National humiliation put down their individual embarrassment and changed their attitude. Shared experiences as Chinese in the United States also brought students and other New Yorkers together. On December 27, 1937, New York's Chinese students responded enthusiastically to the appeal for a cooperative street drive initiated by the American Medical Aid to China. An estimated $4,500 was raised by participating students on a five-day drive from December 27 to 31, 1937, and a two-day drive from January 3 to 4, 1938.[53]

These successful street drives encouraged Chinese students. Bliss Kao, a Chinese student at Columbia University, told a newspaper reporter:

> It was our first time in such a role in an American city. We felt a little timid, even embarrassed . . . but we soon got used to the situation and began to appeal either verbally or by shaking our containers, which began to full up and growing heavy.[54]

Again, in January 1938, over one hundred of New York's Chinese students took part in a seven-day street drive sponsored by the American Bureau for Medical Aid to China to raise funds for China's relief work. Standing in the cold January weather, holding badges, containers, and placards for donations in the busy sections of Time Square, Grand Central, 34th Street, and Wall Street, they achieved more. By the end of the seven-day campaign, $4,444.09 had been raised by the Chinese students in Times Square alone.[55]

In addition to participating in fundraising campaigns organized by Chinese community organizations, students also successfully organized their own campaigns. In a five-day street drive organized by the CSL in Manhattan from October 6 to 10, 1938, students collected a large sum of money that enabled them to purchase three ambulances needed in China. In another street drive, this student body raised $3,377.92.[56]

The successful fundraising street drives were the result of the consolidated effort of New York's Chinese community. Many Chinese restaurant owners and merchants, as well as ordinary workers, were involved. Downtown Chinese restaurants near Wall Street offered the students places to rest, and provided free meals for them.[57] "Canton Village," a Chinese restaurant in midtown Manhattan, served as the campaign headquarters with its convenient location at 49th Street and Broadway.[58]

New York Chinese students' effort to support China's defense inspired those in other areas of the United States. Students in Boston, Iowa, and Chicago were also involved in similar activities.[59]

The ardent support of Chinese students for a strong China received the recognition of the Chinese people. On May 3, 1939, Madam Chiang Kai-shek (Jiang Jieshi) wrote a letter to the Chinese Christian Students' Association in New York to express her appreciation to Chinese students in the United States for their "splendid response" and contributions to the Chinese resistance war.[60]

> Such splendid response has been made by our compatriots overseas that we lose no opportunity to thank them and express appreciation of their patriotism and helpfulness. Our country is determined to continue the resistance. . . . We have now been fighting for 22 months. . . . The Japanese bomb us, but while bombing does terrible destruction to human bodies and property, it will not win the war. . . . We can survive and . . . beat our enemy with the help of our overseas countrymen.[61]

The movement to support a war of resistance against the Japanese invasions contributed to the cohesiveness of the Chinese community in New York. For example, the establishment of the China Aid Information Exchange, which included more than twenty organizations, demonstrated the unity and cooperation among New York Chinese. The Chinese Women's Relief Association, the Chinese Students' League, the Chinese Students' Christian Association, the Federal Council of Churches, and the Committee for Boycott and against Japanese Aggression were members of the association.[62]

Such a coordinating agency, a local Chinese newsletter commented, "filled a long felt need among the scores of organizations which have sprung up to aid relief in China."[63] David Tong, president of the Chinese Students' Christian Association, praised the profound unity of the Chinese community and the "Golden Doctrine of Cooperation" developed among New York's Chinese residents. He contended that members of the Chinese community had "become champions of unity and cooperation" in the cause to support China.[64]

Americans' Support for Chinese New Yorkers

Chinese Americans' enthusiastic support of China during the Japanese invasions brought important acknowledgment from the American society at large. By the end of the 1930s, a different attitude in American society showed a respect for Chinese Americans. Ordinary New Yorkers demonstrated their sympathy and support for students' street collections for the Chinese defense cause. Politicians also publicly endorsed their efforts. Mass demonstrations were held to protest Japanese cruelty as well. Clearly, the Japanese invasion of China and Chinese American support of China's defense brought about coalitions between Chinese New Yorkers and other Americans.

Americans were outraged by the Japanese invasions. In their sympathetic support for the Chinese, even the poorest New Yorkers contributed whatever they could to help. "We're all for you," one New Yorker told a Chinese student after he put a coin in a can in a street drive. "Good luck to you" was a common wish from New York's residents. On one occasion, a "shabbily-dressed" man said to a student, "I wish I could give more," when he took out some pennies. Another man explained that he was skipping a meal when he gave a nickel to a student.[65] A correspondent of the *Chinese Christian Student* reported a "remarkable thing" that happened during their street campaigns: "The people who actually put money into the cans belonged to the lower classes." Their "kind hearts" and "intelligent words" demonstrated that they were the most supportive people. Suffering from hard times during the Depression, their selfless contributions for the desperate in China moved Chinese students the most.[66]

Many donors were "push-cart vendors," "kind-hearted cops," and taxi drivers, according to a Chinese student newsletter. A Japanese man also contributed to the campaign when he passed the students. Some unusual items, including rings and an overcoat, were donated by unknown New Yorkers. An American veteran gave a bullet to a student, saying that he hoped it would "help fight the Japs." Some New Yorkers found other ways to contribute to the fund drive. A "kind old man" offered a female student a cup of hot chocolate, which was "much-needed in the cold weather."[67] The fundraising campaigns for China's defense also received sympathetic and encouraging support from New York City's government. The city's Department of Public Welfare issued the organizers a special license permitting them to carry on their street collections in four of New York's busiest districts.

Big demonstrations were organized in New York, as well. On October 1, 1937, ten thousand New Yorkers—a broad coalition of Chinese New Yorkers and other New York residents—gathered at Madison Square Garden protesting the Japanese occupation of China. Condemning the ruthlessness of the Japanese troops in China, the rally urged a boycott of Japanese goods in America. Rev. Harry F. Ward, professor of Christian ethics at Union Theological Seminary and chairman of the American League against War and Fascism, presided over the rally.[68]

Fifty-one prominent labor, civic, and religious leaders participated in the rally. Joseph Curran, general organizer of the National Maritime Union, Rabbi Stephen S. Wise, and Bishop G. Bromley Oxnam spoke at the rally.[69] Professor John L. Childs of Teachers College at Columbia University; Philip Jaffe, managing editor of *Amerasia*; Dr. Cho-ting Chi, a noted lecturer and writer; Robert N. Baldwin, director of the Civil Liberties Union; D. Willard Lyon, former national secretary of the Y.M.C.A. in China; and William E. Dodds, American ambassador to Germany were among the prominent participants.[70]

Dr. Tsune-chi Yu, consul general of the Chinese Republic, was invited as a special guest to address the rally. Expressing his gratitude for the American people's support on behalf of China, Yu told his audience that "never before had the Chinese people had American sympathy and friendship so much as now." "Chinese did not want one drop of American blood spilled in defense of China," Yu announced. "All that we ask is China's territorial and administrative integrity." Appealing for human justice, Yu urged an American action against the Japanese, particularly an American arms embargo.[71]

Luise Raner, the star of the film *The Good Earth*, also spoke at the rally. "As a human being and as an artist," she announced, "I protest what the Japanese are doing in China."[72] The rally reached its peak when a Chinatown orchestra and the Chinese Boy Scouts performed. The audience was moved by songs such as "In Defense of Peace" and "From the Blood Soaked Earth," and many of them joined in the singing to express their sympathetic feelings for the Chinese in China.

A five-point resolution was reached by the end of the rally. Protesting the Japanese occupation in China, it called on all American citizens to take actions to stop buying Japanese goods, support organized labor in refusing to handle shipments to and from Japan of any war material, embargo all materials for Japan, demand that China be permitted to buy here anything she needs under conditions that will not involve the United States in war, and demand that the United States fulfill her international obligation by proclaiming Japan a violator of the Kellogg-Briand Pact and the Nine-Power Treaty.[73]

In order to convey the sentiments of the rally, the resolution was telegraphed to President Roosevelt, to Secretary of State Cordell Hull, and to C. T. Wang, the Chinese ambassador. An estimated $3,500 in cash was collected during the rally. Like the Chinese American women's organizations, this money was also sent directly to Madam Chiang Kai-shek (Jiang Jieshi) as well as to Madam Sun Yat-sen (Sun Zhongshan). The rally generated so much excitement that members of audience voluntarily pledged $1,600.[74]

On May 9, 1938, more than twelve thousand Chinese from New York and other eastern cities of Newark, Jersey City, Boston, and Philadelphia came together for an unprecedented parade in New York City. Significantly, sympathetic New Yorkers also joined in the march. Volunteer American bands, such as the Negro Band from the Eureka Lodge of the Grand Order of Odd Fellows, the Bay Ridge Boys' Club of Brooklyn Band, and a woman's band from the Dern Post of the Veterans of Foreign Wars, were ardent supporters of the event.[75] Though no appeal was made for funds, according to a local Chinese newsletter, spectators along the streets "began showering nickels and dimes and even dollar[s]" as the parade passed by. About $600 had been collected by the end of the demonstration against the Japanese.[76]

Inspired by the spirit of the rally, more joint activities were organized in New York. On December 10, 1938, the American Friends of the Chinese People organized a big parade in support of the movement to boycott Japanese goods. On December 13, 1938, the Chinese Aid Association also held a rally in support of China's defense.[77]

Mass rallies were held simultaneously in Washington, D.C., Pittsburgh, and Boston, demanding similar boycott actions.[78] Thus, the movement for Chinese defense was no longer simply the business of Chinese Americans. It spread from New York to other eastern cities, obtaining ardent support from the society at large.

The government of New York also endorsed the people's protest against Japanese occupation in China. Mayor Fiorello La Guardia openly supported the anti-Japanese movement: "We wish to raise our voices in world wide protest against ruthless bombing of open towns." He said, "We extend our fullest sympathy and join in your protest and pledge support to all efforts to halt these brutalities before they overwhelm us all."[79]

New York City became a center of national China relief organizations. The China Emergency Civilian Relief Organization, the China Famine Relief U.S.A. Inc., the Associated Boards for Christian Colleges, and the Harmon Foundation were among the important institutions to collect money in support of China's relief.[80]

The China Emergency Civilian Relief Organization was created to cooperate with the American Red Cross to provide emergency relief supplies for war victims in China. With Theodore Roosevelt Jr. as its chairman, the organization was headquartered at 40 Wall Street in New York.[81] During the years when the Chinese were suffering from wars, the China Emergency Civilian Relief Organization raised funds to provide war victims with financial aid. In February 1938, it conducted a big campaign to collect donations in New York; sympathetic residents contributed greatly.[82]

The China Famine Relief U.S.A. Inc. was another relief organization in New York. Located at 105 East 22nd Street, this organization was under the leadership of its treasurer, Mr. James M. Speers, and its executive director, Mr. J. A. Thomas. Funds raised by this organization were distributed in part under the auspices of the International Red Cross at Shanghai. In a short period of a few months in 1938, it raised $60,000 for Chinese civilians in need of food, shelter, clothing, and medical assistance.[83]

Religious organizations, as well, participated in the secular efforts of the larger society to support Chinese defense and aid Chinese civilian relief work. The Associated Boards for Christian Colleges was one of such institutions. With its general office in Room 903 at 150 Fifth Avenue in New York, and with Mr. B. A. Garside as its general secretary and George W. Davison as its treasurer, this organization consisted of twelve Christian universities in China supported by twenty-one mission boards in the United States, Great Britain, and Canada.[84] As early as 1937, when Japanese attacked Beijing, this organization undertook a task to raise an emergency fund of $300,000 to assist colleges in meeting emergency expenses created by the war in China. On October 10, 1937, it organized a big forum on China issues in New York. Dr. Philip S. Chen, a professor of chemistry at Madison College, spoke on Sino-Japanese relations. His speech aroused the audience. On December 7, 1937, this organization launched a fundraising campaign in New York. Sympathetic New Yorkers participated.[85]

The Harmon Foundation was an example of yet another type of organization supporting China's defense. The Harmon Foundation was one of the first American organizations to report on anti-Japanese war in Chinese Communist controlled regions. Motion pictures of the 8th Route Army in action, made by Frances Roots, were shown at its headquarters in New York to draw the attention of the audience to the popular resistance against Japanese occupation of China.[86] During the years of war, it constantly sent motion pictures filmed in China to the United States to arouse American citizens. In the middle of 1938, Logan Roots, a member of the foundation, was reportedly on his way home to the United States from Hankow, a city attacked by the Japanese. He brought with him footage to be screened at the Harmon Foundation.[87]

American organizations and their activities to support China and to endorse Chinese American efforts for China's defense demonstrated both shifting attitudes in American society towards Chinese Americans and American concern about justice and freedom in the troubling world. While the United States remained neutral, New York was departing from neutrality. This departure was reflected by Representative Francis I. Culkin's proposal to ensure adequate financial support for Chinese relief. In the proposal, Mr. Culkin from New York introduced a bill in the U.S. House of Representatives to appropriate $5,000,000 for the relief of the destitute and homeless Chinese in the war zone that eventually pushed President Roosevelt in his proposal to urge American citizens to give $1,000,000 for those suffering in China.[88]

New York Chinese's Response to the Global Crisis

World War II involved countries in Asia, Africa, and Europe that left over sixty million soldiers and civilians dead from bombings, disease, starvation, and genocidal campaigns of extermination. The horrors of the Holocaust and the Rape of Nanjing left a deep scar upon the mind of humanity.

Historians believe that the outbreak of the war had its roots in World War I and in the peace terms of Versailles for leaving territorial issues unresolved. Scholars also contend that the global conflict was a consequence of the uncontrolled expansion of imperialism, nationalism, fascism, and militarism.[89]

World War II cut a gash across the surface of American history. Faced with an unstable world during the decades of the 1920s and 1930s, the United States turned away from international collective action for peace. In rejecting League of Nations membership, Americans deliberately declined to involve themselves in world affairs. In 1935, Congress passed the Neutrality Act. In the next two years, Congress upheld the renewed neutrality legislation of 1936 and 1937, insisting on "protection of neutral rights" for Americans.

New York's Chinese opposed the American neutrality policy in foreign affairs, particularly its policy toward China, warning that the failure of American intervention would lead to more Japanese aggression.[90] They challenged the policy by participating in activities to support China against Japan's invasion. Their rhetoric was not merely nationalistic. More than that, their support of China's defense had a strong internationalist aspect. The declaration of a Chinese American organization revealed Chinese New Yorkers' concern about global peace. Announcing their support of China "in the name of human justice" and for "the cause of international justice and peace," New York's Chinese defined their activities as defending "the most sacred rights of humanity."[91]

The desire of New York's Chinese for world peace was also demonstrated as they joined other ethnic groups to oppose fascism and the expansion of German and Italian military occupations in Europe.

New York Chinese's Support of Other Resistance Movements

Throughout the 1930s, the Great Depression concentrated the attention of New York's Chinese on domestic economic issues. But events in the world also engaged them. In 1935, Mussolini launched his long-anticipated attack on Ethiopia in Africa, Franco revolted in 1936 against the existing republican government in Spain, and the Japanese assaulted Beijing in 1937. Chinese New Yorkers participated in protests with other ethnic groups in New York against imperialist expansion. European ethnic immigrant groups in New York opposed the spread of fascism. As Hitler's army overran Poland in September 1939, an estimated one hundred thousand Polish Americans in New York protested against the Nazi conquest of Poland.[92] The Czechs in New York also openly expressed their opposition to Nazi Germany. They enthusiastically supported their people's military resistance when Nazi Germany invaded the Czechs' homeland.[93] New York Jews initiated civilian drives and activities to protest the mass persecutions of the Holocaust. They held several rallies at Madison Square Garden, calling for aid to their people in escaping European death camps.[94]

New York's Chinese showed much concern about the war in Europe. As early as 1936, when Fascists launched a civil war in Spain, Chinese American volunteers in New York cooperated in campaigns to support the republic. They participated in fundraising activities for the relief of refugees. The American Student Union was established to meet the needs of Spanish civilians, especially students.[95] The All American Anti-Imperialist League, another Chinese American organization was also formed especially for the purpose of supporting anti-imperialist movements of other ethnic groups. On October 10, 1938, the league organized a big demonstration. Two thousand of New York's Chinese residents participated in this event denouncing the German occupation of Poland. Dr. Frank Lee, China's ambassador to Poland, was invited to speak on the situation in Poland.[96]

Informal forums on wars in Europe were also held in Chinatown to demonstrate Chinese New Yorkers' interest in the global crisis. On an occasion, five hundred Chinatown residents gathered at the corner of Mott and Pell Streets to discuss political events in Europe. The discussions were so intensive that, according to a Chinese American newsletter, no participants felt the heat of the scorching sun.[97]

The anti-Axis activities of various immigrant groups forged a movement that created a new climate committing the country toward intervention in world affairs. The active participation of New York's Chinese residents in the movement demonstrated their opposition to the worldwide imperialist expansions and their stance for freedom and justice.

New York's Chinese Advocates for American Involvement in War

Joining the growing voices of those opposing the spread of fascism, New York's Chinese also openly challenged the American neutrality policy in foreign affairs. Calling it the American diplomatic policy of repudiating American international responsibility, they appealed for American involvement in the war. More significant, they continued their support of China and considered their endorsement to be the Americans' obligation in world affairs. Thus, once again, they reinforced their dual identity as Chinese Americans.

New York's Chinese strongly opposed the American neutrality policy in foreign affairs, particularly its policy towards Japan's invasion of China. They denounced the so-called American Neutrality Acts as a policy to help Japan destroy China, as American scrap iron sold to Japan was "to be turned into ammunition to blow Chinese villages to pieces."[98] Referring to the selling of American oil to Japan as "a drop of oil means a drop of blood," they claimed that America's policy of neutrality was only helping the Japanese bomb more Chinese cities and kill more Chinese citizens.[99] Challenging the American neutrality policy, New York's Chinese warned of the possible consequences of Japanese military expansion and appealed for American involvement in the war against Japan:

> Japanese imperialists . . . have been exercising more and more coercion in their attempt to realize their sinister ambition—[from] the exploitation of China [to] the domination of the Far East. . . . The failure of [the international agreements to secure the active support of the signatories] has encouraged the Japanese imperialists to take even more aggressive action. [Therefore], we advocate forceful resistance to the ruthless invasion.[100]

During the years of advocating American involvement in war, New York's Chinese held a strong identity as Chinese Americans. They described their support of resistance to the worldwide imperialist expansions as "American spiritual and material help,"[101] and considered it a necessary responsibility of Chinese Americans. In his essay, "American-Born Chinese and Chino-Japanese Crisis," Lim P. Lee clearly announced the position and stance of Chinese Americans in the war as Americans. "As citizens of the United States," he said, American-born Chinese should remain neutral to avoid any conflict with a belligerent nation as "the United States government's policy was neutral."[102] But when people in Europe as well as the Far East were "fighting with their backs to the walls for freedom and liberty against fascism," Chinese Americans could not remain silent. "We should support resistance wars" against military expansion worldwide, "so that the victims of the war would not think of Uncle Sam's neutrality policy as cold blooded," but of the fact that there was justice "to guide American actions" to maintain world peace.[103]

Conclusion

Throughout the 1930s and early 1940s when the United States remained neutral, New York's Chinese advocated American involvement in the war. Their active participation in the movements to support China against Japan's invasion and to endorse other ethnic groups' protest of German fascism demonstrated their stance for peace in the world.

Their appeal for global peace and stability brought the sympathetic support of Americans and changed their attitudes toward the Chinese in the United States. More important, New York's Chinese considered their support activities to be Americans' responsibilities in world affairs, thus reinforcing their identity as Americans. A similar consciousness-raising was to take place when the United States declared war against Japan after Pearl Harbor. During the war, New York's Chinese were involved in activities, both on the home front and the war's front line, to protect the United States, a country they called home.

Notes

1. H. M. Lai, *The Chinese of America, 1785–1980* (San Francisco: Chinese Cultural Foundation, 1980); also see Lowell Dittmer and Samuel S. Kim, ed., *China's Quest for National Identity* (New York: Cornell University Press, 1993).

2. Gloria H. Chun, "'Go West . . . To China': Chinese American Identity in the 1930's," in *Claiming America: Constructing Chinese American Identities during the Exclusion Era*, ed. K. Scott Wong and Sucheng Chan (Philadelphia: Temple University Press, 1998); also see L. Eve Armentrout Ma, *Revolutionaries, Monarchists and Chinatowns: Chinese Politics in the Americas and the 1911 Revolutions* (Honolulu: Hawaii University Press, 1990); Ronald Takaki, *Strangers from a Different Shore: A History of Asian Americans* (New York: Penguin Books, 1989).

3. *Chinese Christian Student*, Dec. 10, 1935.

4. According to a Chinese newspaper reporter, a Chinese American Aviation School cadet, whose father had a laundry on Madison Avenue, flew overhead during

the demonstration. Arthur Bonner, *Alas! What Brought Thee Hither? The Chinese in New York, 1800–1950* (Madison, N.J.: Fairleigh Dickinson University Press, 1996), 173.

5. Ibid.

6. *Chinese Christian Student*, June 1939, 3.

7. The Anti-Japanese Association of Chinese Residents of New York had been active since its establishment. It was responsible for the May 1928 mass demonstration and the mass gathering to celebrate the victory of the Northeast Army. *Chinese Christian Student*, Feb. 1938, 3, 5.

8. Ibid., 3.

9. According to the memo of General Tsia's grandson, Chinese soldiers of the local armies fought bravely against the Japanese invaders. Both sides suffered great casualties. During the Shanghai defense war, Japanese troops were assigned three different commanders. The fighting spirit of the local troops encouraged the Chinese people in the future of China's war against Japan. Wang Zhijuan, "Tsia Tingkai, the Characteristics of a Soldier," *Global People*, October 2008.

10. *Chinese Nationalist Daily*, Sept. 1, 1932.

11. *Chinese Nationalist Daily*, Aug. 30, 1932.

12. *Chinese Nationalist Daily*, Aug. 18, 1932.

13. Ibid.

14. Ibid.

15. Ibid.

16. *Chinese Nationalist Daily*, Aug. 11, 1932.

17. Ibid.

18. *Chinese Nationalist Daily*, Aug. 22, 1932.

19. Ibid.

20. Theodora Chan Wang, *Chinese Women's Association*, *Condensed Report for the Years of 1932–1936*; Judy Yung, Gordon H. Chang, and Him Mark Lai, ed., *Chinese American Voices: From the Gold Rush to the Present* (Berkeley: University of California Press, 2006), 189.

21. *Chinese Nationalist Daily*, June 9, 1935.

22. *Chinese Nationalist Daily*, June 10, 1935.

23. *Chinese Nationalist Daily*, Sept. 21, 1932. Most Chinese Americans remained neutral in the dispute between the National Party and the Chinese Communist Party in China. Instead of taking sides with either party, they appealed for military defense, national unity, and a united front for China.

24. *Chinese Nationalist Daily*, Sept. 21, 1932.

25. Hua Liang, "Fighting for a New Life: Social and Patriotic Activism of Chinese American Women in New York City: 1900–1945," *Journal of American Ethnic History* 17, no. 2, (Winter 1998): 22.

26. Betty L. Sung, *Mountain of Gold: The Chinese in America* (New York: The Macmillan Company, 1967), 155. The sex ratio is 26.8 to 1 in Harry Kitano and

Roger Daniel's book, *Asian Americans, Emerging Minorities* (Upper Saddle River, N.J.: Prentice Hall, 2001), 25.

27. Louis J. Beck, *New York's Chinatown* (New York: Bohemia Publishing Company, 1898).

28. Hua Liang, "Fighting for a New Life: Social and Patriotic Activism of Chinese American Women in New York City: 1900–1945," *Journal of American Ethnic History* 17, no. 2, (Winter 1998): 22.

29. Roger Daniels, *Asian America: Chinese and Japanese in the United States since 1850* (Seattle: University of Washington Press, 1988), 69.

30. Judy Yung, Gordon H. Chang, and Him Mark Lai, ed., *Chinese American Voices: From the Gold Rush to the Present* (Berkeley: University of California Press, 2006), 186.

31. Theodora Chan Wang, *Chinese Women's Association, Condensed Report for the Years of 1932–1936*; Ibid., 194.

32. Ibid., 186.

33. Ibid., 186.

34. Ibid., 189.

35. *Chinese Christian Student*, Feb. 1938. Deng Zuyin was the first president of the organization.

36. Ibid.

37. Arthur Bonner, *Alas! What Brought Thee Hither? The Chinese in New York, 1800–1950* (Madison, N.J.: Fairleigh Dickenson University Press, 1996), 173.

38. *Chinese Nationalist Daily*, Oct. 10, 1933. In the event, Deng Zuyin, the president of the organization, and Kuan Bingxi appealed for more support for Chinese relief work.

39. Pearl S. Buck, "Western Weapons in the Hands of the Reckless East," *Asia*, Oct. 1937, 672.

40. Ibid. For the cruelty of Japanese war against China, see Iris Chang, *The Rape of Nanking: The Forgotten Holocaust of World War II* (New York: L.L.C. Basic Books, 1997).

41. Paul Siu, *The Chinese Laundryman: A Study of Social Isolation* (New York: New York University Press, 1953, 1987), 139.

42. Ibid.

43. Arthur Bonner, *Alas! What Brought Thee Hither? The Chinese in New York, 1800–1950* (Madison, N.J.: Fairleigh Dickenson University Press, 1996), 173.

44. *Chinese Christian Student*, Feb. 1938.

45. Ibid

46. The money was sent directly to Madam Chiang Kai-shek (Jiang Jieshi). In order to set up a direct aid relation with China, this organization asked Madam Chiang Kai-shek (Jiang Jieshi) to be its honorary president. According to the *Chinese Christian Student*, C. H. Wang was the first president of the Chinese Women's Relief Association, while K. C. L. was selected as its vice president. Ibid.

The nonresistance policy of Chiang Kai-shek toward the Japanese invasions received fierce criticism in China as well as among the Chinese in the United States. General Young Hucheng and Zhang Xueliang rebelled and arrested Chiang in Xian in June 1936. The crisis was eased when Chiang promised to take military actions against the Japanese. He was eventually released and resumed his title as commander-in-chief as a consequence of a series of negotiations in which Madam Chiang was also involved. The Chinese women's association believed that it was the best way to send the money directly to her, as it trusted Madam Chiang.

47. *Chinese Christian Student*, Feb. 1938.

48. *Far Eastern Magazine* 1, no. 2, (Dec. 1937): 66.

49. *Directory of Chinese Students in America* (*Liou Mei Qing Nian*) (New York: Chinese Student Christian Association in North America, 1937); *Chinese Christian Student*, Feb. 1937, No. 4.

50. *Chinese Christian Student*, Feb. 1937, No. 4.

51. *Chinese Christian Student*, Feb.–Mar. 1936, 15.

52. *Chinese Christian Student*, Oct. 1937; *Chinese Digest*, Sept. 1937.

53. The American Bureau for Medical Aid to China was a Chinese American medical organization. Located at 40 East 34th Street in New York, it was formed in December 1937 by a group of prominent medicine professionals with Dr. Co Tui as its chairman and Dr. Farn B. Chu as its vice chairman. This organization raised a considerable sum of money, which enabled it to purchase medical equipment and supplies for China.

The badly needed medical supplies were shipped to Hong Kong, the then-British colony, and reshipped to mainland China where thousands of "stricken civilian men, women and children were waiting . . ." "for a merciful chance for life." The effort of New York's Chinese medical professionals to provide aid for China elicited a wholehearted response from the Chinese community, which was eager to save as many of the lives of the wounded as possible. *Far Eastern Magazine*, Nov. 1937–June 1938, 138–40.

54. *Chinese Christian Student*, Feb. 1938, 5.

55. The $4,444.09 helped the organization purchase six "well-equipped medical and surgical machines" needed in China. *Chinese Christian Student*, Feb. 1938, 5.

56. It lasted from February 19 to 24, 1939. *Chinese Student League of Greater New York*, May 1939, 46.

57. Ibid.

58. When they had a break, according to a local Chinese newsletter, the "shivering Chinese students" came into the restaurant to warm themselves "with a cup of hot tea." Over the tea, they exchanged notes and interesting experiences. Ibid.

59. *Chinese Christian Student*, Feb. 1939, 3.

60. See the second part of note 46 for information on the change of the Chinese government policy.

61. *Chinese Christian Student*, June 1939, 3.

62. They met at the Hotel Lexington in New York on April 21, 1938. Delegates from the American Red Cross and the Associated Boards of Christian Colleges in China also participated in the meeting. *Chinese Christian Student*, May–June 1938, 10.

63. Ibid.

64. *Chinese Christian Student*, Nov. 1938.

65. *Chinese Christian Student*, Feb. 1938, 5.

66. Ibid.

67. Ibid.

68. The League against War and Fascism and the American Friends of the Chinese People were major organizers of the rally. *Chinese Christian Student*, Oct. 1937.

69. Arthur Bonner, *Alas! What Brought Thee Hither? The Chinese in New York, 1800–1950* (Madison, N.J.: Fairleigh Dickenson University Press, 1996), 173.

70. *Chinese Christian Student*, Oct. 1937, 7.

71. Ibid.

72. Ibid.

73. Ibid.

74. Ibid.

75. The parade was considered "the biggest mass demonstration ever staged by Chinese in Eastern United States." "Great Chinese Parade in Eastern United States," *Chinese Christian Student*, May–June 1938. This event was also reported by the *New York Times* and the *Far Eastern Magazine* under the title "12,000 Chinese in Protest Parade."

76. *Chinese Christian Student*, May–June 1938.

77. *Chinese Student League of Greater New York*, May 1939.

78. *Chinese Christian Student*, Oct. 1937, 7.

79. *Chinese Student League of Greater New York*, May 1939.

80. Organizations to aid Chinese relief work were also formed on the West Coast. The China War Relief Association was one of the biggest China relief organizations on the West Coast of the United States. Consisting of ninety-one overseas Chinese organizations, this organization was established on August 19, 1937, one month after the Japanese attacked Beijing. For the purpose of raising money for civilian refugee relief and medical relief for the wounded soldiers in China, the China War Relief Association had raised over three million Chinese dollars by early February 1938. In addition, fifteen thousand pieces of new clothing had been sent to the wounded, and fifty thousand pounds of old clothes had been sent to the war refugees in Shanghai and Canton. According to a local Chinese newsletter, thirty thousand individuals contributed to the fundraising efforts. Three percent of these donors were American friends. They were all volunteers. See "Active China Relief Organizations in America," *Chinese Christian Student*, Feb. 1938.

81. Lyman Pierce and H. B. R. Bugess were the executives of this organization. *Chinese Christian Student*, Feb. 1938.

82. *Chinese Christian Student*, Feb. 1938.

83. Ibid.

84. Ibid.

85. *Chinese Christian Student*, Dec. 1937.

86. Frances Roots was a daughter of Bishop Logan Roots. *Chinese Christian Student*, May–June 1938.

87. *Chinese Christian Student*, May–June 1938.

88. Siuwein Yu, "American Goodwill to China," *Far Eastern Magazine* 1, no. 4, (Feb. 1938): 195.

89. Gerald Feldman, ed., *German Imperialism, 1914–1918* (New York: Wiley, 1972), and Andreas Hillgruber, *Germany and the Two World Wars* (Cambridge, Mass.: Harvard University Press, 1981), approach the debate over Germany's guilt and aggression. W. G. Beasley's *Japanese Imperialism, 1894–1945* (New York: Oxford University Press, 1992) is a good book on Japanese expansion. Akira Iriye, *The Origins of the Second World War in Asia and the Pacific* (London and New York: Longman, 1987), covers the race to war. Eric Hobsbawm's *The Age of Extremes: A History of the World, 1914–1991* (New York: Pantheon Books, 1996) is a recent interpretation with a good discussion of war and revolution.

90. *Chinese Christian Student*, Dec. 10, 1935.

91. *Chinese Christian Student* Jan. 1936, 7.

92. Joseph A. Wytrawal, *Poles in America History and Tradition* (Detroit: Endurance Press, 1969), 386–87; Frederick M. Binder and David Reimers, *All the Nations under Heaven: An Ethnic and Racial History of New York City* (New York: Columbia University Press, 1995), 191.

93. Frederick M. Binder and David Reimers, *All the Nations under Heaven: An Ethnic and Racial History of New York City* (New York: Columbia University Press, 1995), 191.

94. However, these activities had little impact upon federal government policies. For more information, see Richard Lingeman, *Don't You Know There Is a War On? The American Home Front, 1941–1945* (New York, 1970), 331; David Wyman, *The Abandonment of the Jews: America and the Holocaust, 1941–1945* (New York: Pantheon Books, 1984); Frederick M. Binder and David Reimers, *All the Nations under Heaven: An Ethnic and Racial History of New York City* (New York: Columbia University Press, 1995), 192–93.

95. Its headquarters was situated at 112 West 19th Street. It was originally founded with special emphasis on the needs in Spain as Spain was undergoing a bloody civil war. Cooperating with International Student Service in its Chinese university relief fund, certain chapters of this organization were also designated to contribute funds to China war relief. See *Chinese Christian Student*, Feb. 1938.

96. Frank Lee was a son of Tom Lee, who was a Chinese community leader. *Chinese Christian Student*, Feb. 1938, 3.

97. Ibid.

98. *Chinese Christian Student*, Oct. 1937, 5.

99. "Japanese Import of Oil," *Far Eastern Magazine* I, no. 4 (Feb. 1938).

100. Manifesto of the *Chinese Students League of Greater New York*, *Chinese Christian Student*, Dec. 10, 1935.

101. *Chinese Christian Student*, Oct. 1937, 5.

102. Lim P. Lee, "American-Born Chinese and Chino-Japanese Crisis," *Chinese Christian Student*, Oct. 1937, 5.

103. Ibid.

CHAPTER SIX

Pearl Harbor and Its Aftermath

Throughout the 1930s, the United States attempted to remain isolated from international affairs while the troubled world continued to suffer from imperialist expansion. However, efforts to keep formal neutrality could not protect the United States from the spread of fascism and militarism. On December 7, 1941, Japanese bombers suddenly attacked the U.S. naval base at Pearl Harbor. Consequently, the United States was forced into war. This chapter describes the attack on Pearl Harbor and its impact on Americans. It focuses on the response of New York's Chinese Americans to this attack.

In their studies on the change of the American reception of the Chinese in the United States, scholars generally agree that the wartime corporation between the United States and China due to the Pearl Harbor attack created a momentum for the Chinese in the United States to advance in society. John Dower maintains that the war changed the attitude of Americans toward Chinese Americans as they suddenly found themselves on the same line with China against Japan.[1] Fred W. Riggs suggests that in order to defeat Japan, the United States allied with China. This war strategy affected the longstanding anti-Chinese legislation and eventually brought an end to the Chinese exclusion laws.[2] This chapter argues that the Chinese in the United States, particularly New York's Chinese, played a crucial role in changing American attitudes toward the Chinese people. It was the involvement of Chinese Americans, both men and women, in the war effort to oppose Japan that changed American attitudes. And that eventually brought the end of the sixty-one years of Chinese exclusion laws.

The identity gained as Chinese Americans during the war in support of China against Japan was reinforced when Japan attacked the United States. They were "Americans First," as scholar K. Scott Wong described.[3] The commitment of the Chinese in the United States, particularly Chinese New Yorkers, to the war effort and their sacrifice for the cause to protect the country proved them to be patriotic American citizens. Their engagement in military services, wartime industrial production, and civilian activities such as fundraising, war bond purchase, and blood donation was part of the mainstream effort to support the American war against injustice forced upon them. Repeal of the exclusion legislation proved perhaps the most important consequence of their varied efforts to integrate as American citizens and claim their rights as American citizens.

Chinese Americans and the War Front

Japanese bombers suddenly attacked the U.S. naval base at Pearl Harbor on December 7, 1941. Within two hours, the United States lost 8 battleships, 3 cruisers, 4 other vessels, 188 airplanes, and several vital shore installations. More tragically, more than two thousand soldiers died, and another one thousand were injured. The deficiency of the American policy in global affairs crippled the dignity of Americans. On the day after the Pearl Harbor attack, the United States finally declared war against Japan, thus marking the beginning of the U.S. military engagement in World War II.

For years, Americans have tried to evaluate the ramifications of the attack. Traditional interpretations suggest that President Roosevelt deliberately suppressed the information of the forthcoming attack in the belief that a surprise attack would arouse the nation and thus lead American people to support the United States' participation in World War II. Disagreeing with this interpretation, revisionists argue that the success of the Pearl Harbor raid demonstrated American political and bureaucratic failure to access advance warning of the attack. Other scholars attribute the raid to American indifference to Japanese military expansion and the worldwide war crisis.[4]

The debate over Pearl Harbor has never fully subsided. But apparently, because of the attack, an epoch of isolationism in American history finally came to an end. Americans learned a hard lesson from the Pearl Harbor attack, which demonstrated the inadequacy of American isolation as a policy in a moment of such global trouble. "We must begin the great task that is before us," President Franklin Roosevelt announced, to abandon "once and for all the illusion that we can ever again isolate ourselves from the rest of humanity."

The Pearl Harbor attack dealt a big blow on the Americans. Being awakened by the sudden invasion, the whole country was mobilized. Thousands upon thousands of Americans were inspired to join the military forces to defend the United States. According to the *New York Times*, 17,717 enlisted in the army in the first week after the Pearl Harbor attack. Enlistment increased to 28,363 in the following week.[5] Fifteen million men and women nationwide were drafted into the military forces during the war.

Chinese Americans were indignant over the Pearl Harbor attack. They saw it as an excessive assault against their land. The attack aroused their patriotism like everyone else. Inspired by the declaration of war, Chinese Americans ensured the full endorsement of the defense of the country. Representing the Chinese in the United States, Chinese community leaders throughout the nation took a joint action to send a telegram to President Roosevelt to express their support. "For the sake of our country," the telegram declared, "we whole-heartedly support the American declaration of war."[6]

Individual organizations formed particularly to support China defense against Japan in the 1930s were encouraged by the American declaration of war in New York. For years they had lobbied American politicians to take actions to engage the United States in war to contain the spread of fascist aggressions. They immediately sent telegrams to Congress to express their endorsement of the decision of the government to declare war against Japan. The New York Overseas-Chinese Anti-Japanese Association was one of such organizations. In its message to Congress on December 20, this organization expressed its endorsement of American involvement in the war: "We are more than happy to hear that the United States is finally getting into the war for peace."[7]

Military programs were established by New York Chinese in response to the war. A special naval personnel training school, the New York Chinatown Naval Academy, for example, was set up to assist the war efforts. This was an unusual military program created and sponsored by the Chinese in New York. New York Chinese were ardent supporters of military defense in the 1930s when China was attacked by Japan. They organized and sponsored aviation training programs such as the Save-China Aviation Association (SCAA),the New York Chinese American Aviation Volunteers, and the East Coast General Committee of Overseas Chinese Aviators to meet the desperate needs of China for professional, trained pilots in its war against Japan.[8] When the United States was attacked at Pearl Harbor, New York Chinese joined together once again to create naval training programs to meet the devastating needs of the United States to fight back against Japan as the U.S. Navy suffered a great loss during the attack. Thousands of marine soldiers died in the attack as well. The New York Chinatown Naval Academy was established to train naval personnel. It recruited sixteen young Chinese Americans as its first-term cadets. It provided two basic courses: naval navigation and mechanics. In addition, it emphasized field drills to ensure qualified naval personnel for the war.[9] Although it was a small training program, it demonstrated the determination of Chinese New Yorkers in their effort to defend the country.

Like every American citizen, Chinese Americans also joined the American military to defend America. Approximately 13,311 Chinese Americans—nearly 22 percent of adult Chinese males across the country—were drafted into the armed services. An unknown number, perhaps several thousands, volunteered for military service.[10] Joining with other American soldiers, they were deployed to war zones in all parts of the world serving in the Third and Fourth Infantry Divisions in the European war front, and in the Sixth, Thirty-second, and Seventy-seventh in Asia and the Pacific. Twenty-five percent of Chinese American recruits served in the American air force.[11] Many served in the navy.[12]

New York's Chinese had longed for American military engagement in the war. When the United States entered the war after the Pearl Harbor attack, they became ardent supporters. They were among the approximately nine hundred thousand New Yorkers who entered the armed forces.[13] "New York's Chinatown cheered itself hoarse when the first draft numbers drawn were for Chinese Americans," an observer reported.[14] By 1945, an estimated four thousand young Chinese Americans from the New York–New Jersey metropolitan area were drafted.[15]

To support the American war effort, New York's Chinese Americans, both men and women, enlisted. February 15 was the traditional Chinese New Year's day. Around this time of the year, residents of Chinatown would go shopping, clean the house, and cook the food to prepare for the annual Spring Festival celebration. Families and friends would pack the streets. However, 1942 was such a different year as the country needed its citizens to fight for its survival. The *Chinese Nationalist Daily* reported that the military recruitment service station in New York's Chinatown was very crowded.[16] Even though the traditional Chinese New Year was only days away, Chinese New Yorkers were in line at the station, eager to register as they considered enlisting more urgent than preparing for holiday festivities.[17]

The American government recognized the enthusiasm of New York Chinese to join the military to fight for the country. The American military service decided to put Chinese American veterans in charge of recruitment in the Chinese community to encourage more Chinese Americans to join military forces.[18] Sing Keel, a World War I veteran, was named chairman of the Selective Service Board in New York's Chinatown.[19] Lee Yinghuei was appointed to be in charge of recruiting Chinese American women at 40 Mott Street in Chinatown.[20]

The war brought diverse New York Chinese together for the purpose of defending the country. New York's Chinese American recruits came from varied backgrounds. Some were college students, engineers, and newspaper editors; others were butchers, grocers, and restaurant workers. Farmers from Long Island were also part of the recruits. They "poured into the draft office at P.S. 23 in New York's Chinatown," as a local newspaper reported.[21]

Like other American soldiers, New York's Chinese fought in various war fronts. Chen Long and Chen Chongmin, among other Chinese American soldiers from New York, served on Sicily's war front.[22] Peter Lee, a 1941 Columbia University graduate, served with the Flying Tigers of the U.S. Fourteenth Air Force to China under the command of Major General Claire Lee Chennault.[23]

The U.S. Fourteenth Air Force was established in the spring of 1942 to cope with the anti-Japanese war in Asia. Originally formed as the American Volunteer Group in December 1940 to aid in the defense of China, it soon reorganized as China Air Task Force. By late 1942, it had become the U.S. Fourteenth Air Force combating in the China-India-Burma military theater. The air force was, as K. Wong described, "a unique blend of white American, Chinese American, and Chinese Nationalist service personnel."[24] It consisted of both American pilots and Chinese pilots who were trained by American aviators either in India or at Luck Field and Thunderbird Field near Phoenix, Arizona, in the United States. Chinese American pilots were important components of the combats. Started as a small air force unit, the Fourteenth Air Force soon developed to be a powerful air force. Members of the air force contributed greatly to the war in China and in Asia. They demolished 234 enemy planes and coordinated successfully with the Allied Power's ground forces during the war.[25]

New York's Chinese women also demonstrated themselves as valuable supporters for the American military defense. The war created an opportunity for Chinese women in the United States to demonstrate themselves as loyal citizens. It also transformed Chinese American women as they departed from traditional female roles and joined the armed forces. As mentioned earlier, because of the cultural tradition and the Chinese exclusion laws, Chinese women in New York had been isolated from the world outside their community. The anti-Japanese war in the 1930s created an opportunity for them to participate in the activities to support China. When Japan launched its war against the United States, they quickly transferred their public responsibilities to engage in the war effort in support of the United States while continuing their commitment to China's war. Their dual identity of being Chinese Americans that developed in the 1930s grew even stronger when they committed themselves to support the United States against Japan in the 1940s.

Like other Chinese Americans, Chinese women New Yorkers vied with each other to join the army in response to the call of supporting Uncle Sam.[26] The *Chinese Nationalist Daily* reported about the busy military recruitment service station in New York's Chinatown that demonstrated the eagerness of New York Chinese, both men and women, to engage in the war.[27] Chinese women sometimes found it difficult to be recruited as they were considered to be too small to be soldiers. The difficulties for women were exemplified by Emily Lee Shak, the first Chinese woman to join the army. She had lived on a special Chinese diet to reach the 105-pound minimum weight requirement to join the army.[28]

Chinese American women participated in military services. They served both in the army and in the air force. Hazel Toy was one of the first Chinese American women volunteers enlisted in the air unit of the Women's Army Corps in 1943.[29] Maggie Gee became one of the only two Chinese American women accepted by the Women Air Force Service Pilots (WASP). She flew a variety of aircrafts during the war as part of her duty to transport airplanes from one base to another within the United States.[30] Chinese American women also voluntarily joined the army as nurses.[31] Ruth Chang Jang joined the Women's Air Corps and worked in a hospital as a secretary to the nurses at Mitchell Field, Long Island, in New York.[32] Miss T, a daughter of a Euro-Chinese marriage, became a nursing trainee at Columbia University after her college graduation in 1944. She served in the American army in China between 1945 and 1946.[33]

The active participation of New York's young Chinese women in the war effort received the support of the Chinese community. Farewell parties and ceremonies were held to honor their decisions to join the army. For example, when Lee Ying, an American air force cadet, was leaving for the war front, she was honored by New York's Chinese community.[34]

New York's Chinese American women took opportunities to participate in defending the country during World War II. By answering the nation's call to duty, they were able to venture beyond their own community and establish themselves as patriotic Americans.

Him Mark Lai and Shih-shan Tsai suggest that the zeal of Chinese Americans for American military intervention in global affairs came from their anti-Japanese sentiment.[35] Their military service can be seen as a temporary solution to the devastating effects of unemployment on the Chinese during the Depression as well. However, evidence also demonstrates that Chinese Americans became aware of the significance of the war as a moment for them to participate in mainstream politics. For decades since the exclusion laws of 1882, New York's Chinese had fought to be part of society.

World War II created an opportunity for Chinese New Yorkers to participate as a way of identifying themselves as Americans. "We joined the army for America," Kain Chen, a Chinese American veteran of World War II, said in an interview. "We were not simply fighting for China. Instead, we fought for the United States."[36]

Kain Chen's words reflected a growing consciousness of Chinese New Yorkers to be regarded as American citizens. Fighting along with other American soldiers, they felt proud to be trusted to defend America as their own country. Arthur Wang, a war veteran, recalled that "in those days, you felt privileged to handle a gun to defend your country in World War II."[37] Harold Liu recalled that the period of World War II "was just a whole different era in the community. . . . My own brother went into the service." He said, "We were so proud that they were in uniform" fighting along with other American soldiers.[38] As Chinese and Americans were fighting together against their common enemies, Liu said, "We began to feel very good about ourselves. . . . It was a nice feeling for the big change."[39]

The "nice feeling for the big change" of New York's Chinese indicated a large collective interior transformation in Chinese American self-definition. It was not simply the individuals who enlisted that participated in this radically positive redefinition of community and self, but also parents and neighbors. When the United States declared war against Japan, supportive parents sent their children to the war front for the defense of America. Ng Wing, a resident of Chinatown, sent all three of his sons to the army during the war and was honored as a model Chinese American by the Chinese community.[40] Business owners honored new recruits by providing them with free services. Pong Jiajang, a laundry owner, decided to let all army recruits wash and dry their clothes free of charge. One of his customers was moved to say that he would kill more Japanese enemies in gratitude.[41]

The armed forces became a very important avenue by which the Chinese in the United States achieved a new status in American society. Those who were drafted served in integrated military branches and units that opened up opportunities for them to demonstrate their loyalty to the country. Fighting along with other American soldiers also created chances for them to be better understood. What they contributed was appreciated by their fellow soldiers. "Individually every Chinese man and officer was a human being in his own mold, a complex personality with his own idiosyncrasies, strengths, weaknesses and talents," Kenneth E. Kay described. "They were just like Americans."[42] Serving in an integrated military unit, soldiers began to learn to understand each other. With the myth of pigtailed "John Chinaman" in his mind before joining the army, an American veteran would go home "remembering the little Sergeant Hsieh, the 32nd squadron armorer who worked with more furious intensity than any American in that hard driven section," Kay observed.[43]

However, Chinese American soldiers confronted racial prejudice; some found themselves the victims of racial hysteria during the war years. "Unconvinced that American soldiers could be anything but white, some Euro-Americans exhibited color prejudice toward them," as Wayne Hung Wong experienced.[44] They were often caught between the black-white dyad of race relations as they were perceived as neither American nor minority.[45] Chinese Americans were only eligible to enlist as mess steward or cabin boys under the U.S. Navy's discriminatory policies. Their primary duties would be to serve food in the officer's dining room until the navy eased its restriction on what positions Chinese Americans could hold in May 1942 and they were allowed to enlist as apprentice seamen.[46] Overcoming the prejudice, Chinese Americans committed themselves to the war front and they proved to be among the "best men who ever joined the Navy."[47]

The dedication of and sacrifices by Chinese American soldiers during the war proved them to be patriotic Americans. They endured separation from their families and friends, suffered from the brutality and horror of combat, and were drained by the tensions and strains of military life. Ninety Chinese American soldiers from New York lost their lives to the war. Among them were Lincoln Ng and David Ng, two sons of Wing Ng,[48] Lieutenant A. Fong, and twenty-six-year-old Lieutenant Benjamin Ralph Kimlau, the first Chinese American heavy bomber pilot. They were honored by the Chinese community and their heroic deeds received recognition by the American military forces. Benjamin Ralph Kimlau was honored by the Chinese community as a war hero when he died after his B-24 was shot down in the Battle of Coral Sea in the Pacific in August 1942.[49] A. Fong was awarded a medal for his bravery by the American army.[50]

The highly spirited and substantial support of Chinese New Yorkers for America's military defense also showed itself in various civilian activities. Organized fundraising for the war front, for example, was one of such activities. Led by the Chinese Students Association, the "A Bowl of Rice for War" campaign was launched immediately after the United States officially joined the war. In just one day, it collected $800 from New York Chinese.[51] Organizations that were formed to support China against Japan in the 1930s accelerated their campaigns in support of the Allied Powers when the United States entered the war. On December 16, 1941, the Association in Support of China organized a donation bazaar on Mott Street.[52] On December 24, 1941, the National Association in Support of China made a Christmas pledge to collect $25,000 through sponsoring a benefit show of the "Adventure of Marco Polo."[53] On January 1, 1942, the Association of Chinese American Youth to Support China and the War organized a New Year's parade to collect money. Individual citizens contributed greatly to the fundraising campaign. Lee Diannai, a Chinatown resident, for example, contributed 550 Chinese dollars and Wu Qi, another Chinatown resident, donated 100 Chinese dollars at this event.[54] In March 1942, during a "Chinese Day" parade, New York University students raised $6,000.[55] By September 15, 1943, a total amount of $12,200 in cash had been collected from New York's Chinese for the war front.[56] Fundraising activities banded Chinese New Yorkers together as volunteers to help with the war. Men and women, the old and young, students and businessmen donated what they could afford to support the war. Many of them hoped that what they contributed would also help China in its struggle against Japan, the common enemy of the United States and China, a reflection of their Chinese American identity.

Chinese New Yorkers also launched campaigns for blood donations, another kind of activity to support the war. Many of New York's Chinese contributed to the campaigns to save as many lives of soldiers as possible. Some gave money; others donated blood. In a one-day street drive on June 23, 1943, $1,701 was collected to endorse blood donation drives.[57] Moved by the spirit of the street drive, a twenty-two-year-old Japanese American girl donated her blood to show her solidarity with the Chinese and as a protest against Japanese barbarism.[58] On October 27, 1943, a day set aside as "a day for a drop of blood," more than one hundred of New York's Chinese volunteers donated their blood.[59]

In addition to military service, fundraising, and blood donation, New York's Chinese community also mobilized its people to purchase as many war bonds as possible as a means of supporting the American war effort. "Every Chinese American should buy war bonds for liberty" was a popular slogan in New York's Chinatown during wartime that demonstrated the understanding of the war by Chinese New Yorkers.[60] The United States was the country of their birth, the country of which they were citizens, and the country to which they pledged their loyalty. They were eager to help with the war and to contribute to what the country needed. On September 28, 1943, Chinatown organizations initiated a joint effort to arouse people to purchase war bonds. More than twenty members of the Women Volunteers Association participated to make it a success. Thousands of New York's Chinese residents bought war bonds on that day.[61] When Chen Dayi bought $20,000 worth of war bonds at one time, he was honored by the whole Chinese community.[62] By October 9, 1943, the total amount of war bonds purchased by New York's Chinese residents reached $4,134,075.[63]

World War II opened up opportunities for New York's Chinese Americans to demonstrate their commitment to the nation, a reflection of their long-standing desire to be accepted as part of American society. Their active support of what America needed for the war front proved them to be patriotic Americans. The war also created opportunities for the Chinese in the United States to participate in wartime industrial production, an area which had been previously unavailable to them.

Chinese Americans on the Home Front

The American war engagement boosted the economy and created opportunities for Chinese Americans to move out of traditional service businesses of restaurants and laundries and become engaged in wartime production, which was regarded as a socially valued activity. As early as 1939, President Roosevelt promised that American armaments would be made available to the Allied armies to help them compete against the highly productive German munitions industry. The possibility of making the United States an "arsenal of Democracy" resulted in the revision of 1939 Neutrality Acts, which permitted belligerent nations to purchase American arms on the same cash-and-carry basis that earlier Neutrality Acts had established for the sale of nonmilitary materials. In March 1941, Congress passed a lend-lease bill authorizing the president to sell, lease, or lend war materials to any nation whose defense was considered vital to America's safety.[64]

The new legislation and the demands of wartime production created a boom in the American economy. The gross national product soared from $91 billion in 1939 to $166 billion in 1945. The impact of government spending was most dramatic during the boom. The federal government invested almost $40 billion in factories, military and transportation facilities, highways, and power plants in the West alone. Many new factory complexes were funded directly by the federal government's Defense Plants Corporation. By the beginning of 1944, the output of American factories was twice that of all the Axis countries combined. Constituting a "third front" in the global fighting, the American industrial economy became vital to the war effort. Joseph

Stalin once toasted the wartime American production, saying that without American production, "the war would have been lost."[65]

Historians agree that the war economy provided vital support for the Allies in World War II. Scholars also point to the doubling of job opportunities.[66] As American wartime industry flourished, the demand for labor greatly increased. With fifteen million men and women entering the military forces, seven million Americans who had previously been off the jobs market entered the labor force. Workers who had been unemployed for years found jobs in war-related factories and plants.

The wartime economy employed a large portion of the working population. Because of so many Americans going off to war, the labor shortage opened opportunities for the Chinese and other minorities in the United States to participate in American industrial activities which had excluded them for decades. There are no official statistics on the wartime employment of the Chinese nationwide. However, contemporary Chinese American publications indicated that the Chinese increasingly found jobs in shipyards, airplane factories, and defense plants.[67] In Los Angeles, some three hundred Chinese worked on the construction of the ship *China Victory*.[68] In Douglas, there were approximately one hundred Chinese working at the three defense plants of Santa Monica, Long Beach, and El Segundo.[69] Approximately sixteen hundred Chinese Americans out of a population of eighteen thousand in the San Francisco Bay Area worked in the defense industries, especially shipbuilding in 1942.[70] Chinese workers constituted 15 percent of the shipyard workforce in the San Francisco Bay Area in 1943.[71] Chinese workers also found jobs in the defense industries at the Seattle-Tacoma Shipbuilding Corporation, and in the shipyards of Delaware and Mississippi.[72]

The increasing Chinese work population particularly in shipyards throughout the nation was a result of the wartime labor shortage, combined with federal regulations against discrimination, which made the shipyards quite willing to hire minorities.[73] Shipyards in the Bay Area in particular ran recruiting advertisements in Chinatown newspapers offering government-sponsored free classes in marine sheet metal, pipe fitting, electricity, ship fitting, and drafting to appeal to Chinese Americans. Shipyards in Richmond even announced that they were willing to hire the Chinese in the United States regardless of citizenship status while calling upon Chinese Americans to join the war effort.[74]

Chinese New Yorkers also found jobs in war-related industries. According to the *Chinese Press*, about 30 percent of male Chinese were employed in defense plants by 1942.[75] Because of the increasing demand for laborers, Timing Ship, a shipbuilding factory, reportedly looked for four hundred new workers among the Chinese population in New York.[76] Chinese New Yorkers also found jobs in airplane factories on Long Island. They worked as assemblers, as well as riveters and welders.[77]

However, the workplace was not without racial tensions. Chinese Americans often worked in segregated crews. They were often assigned to do certain jobs that were considered "suitable" only for the Chinese.[78] They were not expected to be promoted to supervisory positions. In spite of such issues, Chinese Americans worked hard, as they felt they were building ships and airplanes to fight the war.[79] They took the job opportunity to expose themselves to the "American work world." Working and serving the country alongside people with whom they had previously had little contact also provided them with an opportunity to integrate into mainstream activities. Venturing outward, beyond their own community, Chinese Americans were exposed to a broader spectrum of social roles and situations during the war.

World War II also changed the pattern of the employment of Chinese American professionals. College-educated Chinese were able to find jobs in their fields of specialization, such as architecture and engineering.[80] Lingchi Wang's study of Chinese employment in the United States in professional and technical jobs from 1940 to 1950 reveals that in 1940, one thousand out of thirty-six thousand employed Chinese held professional and technical jobs. In 1950, some thirty-five hundred out of forty-eight thousand Chinese Americans were employed as professionals and technicians.[81]

The increasing demand for labor during the war also provided job opportunities for Chinese women. According to Rose Hum Lee's research, "Even girls were getting jobs" working as office workers and secretaries during the war.[82] Women constituted one-fifth of the employed Chinese population in 1940. In 1950, the proportion increased to one-third.[83] They were cogs in America's machinery and they were part of "the millions who stand behind the man behind the gun."[84]

The war industries provided opportunities for Chinese Americans. Yet it was the participation of Chinese Americans in wartime production and their dedication to the war effort that changed their image in the eyes of society. New York's Chinese were aware of the importance of the war in enabling them to join the industrial and professional labor force, especially as their participation in wartime production received social recognition. They were promoted at jobs. Arthur Wang, for example, reached managerial levels, climbing the job ladders that were previously unavailable. Wang started out as an assembler at a Curtis-Wright plant, an airplane plant in Long Island. Then he worked as a riveter. By the time he left for the army, he had already been an assistant to a foreman. He had twenty-eight people working for him before he "got drafted by Uncle Sam."[85]

Chinese New Yorkers' active participation in wartime production was a factor contributing to Americans' changing image of them. A Gallup poll taken in 1942 showed that responders characterized the Chinese as "hard-working, honest, brave, religious, intelligent, and practical."[86] As industrial workers in ship and airplane building industries and as specialists in professional fields during the war, Chinese New Yorkers found themselves with the opportunity to become economically assimilated.

Greater participation in mainstream economic activities also provided the impetus for New York's Chinese to integrate into society in other ways. They moved out of their ethnic community in Lower Manhattan and settled in other areas to be close to work. Many settled in Long Island, Queens, and Brooklyn.

As we have seen, the war changed the image of the Chinese in the United States. Their active participation in World War II on both the war front and the home front contributed to the creation of a new image. They were no longer seen as strangers or aliens. Instead, they began to be considered allies. As the war continued, Chinese American political activists in New York grasped the opportunity and opened a new frontier for the legalization of Chinese immigrants in the United States.

The War and the Repeal of the Exclusion Laws

On November 11, 1943, Congress passed a repeal bill that terminated the Chinese exclusion acts, which had barred almost all Chinese immigration since 1882.[87] Historians suggest that the American government's repeal of Chinese exclusion was an emergency war measure to combat Japanese war propaganda. Since China had already been at war against Japan, repeal to some presented a self-interested feature of the war effort to keep China as an ally.[88]

However, repeal was also a legal achievement of the Chinese in the United States, who regained their basic constitutional right to live and to work in the land they chose as home. Their demand for racial equality and their participation in the repeal movement eventually brought an end to the Chinese exclusion laws. The wartime repeal efforts of New York's Chinese reflected their growing political consciousness and their active participation in mainstream activities. Their contributions to the American war effort significantly amplified their demands for legal status in the United States.

The Japanese government had launched a major ideological anti-Anglo-American propaganda offensive before Pearl Harbor. Accusing the United

States and its European allies of mistreating millions of Asian people and exploiting Asian nations, the Japanese Ministry of Education issued a manifesto titled "The Way of the Subject" in August 1941, defining the war as "a struggle between race." Japanese propaganda condemned the United States in particular for its discriminatory laws and, in the bitterest of ironies, for segregating the Chinese in ghettos where they had been relegated to "the most menial of occupations, despised and mistreated."[89]

Like Nazi Germany, Japan used race issues as an excuse for war. Indeed, shaming these spurious Japanese accusations of U.S. racism, around thirty million Chinese civilians were killed by Japanese soldiers between 1937 and 1945.[90] More than 350,000 noncombatant Chinese died in a few weeks alone in late December 1937 and early 1938 during the Nanjing Massacre.[91] In order to combat the Japanese accusation and to convince the world that racial prejudice was unacceptable in the United States, China, as a Chicago newspaper stated, became America's "white hope" in the East.[92]

New York's Chinese took the American war strategy as a means of reaching their own goals intensifying their effort to bring an end to the Chinese exclusion legislation. In early 1943, organizations as well as individuals of New York's Chinese community launched a petition campaign for repeal.

The Chinese Women's Association of New York took the lead in the petition writing campaign. On February 16, 1943, Theodora Chan Wang, president of the Chinese Women's Association of New York, wrote to Eleanor Roosevelt, asking for a revision of the Chinese immigration laws. Denouncing racial discrimination, she firmly demanded equal treatment of the Chinese. What Chinese Americans wanted, wrote Wang, was merely an immigration quota, so that the Chinese would be accorded the privileges enjoyed by "our companions."[93] This request was followed by a strong response from the leading organization of New York's Chinatown, the Chinese Consolidated. On May 4, the Benevolent Association sent a message to Congress demanding the repeal of the exclusion legislation, calling it a most serious violation of the fundamental principles of equality.[94] At the same time, individual Chinese New Yorkers also wrote letters to petition for repeal. George Kin Leung, a New York Chinese resident, wrote to Martin Kennedy, a New York representative to Congress,

> Born in New Jersey . . . and now sojourning in our New York City, you may imagine how keenly I feel on this subject. [The] friendship between China and America . . . must be fed now, before the war ends, to make easy the post-war cooperation.[95]

This letter sent another strong message demanding an immediate termination of the racially based Chinese Exclusion Law. Moreover, Leung also suggested the possible political cooperation between the United States and China for the sake of the world peace, not only during, but also after the war.

Other New York Chinese residents, such as Yu Tang and Li Chenhuei, also urged an immediate termination of the Chinese exclusion laws. There was no reason for the United States to delay repeal, they said; it was "better for the United States to ban the racial laws sooner and for ever."[96]

The voice of Chinese Americans for repeal had increased. On October 21, 1943, the *Chinese Nationalist Daily* published a poll on the issue showing that the majority of Chinese New Yorkers supported immediate repeal.[97] It also revealed their concern about global peace. Yi Jianlong, director of the Blood Donation Committee of New York's Chinatown, told a reporter that in order to combat the racial war propaganda of the Japanese, the United States should neither hesitate to terminate the legislation nor leave any possibilities for Japan to find excuses for war.[98]

The position of New York's Chinese in the repeal campaign demonstrated their political maturity. Clearly articulated as a desire for racial equality and justice, it also showed their understanding that repeal could be advocated as a war measure for the United States and, further, could be used to support their hopes for the future cooperation of the United States and China.

Petitions for the repeal of the exclusion laws received sympathetic support from other New Yorkers who also saw the necessity of reforming racially discriminatory legislation for the benefit of the war. Richard Walsh, a leading political activist in the repeal campaign, argued that Americans must act for "justice toward our Chinese allies," and demanded a fair legal treatment of Chinese within the framework of a quota system.[99]

In May 1943, New York's political activists established a special organization, the Citizens Committee, to lobby for repeal.[100] Headed by Richard Walsh, editor of the magazine *Asia and the Americas*, the committee's agenda was to participate in activities to repeal the Chinese Exclusion Law "with the added objectives of placing Chinese immigration on a quota basis and making Chinese residents eligible for American citizenship."[101]

Although, to a certain degree, the committee's advocacy was within the limit of the unequal immigration quota system, its opposition against the particular racial discriminatory exclusion laws against the Chinese was appealing. Emphasizing the immediate goal of repealing the discriminatory legislation before the war's end, members of the Citizens Committee publicized the destructive racial aspect of the Chinese exclusion laws through various media to draw public attention to the issue. They exerted their influence through newspaper editorials, radio broadcasts, letters to "old China hands," and lobbying in Washington for the recognition of Chinese immigrants' legal status in the United States, advocating that the principle to eliminate "all racial discriminations" from American immigration and naturalization laws should be enhanced.[102] Within three months of its establishment, 223 members of the Citizens Committee wrote editorials for various newspapers such as the *Saturday Evening Post*, the *New York Times*, and fifty-two other newspapers in over twenty-two states. Fourteen radio broadcasting programs relating to the Chinese exclusion issues were made through various stations such as WABC and WNYC.[103]

The committee's effort for repeal received support from various local New York organizations, particularly religious groups and labor unions, including New York's Chinese labor organizations. The Cafeteria Employees Union, local 302 of the American Federation of Labor in New York,[104] the Chinese Women's Association of the CIO, the International Garment Workers Union, and the Federal Council of Churches of Christ in America were among the twenty-five organizations that successively passed resolutions for repeal.[105]

Individual New Yorkers also participated in the petition campaign. Frances W. Butterfield, member of the New York City Alumnae Association at Randolph-Macon College, sent a letter to all alumnae, asking them to work for repeal and to write their congressmen and their friends. As a result, several local club projects for repeal were established.[106]

As the popular campaign for repeal grew, New York legislators also moved to initiate legal action. On February 17, 1943, Representative Martin Kennedy of New York introduced a repeal bill in the House. Thus, the campaign for repeal forced its way onto the national political agenda.

At the same time, Congress was also moving through prominent diplomatic levels towards a favorable solution to the Chinese exclusion laws by inviting Madam Chiang Kai-shek (Jiang Jieshi) to the United States, a clear signal promoting an improved bilateral relationship. On February 18, 1943, Madam Chiang addressed a joint session of Congress. In her speech, she sent a strong message to the United States about what China needed for cooperative support in its anti-Japanese war. "Basically and fundamentally," she said, "we are fighting for the same cause. . . . We have identity of ideals of . . . freedom. . . . I feel that it is necessary for us not only to have ideals," but also to "act to implement them."[107]

Madam Chiang Kai-shek's speech calling for the implementation of "ideals for freedom" raised the issue of the legal status of Chinese immigrants in the United States. At a dinner party on May 15, 1943, Madam Chiang Kai-shek once again indicated the possible impact of the repeal of the Chinese exclusion laws when she talked to several key congressmen about the war in Asia. The repeal of the Chinese exclusion laws, she suggested, would boost Chinese morale and buttress her country's war effort.[108] Although Madam Chiang's words on the repeal were still in the framework of war consideration offered in the pursuit of an effective strategy for the war, they proved an incentive for Congress to move forward and place the repeal issue on its agenda. In mid-May, Congress called the Immigration and Naturalization Committee of the House to begin public hearings on various bills relating to the repeal of the Chinese exclusion laws.[109]

During hearings, the Chinese in the United States played a vital role in providing evidence to convince legislators of the destructive nature of the racial legislation. Individual citizens such as Lin Min Hin, a medical doctor, and Paul Yee, an electronics engineer, among other Chinese as well as Asian Americans testified before the House hearings.[110] Chinese communities throughout the United States provided financial support. They raised money to endorse lobbying in Congress. According to the statistics, one-fourth of the funds ($1,116) received by the Citizens Committee was from the Chinese community in Hawaii.[111]

However, the repeal campaign and efforts to rally support for the proposed legislation still faced familiar obstacles of fear and anti-Chinese hostility. The American Federation of Labor again raised the specter of an invasion of an army of laborers from China. An immigration quota for the Chinese, the union warned, would lead to pressures to open the gates even wider: If England with a population of one hundred million had a quota of sixty-five thousand, then China with a population of four hundred million could demand and get U.S. annual quotas of over one million.[112] The influx, the union argued, would jeopardize the position held by the American workers.

Nevertheless, the commonplace and predictable specter of labor tension caused by the influx of Chinese immigrants could not hold the national political floor in the time of the war. On October 7, 1943, after several hearings, the Committee of Immigration and Naturalization favorably reported on H.R. 3070, recommending the repeal of the exclusion laws. After serious debates, the Senate Immigration Committee passed the repeal bill with a unanimous recommendation.[113]

On October 11, 1943, President Roosevelt sent a message to Congress favoring the repeal bill. "China is our ally," Roosevelt wrote. "For many long years she stood alone in the fight against aggression. Today we fight at her side. She has continued her gallant struggle against very great odds."[114]

In addition to the strategic consideration of maintaining China as a wartime ally, the president also saw the historical importance of the repeal for the achievement of racial equality within the American society. He urged equal treatment of the Chinese while expressing his gratitude for the contributions of Chinese immigrants to the cause of freedom and justice in the United States. President Roosevelt addressed Congress in October 1943, urging them to "be big enough" to acknowledge and correct an error of the past. "By the repeal of the Chinese exclusion laws," he said,

> We can correct a historic mistake and silence the distorted Japanese propaganda. The enactment of legislation now pending before Congress would put Chinese immigrants on a parity with those from other countries. . . . While it would give the Chinese a preferred status over a certain Oriental people, their great contribution to the cause of decency and freedom entitle them to such preference.[115]

On December 17, the president signed the repeal bill into law, thus terminating the legislation that had racially barred Chinese immigration for sixty-one years.

The 1943 repeal of the exclusion law was in part a consequence of American war efforts to combat the Japanese. However, the repeal was also a result of demands of the Chinese in the United States for racial equality. The active and sustained participation of New York's Chinese in the repeal campaign played an important role in ending the legislation. The repeal of the Chinese exclusion laws served, in turn, as a milestone in the history of New York's Chinese community. The persistent efforts of New York's Chinese to win their constitutional right to live and to work in the United States were finally realized.

However, the repeal only marked an historical turning point; discrimination declined slowly. When Chinese American soldiers returned from the war, they found they were not welcomed as American heroes and were, like black Americans, still subjected to racial discrimination. "I felt so frustrated that I was denied American citizenship when I came back home after fighting in Italy and France for the United States," a World War II veteran from New York recalled.[116] Kain Chin, another war veteran, also expressed his resentment when he realized that his family was still suffering from racial antagonism after he came back home from the war front. "My family had been in this country for almost a century, and I served in the American army," he said. But "we were still treated like aliens."[117]

The repeal did not lead to a great increase in Chinese immigration, either. In one respect, the repeal consolidated America's restrictive immigration policy. The annual quota of 105 barred large numbers of Chinese immigrants from getting into the country. Thomas Kessner argues that, strictly speaking, the repeal was only a public relations gesture. It was a necessary step in undercutting Japanese propaganda accusing the United States of prejudice against Asians. The idea of dropping the bar to Chinese immigrants never represented a change of heart of the American immigration policy.[118]

Nevertheless, with the repeal of both the exclusion laws and the naturalization prohibition, Chinese immigrants were granted legal opportunities to build normal lives in America. When the war was over, more Chinese women were permitted to come to the country to join their husbands and families as a result of a new law that extended non-quota immigration status to Chinese wives of citizens, admitting these Chinese wives to the United States without regard to the annual quota.[119] From 1945 to 1948, four thousand Chinese women entered the United States under the War Bride and GI Acts. As a result, the male-to-female ratio approached parity and the number of families increased.[120] The old bachelor society was being replaced by a newly structured social order and family system that was to become a mainstay of the stability of the Chinese community. By 1960 there were 134,549 males to 101,743 females of Chinese origin living in the United States.[121]

The repeal bill, of course, also affected New York's Chinese community. By the end of the 1940s, New York's Chinese population reached 20,171.[122] The influx of women and children changed the life of the Chinese community. Former Chinatown residents recalled that for the first time, they saw young Chinese women and children living in New York's Chinatown during the period right after the war.[123] Optimistic for their future life in the United States, Chinese New Yorkers continued to struggle for racial equality and to work hard for their own prosperity.

Conclusion

World War II changed the life of the Chinese in New York. With the U.S. entry into the war, New York's Chinese community, like the rest of the nation's Chinatowns, underwent an important transformation. For the first time in history, significant numbers of Chinese Americans, including Chinese American New Yorkers, served in military forces and other defense-related enterprises. With many American citizens entering the armed forces, members of formerly excluded racial minorities entered the workforce in unprecedented numbers as well. Chinese New Yorkers were able to leave the restaurants, laundries, gift shops, and other service businesses and become part of the mainstream industrial labor force. Chinese American women also had the opportunities to join the armed forces and participate in war-related activities.

World War II created opportunities allowing Chinese Americans to express their American patriotism and their concerns for China. They demonstrated themselves as loyal American citizens while maintaining their ethnic identity.

Shared experiences of fighting for justice and for the defense of the United States banded Chinese American New Yorkers together. Their sincere and continuous efforts to support the war against Japan's invasion eventually won the recognition of the American people.

Repeal was a good example of the change of the attitude of the Americans towards Chinese. The active participation of New York's Chinese on both war and home fronts demonstrated their desire and determination to gain recognition as American citizens. This growing political consciousness was reflected in their demand for the repeal of the exclusion laws. Their participation in mainstream politics as responsible American citizens and their efforts for racial equality and justice received a newfound acceptance from American society.

Notes

1. John Dower, *War without Mercy: Race and Power in the Pacific War* (New York: Pantheon Books, 1993).

2. Fred W. Riggs, *Pressures on Congress: A Study of the Repeal of Chinese Exclusion* (Westport, Conn.: Greenwood Press Publishers, 1950).

3. K. Scott Wong, *Americans First: Chinese Americans and the Second World War* (Cambridge, Mass.: Harvard University Press, 2005).

4. Charles Beard's *President Roosevelt and the Coming of the War 1941: A Study in Appearances and Realities* (New Haven, Conn.: Yale University Press, 1948, 1968) is a classic interpretation of the president's decision to join the war. Basil Rauch, *Roosevelt from Munich to Pearl Harbor* (New York: Creative Age Press, 1950); Roberta Wholstetter, *Pearl Harbor: Warning and Decision* (Stanford, Calif.: Stanford University Press, 1962); and Gordon W. Prange, *At Dawn We Slept* (New York: McGraw-Hill, 1982), analyze the decisions of Roosevelt and his administration in war policy. Dorothy Borg's *The United States and the Far Eastern Crisis of 1933–1938: From the Manchurian Incident through the Initial Stage of the Undeclared Sino-Japanese War* (Cambridge, Mass.: Harvard University Press, 1964) is a basic work on American foreign policy in the Far East in war crisis. Herbert Feis in *The Road to Pearl Harbor* (Princeton, N.J.: Princeton University Press, 1950) assesses Japanese problems from various angles. Selig Adler, *The Isolationist Impulse: Its Twentieth Century Reaction* (London and New York: Abelard-Schuman, 1957) and Manfred Jonas, *Isolationism in America 1935–1941* (Ithaca, N.Y.: Cornell University Press, 1966) are informative on American isolationism. Also see Hilary Conroy and Harry Wray, ed., *Pearl Harbor Reexamined: Prologue to the Pacific* (Honolulu: University of Hawaii Press, 1990).

5. *New York Times*, Dec. 24, 1941.

6. According to the *Chinese Nationalist Daily*, twenty-six Chinese American associations, including the ones from New York, sent the telegraph to the president of the United States on December 10. On December 24, President Roosevelt sent back a message of appreciation for the support. *Chinese Nationalist Daily*, Jan. 24, 1942.

7. *Chinese Nationalist Daily*, Dec. 20, 1941.

8. See chapter 5.

9. *Chinese Nationalist Daily*, Dec. 30, 1941.

10. Wayne Hung Wong, *American Paper Son: A Chinese Immigrant in the Midwest* (Urbana and Chicago: University of Illinois Press, 2006), 13.

There are some differences in the figures. According to another account, altogether 13,499 Chinese Americans enlisted in the U.S. armed forces. Twenty percent of Chinese Americans across the country served in the American military forces. Diane Mei Lin Mark and Ginger Chin, A *Place Called Chinese America* (Dubuque, Iowa: Kendall Hunt Pub. Co., 1982), 97.

11. Thomas Chinn, *Bridging the Pacific: San Francisco Chinatown and Its People* (San Francisco: Chinese Historical Society of America, 1989), 147–50; Sucheng Chan, *Asian Americans: An Interpretive History* (Boston: Twayne Publishers, 1991), 122.

12. According to the *Chinese Press* on March 20, 1942, the U.S. Navy wanted five hundred Chinese to be recruited. This newspaper applauded the change of the previous discriminatory policies that Chinese Americans could only enlist as mess stewards or cabin boys on ships. K. Scott Wong, *Americans First: Chinese Americans and the Second World War* (Cambridge, Mass.: Harvard University Press, 2005), 60.

13. Frederick M. Binder and David M. Reimers, *All the Nations under Heaven: An Ethnic and Racial History of New York City* (New York: Columbia University Press, 1995).

14. K. Scott Wong, *Americans First: Chinese Americans and the Second World War* (Cambridge, Mass.: Harvard University Press, 2005), 59.

15. Him Mark Lai, *The Chinese of America: 1785–1980* (San Francisco: Chinese American Organization, 1980), 67. It was more than 33 percent of New York's total Chinese population. My estimate is based on the statistics Ira Rosenwaike provided. There were 12,753 Chinese living in New York in 1940. *Population History of New York City* (Syracuse, N.Y.: Syracuse University Press, 1972).

16. *Chinese Nationalist Daily*, Jan. 12, 1942.

17. *Chinese Nationalist Daily*, Jan. 17, 1942.

18. In fact, young Chinese Americans joined the army before the United States officially entered the war. According to the *Chinese Nationalist Daily*, almost one hundred Chinese American New Yorkers were registered in the four U.S. Army recruiting stations in New York in 1935. When another registration of the draft began in October 1940, "men from New Jersey and Long Island farms poured into the draft office at P.S. 23 in New York's Chinatown." *Chinese Nationalist Daily*, Apr. 9, 1942.

19. Sing was rewarded the Distinguished Service Cross medal for his bravery in World War I in his continuous running of a message center during a gas attack in Argon Forese. Arthur Bonner, *Alas! What Brought Thee Hither? The Chinese in New York 1800–1950* (Madison, N.J.: Fairleigh Dickinson University Press, 1997), 175.

20. *Chinese Nationalist Daily*, Oct. 21, 1943.

21. *Chinese Nationalist Daily*, Apr. 9, 1942.

22. *Chinese Nationalist Daily*, Sept. 28, 1943.

23. Chinatown History Project, Museum of Chinese in America.

24. K. Scott Wong, *Americans First: Chinese Americans and the Second World War* (Cambridge, Mass.: Harvard University Press, 2005), 61.

25. Anna Chennault wrote an autobiography, *The Education of Anna* (New York: Time Books, 1980). In her book, she traced the history of the U.S. Fourteenth Air Force (better known as the "Flying Tigers"). According to Anna, the air force was the smallest American air force ever to be commanded by a general. Yet it contributed greatly to assisting China in her defense. Started with two hundred men and a few dented planes under the leadership of General Chennault, it had grown to thirty thousand men and one thousand planes by 1945.

26. For the active participation of Chinese American women, particularly on the West Coast, see Judy Yung, *Unbound Voices: A Documentary History of Chinese Women in San Francisco* (Berkeley: University of California Press, 1999).

27. See note 18.

28. Florence Gee, "I Am an American: How Can I Help Win This War?" *Chinese Press*, May 15, 1942; "Women in the War," *Chinese Press*, Mar. 24, 1943; "First Chinese WAAC: New York's Emily Lee Shak," *Chinese Press*, Sept. 25, 1942; Ronald Takaki, *Strangers from a Different Shore: A History of Asian Americans* (Boston: Little, Brown and Company, 1989), 373.

29. Diane Mei Lin Mark and Ginger Chin, *A Place Called Chinese America* (Dubuque, Iowa: Kendall Hunt Pub. Co., 1982), 96.

30. Ah Ying was another Chinese American woman accepted by WASP. She completed flight instruction and was assigned to China with her brother. While her brother flew combat missions she taught in a village school in southern China where her father originally came from. She eventually flew with the WASP when she came back to the United States. Judy Yung, *Unbound Voices: A Documentary History of Chinese Women in San Francisco* (Berkeley: University of California Press, 1999); K. Scott Wong, *Americans First: Chinese Americans and the Second World War* (Cambridge, Mass.: Harvard University Press, 2005), 55.

31. *Chinese Nationalist Daily*, Apr. 9, 1942.

32. While in military service, Ruth C. Jang also gave lectures on Chinese culture. American-born, she did not know much about Chinese cultures. But she used the base library to get information. Ruth saw herself as American when she told her audience that in the war "China was on our side." She was promoted for her two years of excellent service. After the war, she used the GI bill to go to

community college. "I came to feel much better about myself," she said, as there were so few Chinese American women serving in the military. In December 1997, Ruth's husband, First Lieutenant Harry Jang, a recipient of the Distinguished Flying Cross for his service in World II, suffered a stroke and passed away. He was buried with full military honors at Arlington National Cemetery. A spot has been reserved for Ruth to be buried beside him. Judy Yung, *Unbound Voices: A Documentary History of Chinese Women in San Francisco* (Berkeley: University of California Press, 1999), 492. Also see Marianne Verges, *On Silver Wings: The Women Air Force Service Pilots of World War II* (New York: Ballantine Books, 1997); *Chinese Press*, Apr. 2, 1943.

33. *Margaret Mead Papers*, Vol. 18; Judy Yung, *Unbound Voices: A Documentary History of Chinese Women in San Francisco* (Berkeley: University of California Press, 1999), 492. Also see Marianne Verges, *On Silver Wings: The Women Air Force Service Pilots of World War II* (New York: Ballantine Books, 1997).

34. *Chinese Nationalist Daily*, Aug. 7, 1943.

35. Him Mark Lai, *The Chinese of America: 1785–1980* (San Francisco: Chinese American Organization, 1980); Shih-shan Tsai, *China and the Overseas Chinese in the United States* (Fayetteville: University of Arkansas Press, 1983).

36. My interview with Kain Chin in the symposium "Allies and Enemies: The Dilemma of Asian-Americans during World War II," New York, Dec. 1996.

37. An interview with Arthur Wang in Joan Morrison and Charlotte Fox Zabusky, *American Mosaic: The Immigrant Experience in the Words of Those Who Lived It* (New York: E.P. Dutton, 1980), 77.

38. Diane Mei Lin Mark and Ginger Chin, *A Place Called Chinese America* (Dubuque, Iowa: Kendall Hunt Pub. Co., 1982), 98.

39. Ibid.

40. Arthur Bonner, *Alas! What Brought Thee Hither? The Chinese in New York 1800–1950* (Madison, N.J.: Fairleigh Dickinson University Press, 1997), 176.

41. *Chinese Nationalist Daily*, Jan. 20, 1942.

42. K. Scott Wong, *Americans First: Chinese Americans and the Second World War* (Cambridge, Mass.: Harvard University Press, 2005), 64.

43. Kenneth E. Kay wrote the unit history of the Third Fighter Group of the Chinese American Composite Wing (CACW) established in 1943. CACW was operated through the lend-lease program whereby planes and supplies would be sent to the Chinese air force and their pilots would be trained by American aviators. Ibid., 61.

44. Wayne Hung Wong, *American Paper Son: A Chinese Immigrant in the Midwest* (Urbana and Chicago: University of Illinois Press, 2006), 14.

45. Ibid.

46. K. Scott Wong, *Americans First: Chinese Americans and the Second World War* (Cambridge, Mass.: Harvard University Press, 2005), 60.

47. *Chinese Press*, Mar. 20, 1942; Ibid.

48. Arthur Bonner, *Alas! What Brought Thee Hither? The Chinese in New York 1800–1950* (Madison, N.J.: Fairleigh Dickinson University Press, 1997), 176.

49. Ibid., 175.

50. His seventy-five-year-old father, Fong Zhou, took the honor to receive a medal from the American army for his bravery. *Chinese Nationalist Daily*, Aug. 31, 1943. Other Chinese American veterans of World War II were also honored. First Lieutenant Harry Jang received a metal of the Distinguished Flying Cross for his service in the war and was buried with full military honors at Arlington National Cemetery in 1997.

51. *Chinese Nationalist Daily*, Dec. 16, 1941.

52. *Chinese Nationalist Daily*, Dec. 19, 1941.

53. *Chinese Nationalist Daily*, Dec. 26, 1941.

54. *Chinese Nationalist Daily*, Jan. 5, 1942.

55. *Chinese Nationalist Daily*, Mar. 5, 1942.

56. *Chinese Nationalist Daily*, Sept. 15, 1943.

57. *Chinese Nationalist Daily*, July 19, 1943.

58. *Chinese Nationalist Daily*, July 20, 1943.

59. *Chinese Nationalist Daily*, Oct. 27, 1943.

60. Ibid.

61. *Chinese Nationalist Daily*, Sept. 28, 1943.

62. *Chinese Nationalist Daily*, Sept. 29, 1943.

63. *Chinese Nationalist Daily*, Oct. 9, 1943.

64. For the brief description of the prewar diplomacy, see Warren Kimball, *The Most Unsordid Act: Lend-Lease, 1939–1941* (Baltimore: Johns Hopkins University Press, 1920, 1969); Joseph Lash, *Roosevelt and Churchill* (New York: Norton, 1976); and David Reynold, *The Creation of the Anglo-American Alliance, 1937–1941* (Chapel Hill: University of North Carolina Press, 1982). Robert Dallek's *Franklin D. Roosevelt and American Foreign Policy, 1933–1945* (New York: Oxford University Press, 1979) is more comprehensive and covers the war years.

65. Edward E. Bennett, *Recognition of Russia* (Waltham, Mass.: Blaisdell, 1970); Robert Browder, *The Origins of Society—American Diplomacy* (Princeton, N.J.: Princeton University Press, 1953). For war mobilization, see Paul A. C. Koistinen, *The Military-Industrial Complex: A Historical Perspective* (New York: Praeger, 1980); Donald Nelson, *Arsenal of Democracy* (New York: Harcourt, Brace and Company, 1946).

66. David Brinkley's *Washington Goes to War* (New York: A.A. Knopf, 1988) is informative on the home front. But for a broader treatment see John Blum, *"V" Was for Victory* (New York: Harcourt, Brace and Jovanevich, 1976) and Richard Polenberg, *War and Society: The United States, 1941–1945* (Philadelphia: Lippincott, 1972).

67. Him Mark Lai, *The Chinese of America: 1785–1980* (San Francisco: Chinese American Organization, 1980); Lingchi Wang, "The Politics of Assimilation and Repression" (unpublished manuscript); Sucheng Chan, *Asian Americans: An Interpretive History* (Boston: Twayne Publishers, 1991); K. Scott Wong, *Americans*

First: Chinese Americans and the Second World War (Cambridge, Mass.: Harvard University Press, 2005); Judy Yung, Gordon H. Chang, and Him Mark Lai, ed., *Chinese American Voices: From the Gold Rush to the Present* (Berkeley: University of California Press, 2006).

68. *The Chinese Press*, Apr. 2, 1943; Ronald Takaki, *Strangers from a Different Shore: A History of Asian Americans* (Boston: Little, Brown and Company, 1989), 374.

69. Ibid.

70. K. Scott Wong, *Americans First: Chinese Americans and the Second World War* (Cambridge, Mass.: Harvard University Press, 2005), 50.

71. *The Chinese Press*, Apr. 2, 1943; Ronald Takaki, *Strangers from a Different Shore: A History of Asian Americans* (Boston: Little, Brown and Company, 1989), 374.

72. *The Chinese Press*, Apr. 2, 1943.

73. K. Scott Wong, *Americans First: Chinese Americans and the Second World War* (Cambridge, Mass.: Harvard University Press, 2005), 49.

74. Ibid., 50.

75. "All Chinatown Responds to War Needs," *Chinese Press*, Jan. 2, 1942; Ronald Takaki, *Strangers from a Different Shore: A History of Asian Americans* (Boston: Little, Brown and Company, 1989), 374.

76. *Chinese Nationalist Daily*, Oct. 29, 1943.

77. Him Mark Lai, *The Chinese of America: 1785–1980* (San Francisco: Chinese American Organization, 1980).

78. K. Scott Wong, *Americans First: Chinese Americans and the Second World War* (Cambridge, Mass.: Harvard University Press, 2005), 53.

79. Ibid., 53.

80. Ronald Takaki, *Strangers from a Different Shore: A History of Asian Americans* (Boston: Little, Brown and Company, 1989), 374.

81. Lingchi Wang, "The Politics of Assimilation and Repression" (unpublished manuscript); Sucheng Chan, *Asian Americans: An Interpretive History* (Boston: Twayne Publishers, 1991), 123.

82. Rose Hum Lee, "Chinese in the United States Today, the War Had Changed Their Lives," *Survey Graphic*, Oct. 1942; Ronald Takaki, *Strangers from a Different Shore: A History of Asian Americans* (Boston: Little, Brown and Company, 1989), 375.

83. Lingchi Wang, "The Politics of Assimilation and Repression" (unpublished manuscript); Sucheng Chan, *Asian Americans: An Interpretive History* (Boston: Twayne Publishers, 1991), 123

84. Theodora Wong, "Chinese Career Girls: They Help Run the Vital 'Behind-the-Lines' Business of the United States at War," Report, Spring 1942; K. Scott Wong, *Americans First: Chinese Americans and the Second World War* (Cambridge, Mass.: Harvard University Press, 2005), 47.

85. An interview with Arthur Wang in Joan Morrison and Charlotte Fox Zabusky, *American Mosaic: The Immigrant Experience in the Words of Those Who Lived It* (New York: E.P. Dutton, 1980), 77.

86. Harold R. Isaacs, *Images of Asia: American Views of China and India* (New York: Harper and Row, 1972), xviii–xix (originally published in 1958 under the title *Scratches on Our Mind*); Sucheng Chan, *Asian Americans: An Interpretive History* (Boston: Twayne Publishers, 1991), 121

87. See chapter 1 for the information on Chinese exclusion laws.

88. For information on the Japanese war propaganda, see John Dower's book *War without Mercy: Race and Power in the Pacific War* (New York, Pantheon Books, 1993). Fred W. Riggs, *Pressures on Congress: A Study of the Repeal of Chinese Exclusion* (Westport, Conn.: Greenwood Press Publishers, 1950), provides adequate materials of the debates on repeal.

89. John Dower, *War without Mercy: Race and Power in the Pacific War* (New York: Pantheon Books, 1993).

90. Xuoling Pen, *History of Chinese Revolution* (Beijing: Chinese Higher Education Press, 1995), 190.

91. Iris Chang, *The Rape of Nanking: The Forgotten Holocaust of World War II* (New York: L.L.C. Basic Books, 1997).

92. John Dower, *War without Mercy: Race and Power in the Pacific War* (New York: Pantheon Books, 1993), 164.

93. Fred W. Riggs, *Pressures on Congress: A Study of the Repeal of Chinese Exclusion* (Westport, Conn.: Greenwood Press Publishers, 1950), 111.

94. Ibid., 376.

95. Ibid., 112–13.

96. Ibid., 113.

97. *Chinese Nationalist Daily*, Oct. 21, 1943.

98. Ibid.

99. Richard Walsh, "Report to the Members of the Citizens Committee," Citizens Committee archives, Sept. 10, 1943. "Citizens Committee, to Repeal Chinese Exclusion and Place Immigration on a Quota Basis," New York's Public Library archives.

100. Political advocates in other states were also active in the campaign. In 1942, the California League of Women Voters of San Francisco initiated an educational campaign for the removal of racial discrimination from the immigration law.

101. "Citizens Committee, to Repeal Chinese Exclusion and Place Immigration on a Quota Basis," May 1943, New York's Public Library archives.

102. "Citizens Committee, to Repeal Chinese Exclusion and Place Immigration on a Quota Basis," Aug. 15, 1943, New York's Public Library archives.

103. Ibid.

104. The national agenda of the AFL was conservative on the repeal issue.

105. "Citizens Committee, to Repeal Chinese Exclusion and Place Immigration on a Quota Basis," Aug. 15, 1943, New York's Public Library archives.

106. Fred W. Riggs, *Pressures on Congress: A Study of the Repeal of Chinese Exclusion* (Westport, Conn.: Greenwood Press Publishers, 1950), 139.

107. Congressional Record, 78th Congress 1st session, 1943, 1080–81.

108. Ronald Takaki, *Strangers from a Different Shore: A History of Asian Americans* (Boston: Little, Brown and Company, 1989), 376.

109. Samuel Dickstein of New York chaired the committee. His consistent favor for the bills to liberalize the immigration laws played a fundamental role in determining the course of legislation. Fred W. Riggs, *Pressures on Congress: A Study of the Repeal of Chinese Exclusion* (Westport, Conn.: Greenwood Press Publishers, 1950), 177.

110. "A Chinese Youth Meeting," *Chinese Press*, Oct. 1, 1943; Ronald Takaki, *Strangers from a Different Shore: A History of Asian Americans* (Boston: Little, Brown and Company, 1989), 377.

111. Fred W. Riggs, *Pressures on Congress: A Study of the Repeal of Chinese Exclusion* (Westport, Conn.: Greenwood Press Publishers, 1950), 112.

112. Rose Hum Lee, "Chinese in the United States Today, the War Had Changed Their Lives," *Survey Graphic*, October 1942, 444; Ronald Takaki, *Strangers from a Different Shore: A History of Asian Americans* (Boston: Little, Brown and Company, 1989), 375.

113. Fred W. Riggs, *Pressures on Congress: A Study of the Repeal of Chinese Exclusion* (Westport, Conn.: Greenwood Press Publishers, 1950), 182.

114. Congressional Record, 78th, sess. 1, Oct. 11, 1943, 8199–8200.

115. Ibid.

116. An interview with Kem Louei, daughter of the war veteran in the symposium "Silent No More: Asian American Women Speak Out," New York, 1997.

117. Interview with Kain Chin in the symposium "Allies and Enemies: The Dilemma of Asian-Americans during World War II," New York, 1996.

118. Thomas Kessner and Betty Caroli, *Today's Immigrants, Their Stories: A New Look at the Latest Immigrants* (New York: Oxford University Press, 1981), 237.

119. On August 9, 1946, Congress passed the new law.

120. Him Mark Lai, *The Chinese of America: 1785–1980* (San Francisco: Chinese American Organization, 1980), 70.

121. Him Mark Lai, *The Chinese of America: 1785–1980* (San Francisco: Chinese American Organization, 1980), 173; David M. Reimers, *Still the Golden Door: The Third World Comes to America*, second ed. (New York: Columbia University Press, 1992).

122. Decennial censuses, 1950; Betty Lee Sung, *Mountain of Gold: The Story of the Chinese in America* (New York: Macmillan Company, 1967), 112.

123. David M. Reimers, *Still the Golden Door: The Third World Comes to America*, second ed. (New York: Columbia University Press, 1992), 27.

Conclusion

New York's Chinese community, like other ethnic American groups, experienced economic crisis, war, and social upheaval in the period between the 1930s and 1940s. The hardships of the Great Depression reinforced racial discrimination and poverty. However, the devastating situation stirred a new generation of New York's Chinese who actively sought reform and change. The rapid growth of self-reliant and self-determined labor unions and small business associations added to a new generation's changing awareness of and shifting attitudes and practices toward dealing with economic crisis and racial discrimination. No longer constrained within their own ethnic culture for protection, community members moved into mainstream activities as a way of demanding their basic constitutional rights to live and to work in the United States. Active participation in national and local political campaigns demonstrated this new political maturity.

The findings in chapters 2 and 4 detail this new political maturity. Beginning with the Chinese Exclusion Law of 1882, exclusionary legislation barred Chinese immigrants from entering this country and prohibited the naturalization of those who had already been in the United States. Racial discrimination and riots took place in various regions and many Chinese were killed. In order to protect themselves, New York's Chinese stayed in their own ethnic enclave. However, they did not passively accept racial inferiority and enforced isolation. Instead, they resisted. During the years of exclusion, they constantly took their cases to court, an American way of fighting for legal recognition of equality. They also participated in demonstrations seeking public support.

Their persistent resistance underwent tremendous changes during the Depression when laborers, small businessmen, students, women, and other ordinary Chinese New Yorkers organized and participated in mainstream activities. Represented by the Lien Yi Society, the Chinese Unemployed Council, and other organizations, laborers not only independently conducted strikes but also successfully integrated their activities into the mainstream labor movement. Their efforts to reach out to create alliances with other American labor organizations demonstrated the increasing self-consciousness of New York's Chinese to be part of American society.

Like labor organizations, a new type of trade union also emerged during the Depression. The Chinese Hand Laundry Alliance and the Chinese American Restaurant Association of Greater New York were good examples of this new type of organization. Activities such as opposition to the city's discriminatory laundry ordinances and support for New Deal efforts to combat the Depression demonstrated their demand for equal treatment and their desire to involve themselves in mainstream politics.

Although labor unions and small business organizations were originally formed to deal with economic difficulties in the 1930s, their self-determined and self-reliant activities challenged traditional modes of control within the ethnic Chinese community. Their demand for legal protection by the American government and their desire to involve themselves in mainstream politics also effectively challenged the legacy of racist exclusion. Therefore, these organizations were also pioneer Chinese civil rights organizations in New York City.

The formation of political organizations also demonstrated the new political maturity of New York's Chinese. The Chinese American Citizens Alliance, the New York Chinese American Voting League, and the New York Chinese American Committee of the National Democratic Party encouraged Chinese Americans to use their right to vote, thereby marking a new strategy and means of claiming their civil rights as American citizens. Not accepting some historical literature that portrays Chinese Americans as docile and politically indifferent, the new findings of historical evidence have shown the active participation of New York's Chinese in local and national political campaigns, particularly their engagement in the 1933 election for the New York City government and in the 1932 and 1936 presidential elections. Their endorsement of Fiorello H. La Guardia as mayor and of Franklin D. Roosevelt as president characterized their political consciousness and maturity.

World War II generated the momentum to push change forward. The findings in chapter 5 and chapter 6 particularly stress the development of a new Chinese American identity of Chinese New Yorkers. Their participation in support of China's defense against Japan's invasion during the 1930s and their activities endorsing the American war effort after the Pearl Harbor attack demonstrated their nationalistic passion for their homeland, as well as their patriotic zeal for the country where they were born but alienated. During the years of supporting China against Japan's invasion, New York's Chinese not only provided millions of dollars for civilian relief work, but also sent well-trained military personnel to fight along with their compatriots in China. Many died for the freedom of China. However, we cannot simply look to their Chinese ancestry as a way to justify their support. More important, they considered their role to "guide American actions to maintain world peace." They were not simply fighting for China. Instead, they "fought for the United States," and appealed for global peace as Americans. Therefore, Chinese American identity is a more accurate explanation of support for China.

Evidence that demonstrated this Chinese American identity was also presented in their support for the United States after the Pearl Harbor attack. An estimated four thousand Chinese New Yorkers were drafted. Ninety died for the United States. In addition to military service, New York's Chinese participated in other activities of fundraising, war bonds purchasing, and blood donation for the war front. They also participated in wartime production on the home front as a way to claim themselves as Americans and to achieve racial equality. Joining the war as Americans, New York's Chinese continuously endorsed China's efforts against Japan after Pearl Harbor. The New York Chinatown Naval Academy was established during this time and Chinese American pilots served the Flying Tigers of the U.S. Fourteenth Air Force to China.

This Chinese American identity reflected a radical interior transformation in Chinese New Yorkers' self-definition that contributed to their intensified efforts for racial equality. The participation of New York's Chinese, particularly the engagement of the younger generation in cultural activities, as shown in chapter 3, demonstrated their self-consciousness of being Chinese Americans. This dual sense of identity encouraged them to participate in activities that reinforced Chinese cultural heritage while promoting confidence in being Americans. Activities such as Chinese-language learning, essay contests that stressed the future of American-born Chinese in the United States, and outreach through art performances and sports once again characterized the political maturity of New York's Chinese to be part of American society.

The repeal of the exclusion legislation proved to be the most important consequence of their varied efforts and dedications to integrate as American citizens and claim racial equality. New York's Chinese played a crucial role in changing American attitudes towards them. Their demand for racial equality and participation in the repeal process, as shown in their petition to the government, fundraising in support of lobbying in Congress, and testimony before the House hearings, eventually brought an end to the Chinese exclusion laws. The Chinese Women's Association of New York played an unusual role to initiate the petition. The repeal efforts of New York's Chinese once again demonstrated their political maturity.

The participation of New York's Chinese in political, cultural, and social activities laid the groundwork for future involvement and fundamentally altered the traditional means by which social control had once been exercised. American-born Chinese were major participants in these activities. They functioned as a dynamic element to reconstruct a newly structured ethnic community that integrated into society. College students, represented by some of the organizations such as the Chinese Students League of Greater New York and the Chinese Student Christian Association, played an important role in the transformation of the Chinese community as they redefined themselves and turned their attention to the welfare of their community. They helped to overcome the isolation and exclusionary atmosphere of New York's Chinese community.

Chinese New Yorkers' active participation in mainstream activities during the Depression and the war contributed to Americans' changing image of them. Nevertheless, racial prejudice and discrimination still haunt the Chinese. Chinese Americans continue to fight for justice, freedom, and equality as citizens and as people proud of their ethnic heritage. With decades of increasingly successful integration behind them, they are more assured than before.

I hope that my study will contribute to a better understanding of the ways in which the Depression and war were experienced by minority groups who have suffered racial prejudice. Cheryl Lynn Greenberg's book on the experiences of blacks in Harlem in the Great Depression provides another dimension to this aspect of our nation's history.

> Racism created and perpetuated Harlem's poverty—race and class were inextricably linked in the black experience. Yet segregation and discrimination also produced strong social and political networks within the black community. These served not only to meet immediate needs, but also to mobilize thousands to demand a better life. This activism, both organized and spontaneous, demonstrated that a determined people could win effective improvements in their condition.[1]

What Greenberg summarizes also applies to Chinese Americans in New York. Chinese Americans have different cultural traditions and very different histories from African Americans. But they shared comparable experiences of racial prejudice and discrimination and responded similarly in that they did not passively accept designations of racial inferiority. Chinese Americans in New York used a variety of tactics to challenge racism. This struggle for racial equality and against prejudice continues. Further studies of this aspect of our past should help in illuminating the complexity of group experiences.

Notes

1. Cheryl Lynn Greenberg, "*Or Does It Explode?*": *Black Harlem in the Great Depression* (New York: Oxford University Press, 1991), 6.

Bibliography

Primary Sources

Newspapers and Periodicals

Annals of the American Academy of Political and Social Science, Vol. 186–88, 1936.

Asia, 1936, 1937.

Asia Magazine, 1942, 1943.

The Builder, 1945–1946.

China Daily Tribune, 1948.

The China Weekly Review, 1931.

China News Service, New York, Mar. 5–May 20, 1927, 1943.

Chinese Daily News (Zhong Guo Qiao Bao), 1940–1947.

Chinese Digest, 1937–1940.

Chinese Nationalist Daily (Ming Qi Ri Bao), 1927–1942.

Chinese Press Views, No. 1–32, Mar. 1940–Dec. 4, 1941.

Chinese Reform News (Zhong Guo Wei Xing Bao), 1907–1937.

Chinese Vanguard (Xian Fong Bao), 1930–1937.

Classroom Materials, Bureau for Intercultural Education Publications: 1936–1937.

Education for One World, 1948/1949–1953/1954.

The Far Eastern Magazine, 1937.

Journal of American Ethnic History.

Journal of the Young China Association (Shao Nien Chung-Kuo), 1919–1924.

National Reconstruction Journal, Vol. 5, Aug. 1942–July 1947.

New York Daily Tribune, 1869, 1870.

New York Herald, 1870.

New York Times, 1879, 1901, 1937, 1938.
Sociology and Social Research, Vol. 12–76, Sept. 1927–1992.
Young China, Feb. 16–Mar. 31, 1911/Oct.–Dec. 1913.

Pamphlets, Reports, and Student Publications

Annual Report, 1904–1912.
The Builders, 1945.
China Defense League, 1943.
Chinese Affairs, Vol. 1–5, 1928–1933.
Chinese Chambers of Commerce of New York, Inc. 50th Anniversary, 1957.
Chinese Christian Student, monthly, 1930–1957.
Chinese Student Bulletin, Vol. 1, No. 1–3, Mar.–May, 1928.
Chinese Student League of Greater New York, Handbook, 1939.
Chinese Students, Vol. 1–2, No.5, Dec. 1935–June 1938.
Chinese Students' Alliance in the United States of America, No. 2–3, 1921.
Chinese Students' Alliance of Eastern States, U.S.A., Oct. 1907.
Chinese Students' Series on China and the Washington Conferences, 1922.
Chinese Students' Monthly, 1907, 1913, 1918.
Citizens Committee to Repeal Chinese Exclusion and Place Immigration on a Quota Basis, 1943.
Directory of Chinese Students in America, 1934–1939.
The Far Eastern Magazine, 1937.
The New York Chinese School, 1995.

Church Archives

China & the Chinese—Periodical Excerpts, 1916, United Methodist Church.
Chinese Recorder, Vol. 50, 1919, Union Theological Seminary.
Church Federation: Inter-Church Conference on Federation, 1905, United Methodist Church.
Church Missionary Review, 1922, Union Theological Seminary.
The Echo, Spring/Summer, 1973, United Methodist Church.
Engage/Social Action, 1976, 1983, United Methodist Church.
Monthly Echo, 1928, 1937, United Methodist Church.
Outlook, Dec. 27, 1902, United Methodist Church.
The Presbyterian Digest, Vol. 1, 1930, Presbyterian Church in the United States.
Transfiguration Church, a Church of Immigrants 1827–1977, 1977, Transfiguration Church.
Year Book, 1935/1936–1940/1941, 1941/1942–1947, The First Presbyterian Church of New York.

Foundation Archives

Davison Collection, Rockefeller Archives Center, Rockefeller Foundation.
Rockefeller Brother Collection, Rockefeller Foundation.

Museum Archives

Museum Archives (Clippings, Photos, Assorted Materials), Museum of Chinese in America, New York.

New York Municipal Archives

WPA Federal Writers' Project, NYC Unit, Racial Groups in New York I: Chinese in New York, MN #21065, Roll 1–5, 66, Folder 38–56, 1936–1940 (New York City: New York Municipal Archives), Microfilm.

NYC Guide, MN #21026, Roll 27, 28, 1936–1939 (New York City: New York Municipal Archives), Microfilm.

References

Annual Report of the Board of Elections in the City of New York for the Year 1933, New York Election Board Annual Report, 1931–1935.

Concise Dictionary of American Biography, third ed., New York: Charles Scribner's Sons, 1980.

Documents of American History, Vol. 1 and 2, ninth ed., edited by Henry Steel Commager. Englewood Cliffs, N.J.: Prentice-Hall, Inc., 1973.

The Encyclopedia of the Chinese Overseas, Cambridge, Mass.: Harvard University Press, 1999.

Harvard Encyclopedia of American Ethnic Groups, 1981.

New York City Guide: The WPA Guide to New York City: The Federal Writers' Project Guide to 1930's New York. New York: Random House, 1936–1939.

Selected List of References on Chinese Immigration, United States Library of Congress, Division of Bibliography, 1904, Microfilm.

Who's Who in Jurisprudence: A Biographical Dictionary of Contemporary Lawyers and Jurists, 1925.

Secondary Sources

Books and Articles

Adler, Selig. *The Isolationist Impulse: Its Twentieth Century Reaction*. London and New York: Abelard-Schuman, 1957.

Allen, Robert. *Reluctant Reformers: Racism and Social Reform Movements in the United States*. Washington, D.C.: Howard University Press, 1974, 1983.

Anbinder, Tyler. *Five Points: The 19th-Century New York City Neighborhood That Invented Tap Dance, Stole Elections, and Became the World's Most Notorious Slum*. New York: A Plume Book, 2001.

Barth, Gunther. *Bitter Strength—A History of Chinese in the United States 1850–1870*. Cambridge, Mass.: Harvard University Press, 1964.

Beard, Charles. *President Roosevelt and the Coming of the War 1941: A Study in Appearances and Realities*. New Haven, Conn.: Yale University Press, 1948, 1968.

Beasley, W. G. *Japanese Imperialism: 1894–1945*. New York: Oxford University Press, 1992.

Beck, Louis Joseph. *New York's Chinatown: An Historical Presentation of Its People and Places*. New York: Bohemia Publishing Company, 1898.

Bennett, Edward. *Recognition of Russia*. Waltham, Mass.: Blaisdell Publishing Co, 1970.

Bercovici, Konrad. *Around the World in New York*. New York: The Century Co., 1924.

Berger, Mike. "New York Chinatown," Chinese Chambers of Commerce of New York Inc., 50th Anniversary, 1957, 25–34.

Berrol, Selma. *The Empire City: New York and Its People, 1624–1996*. Westport, Conn.: Praeger Publishers, 1997, 2000.

Bevans, Charles, ed. *Treaties and Other International Agreements of the United States of America, 1776–1949*. Washington, D.C.: Department of State, 1971.

Binder, Frederick M., and David M. Reimers. *All the Nations under Heaven: An Ethnic and Racial History of New York City*. New York: Columbia University Press, 1995.

Blackmar, Elizabeth. *Manhattan for Rent, 1785–1850*. Ithaca, N.Y.: Cornell University Press, 1989.

Blum, John M. *"V" Was for Victory*. New York: Harcourt, Brace and Jovanovich, 1976.

Bodnar, John. *The Transplanted: A History of Immigrants in Urban America*. Bloomington: Indiana University Press, 1985.

Bonner, Arthur. *Alas! What Brought Thee Hither? The Chinese in New York 1800–1950*. Madison, N.J.: Fairleigh Dickinson University Press, 1997.

Borg, Dorothy. *The United States and the Far Eastern Crisis of 1933–1938: From the Manchurian Incident through the Initial Stage of the Undeclared Sino-Japanese War*. Cambridge, Mass: Harvard University Press, 1964.

Bornstein, Jerry. "The Old and The New." *Engage/Social Action*. Vol. 4. Washington, D.C.: Board of Church and Society, United Methodist Church. Jan. 1976, 49–51.

Boyer, Paul. *Urban Masses and Moral Order in America, 1820–1920*. Cambridge, Mass: Harvard University Press, 1978.

Breuilly, John. *Nationalism and the State*. Second ed. Chicago: University of Chicago Press, 1994.

Brinkley, David. *Washington Goes to War*. New York: A.A. Knopf, 1988.

Browder, Robert. *The Origins of Soviet American Diplomacy*. Princeton, N.J.: Princeton University Press, 1953.

Buck, Pearl S. "Western Weapons in the Hands of the Reckless East." *Asia*. Oct. 1937, 672.

———. *The Good Earth*. New York: International Collector Library, 1949.

Burrows, Edwin, and Mike Wallace. *Gotham: A History of New York City to 1898*. New York: Oxford University Press, 1999.

Cafferty, Pastora San Juan, et al. *The Dilemma of American Immigration—Beyond the Golden Door*. New Brunswick, N.J.: Transaction Books, 1983.

Cao, Lan, and Himilce Novas, *Everything You Need to Know about Asian-American History*. New York: A Lume Book, 1996.

Chan, Sucheng. *Asian Americans: An Interpretive History*. Boston: Twayne Publishers, 1991.

Chan, Sucheng, and Douglas Henry Daniels, ed. *Peoples of Color in the American West*. Lexington, Mass.: D.C. Heath and Company, 1994.

Chandler, Lester. *America's Greatest Depression: 1929–1941*. New York: Harper and Row, 1970.

Chang, Iris. *The Rape of Nanking: The Forgotten Holocaust of World War II*. New York: L.L.C. Basic Books, 1997.

———. *The Chinese in America: A Narrative History*. New York: Viking, Penguin Groups, 2003.

Chen, Jack. *The Chinese of America*. San Francisco: Harper & Row, 1980.

Chen, Hsiang-shui. *Chinatown No More*. Ithaca, N.Y.: Cornell University Press, 1992.

Chen, Hsiang-shui, and John Kuo Wei Tchen. *Asian/American Center Working Papers: Towards a History of Chinese in Queens*. New York: Queens College, City University of New York, 1989.

Chen, Shehong. *Being Chinese, Becoming Chinese Americans*. Champaign: Illinois University Press, 2002.

Chen, Yong. *Chinese San Francisco, 1850–1943: A Trans-Pacific Community*. Stanford, Calif.: Stanford University Press, 2002.

Cheng, Hsin-I. *Culturing Interface: Identity, Communication, and Chinese Trans-Nationalism*. New York: Peter Lang, 2008.

Cheunault, Anna. *The Education of Anna*. New York: Time Books, 1980.

———. *A Thousand Springs*. New York: Paul S. Ericsson, Inc., 1962.

Chi, Tsung. *East Asian Americans and Political Participation, Reference Handbook*. Santa Barbara, Calif.: ABCCLIO, 2005.

Chinn, Thomas. *Bridging the Pacific: San Francisco Chinatown and Its People*. San Francisco: Chinese Historical Society of America, 1989.

Chiu, Y. T. *Meditations of a Christian Chinese*. New York: Pageant Press, 1956.

Chu, Jennings Pink Wei. *Chinese Students in America: Qualities Associated with Their Success*. New York City: Teachers College, Columbia University, 1922.

Chu, Louis. *Eat a Bowl of Tea*. New York: Lyle Stuart, 1961.

Chun, Gloria Heyung. *Of Orphans and Warriors: Inventing Chinese American Culture and Identity*. New Brunswick, N.J.: Rutgers University Press, 2000.

Cieslak, Edward Charnwood. *The Foreign Students in American Colleges: A Survey & Evaluation of Administrative Problems and Practices*. Detroit: Wayne University Press, 1955.

Clark, Helen. "The Chinese of New York: Contrasted with Their Foreign Neighbor." *The Century Magazine*. Vol. 53, 1896, 104–5.

Clyde, Paul Hibbe. *U.S. Policy toward China*. New York: Russell and Russell, 1940, 1964.

Conroy, Hilary, and Harry Wray, ed. *Pearl Harbor Reexamined: Prologue to the Pacific War*. Honolulu: University of Hawaii Press, 1990.

Conwell, Russel H. *Why and How: Why the Chinese Emigrate, and the Means They Adopt for the Purpose of Reaching America*. Boston: Lee and Shepard, 1871.

Coolidge, Mary Roberts. *Chinese Immigration*. New York: H. Holt and Company, 1909, 1968.

Corsi, Edward. *In the Shadow of Liberty*. New York: Arno Press and the *New York Times*, 1969.

Covel, Ralph R. *Confucius, the Buddha and Christ: A History of the Gospel in Chinese*. New York: Maryknoll: Orbis Books, 1986.

Crahan, Margaret E., and Alberto Vourvoulias-Bush, ed. *The City and the World New York's Global Future*. New York: Council on Foreign Relations, 1997.

Dallek, Robert. *Franklin D. Roosevelt and the American Foreign Policy: 1933–1945*. New York: Oxford University Press, 1979.

Danico, Mary Yu, and Franklin Ng. *Asian American Issues*. Westport, Conn.: Greenwood Press, 2004.

Daniels, Roger. *Asian America Chinese and Japanese in the United States since 1850*. Seattle and London: University of Washington Press, 1988.

Dinnerstein, Leonard, and David M. Reimers. *Ethnic Americans—History of Immigration and Assimilation*. New York: Harper and Row, 1975.

Dittmer, Lowell, and Samuel S. Kim, ed. *China's Quest for National Identity*. Ithaca, N.Y.: Cornell University Press, 1993.

Divine, Robert A. *American Immigration Policy 1924–1952*. New Haven, Conn.: Yale University Press, 1957.

Dower, John W. *War without Mercy: Race and Power in the Pacific War*. New York: Pantheon Books, 1993.

Dubofsky, Melvyn, and Stephen Burnwook, ed. *The Great Depression and the New Deal*. New York: Garland Publishing, 1990.

Elazar, Daniel J. *Community and Polity: The Organization Dynamics of American Jewry*. Philadelphia: The Jewish Publication Society of America, 1980.

Ernest, Robert. *Immigrant Life in New York City, 1825–1863*. New York: Octagon Books, 1979.

Espiritu, Yen Le. *Asian America Women and Men: Labor, Laws, and Love*. Thousand Oaks, Calif.: Sage Publications, 1997.

Fairbank, John King. *The United States and China*. Fourth ed. Cambridge, Mass.: Harvard University, 1983.

———. *The Great Chinese Revolution 1800–1985*. New York: Harper and Row, 1987.

Feis, Herbert. *The Road to Pearl Harbor*. Princeton, N.J.: Princeton University Press, 1950.

Feldman, Gernald, ed. *German Imperialism: 1914–1918*. New York: Wiley, 1972.

Fernando, Shanti Irene. *Race and the City: Chinese Canadian and Chinese American Political Mobilization*. Vancouver: UBC Press, 2006.

Fessler, Loren. *Chinese in America: Stereotyped Past, Changing Present*. New York: Vantage, 1983.

Foner, Nancy, ed. *New Immigrants in New York*. New York: Columbia University Press, 1987.

———. *From Ellis Island to JFK: New York's Two Great Waves of Immigration*. New Haven, Conn.: Yale University Press, 2000.

Foner, Philip S., and Daniel Rosenberg, ed. *Racism, Dissent, and Asian Americans from 1850 to the Present*. Westport, Conn.: Greenwood Press, 1993.

Forest, Robert W. De. *The Tenement House Problem*. New York: Arno Press and the *New York Times*, 1903, 1970.

Freeman, Richard B., and James L. Medorr. *What Do Unions Do?* New York: Basic Books, 1984.

Fung, Eddie. *The Adventures of Eddie Fung: Chinatown Kid, Texas Cowboy, Prisoner of War*. Seattle: University of Washington Press, 2007.

Gabaccia, Donna R. *From Sicily to Elizabeth Street: Housing & Social Change among Italian Immigrants, 1880–1930*. Albany: State University of New York Press, 1984.

Gallbraith, John K. *The Great Crash*. New York: Houghton Mifflin, 1955.

Glick, Carl. *Shake Hands with the Dragon*. New York: Whittlesey House, McGraw-Hill Book Company, 1941, 1971.

Goodrich, Carter. "Internal Migration and Economic Opportunity." *The Annals of the American Academy of Political and Social Science*. Vol. 186–88, 1936, 260–63.

Greenberg, Cheryl Lynn. *"Or Does It Explode?": Black Harlem in the Great Depression*. New York: Oxford University Press, 1991.

Guest, Kenneth J. *God in Chinatown: Religion and Survival in New York's Evolving Immigrant Community*. New York: New York University Press, 2003.

Gulick, Sidney. *American Democracy and Asiatic Citizenship*. New York: Charles Scribner's Sons, 1918.

Gutman, Herbert. *Who Built America? American Social History Project: Working People & the Nation's Economy Politics, Culture and Society*. Vol. 1–2, 1982.

Handlin, Oscar. *The Uprooted: The Epic Story of the Great Migrations That Made the American People*. Boston and Toronto: Little, Brown & Company, 1951, 1973.

Harlow, Alvin F. *Old Bowery Days*. New York: D. Appleton and Company, 1931.

Hart, Robert Lamb, Adam Krivatsy, and William Stubee (Planning Consultants Firm). *Chinatown New York: A Report on the Conditions and Needs of a Unique Community: Prepared for Department of City Planning*. New York: July 1968.

Higham, John. *Strangers in the Land: Patterns of American Nativism, 1860–1925*. New Brunswick, N.J.: Rutgers University Press, 1963.

———. *Send These to Me—Jews and Other Immigrants in Urban America*. New York: Atheneum, 1975.

Hill, Joseph A. "Composition of the American Population by Race and Country of Origin." *The Annals of the American Academy of Political and Social Science*, Vol. 186–88, 1936, 177–84.

Hillgruber, Andreas. *Germany and the Two World Wars*. Cambridge, Mass.: Harvard University Press, 1981.

Hing, Bill Ong. *Making & Remaking Asian America through Immigration Policy 1850–1990*. Stanford, Calif.: Stanford University Press, 1993.

———. *To Be an American: Cultural Pluralism and the Rhetoric of Assimilation*. New York: New York University Press, 1997.

Hobsbawm, Eric J. *The Age of Extremes: A History of the World: 1914–1991*. New York: Pantheon Books, 1996.

Hoffman, Abraham. *Unwanted Mexican Americans in the Great Depression*. Tucson: University of Arizona Press, 1974.

Hollinger, David A. *Postethnic America: Beyond Mulitculturalism*. New York: Basic Books, 1995.

Homberger, Eric. *The Historical Atlas of New York City: A Visual Celebration of Nearly 400 Years of New York City's History*. New York: An Owl Book, 1994.

Hsu, Francis L. K. *The Challenge of the American Dream: The Chinese in the United States*. Belmont, Calif.: Wadsworth Publishing Company, Inc., 1971.

Hu, Shen. *From the Opium War to the May 4th Movement*. Beijing: People's Publisher, 1980.

Hunter, Jane. *The Gospel of Gentility—American Women Missionaries in Turn-of-the-Century China*. New Haven, Conn.: Yale University Press, 1984.

Hutchison, William R. *Errand to the World—American Protestant Thought and Foreign Missions*. Chicago: The University of Chicago Press, 1987.

Iriye, Akira. *The Origins of the Second World War in Asia and the Pacific*. London and New York: Longman, 1987.

Isaacs, Harold R. *Images of Asia: American Views of China and India*. New York: Harper and Row, 1972.

Jonas, Menfred. *Isolationism in America: 1935–1941*. Ithaca, N.Y.: Cornell University, 1966.

Kessner, Thomas. *Fiorello H. La Guardia and the Making of Modern New York*. New York: McGraw-Hill Publishing Company, 1989.

———. *The Golden Door: Italian and Jewish Immigrant Mobility in New York City, 1880–1915*. New York: Oxford University Press, 1977.

Kessner, Thomas, and Betty Caroli. *Today's Immigrants, Their Stories: A New Look at the Latest Immigrants*. New York: Oxford University Press, 1981.

Kibria, Nazli. *Becoming Asian Americans: 2nd Generation Chinese and Korean American Identities*. Baltimore: Johns Hopkins University Press, 2002.

Kim, Samuel, ed. *China's Quest for National Identity*. Ithaca, N.Y.: Cornell University Press, 1993.

Kimball, Warren. *The Most Unsordid Act: Lend-Lease, 1939–1941*. Baltimore: Johns Hopkins University Press, 1969.

Kindleberger, Charles. *The World in Depression*. Berkeley: University of California Press, 1973.

Kingston, Maxine Hong. *China Men*. New York: Knopf, 1980.

Kitano, Harry H. L., and Roger Daniels. *Asian Americans, Emerging Minorities*. Third ed. Upper Saddle River, N.J.: Prentice Hall, 2001.

Koistinen, Paul. *The Military-Industrial Complex: A Historical Perspective*. New York: Praeger, 1980.

Kung, S. W. *Chinese in American Life: Some Aspects of Their History, Status, Problems, and Contributions*. Seattle: University of Washington Press, 1962.

Kuo, Chia-ling. *Social and Political Change in New York's Chinatown: The Role of Voluntary Associations*. New York: Praeger Publishers, 1977.

Kwong, Peter. *Chinatown, New York: Labor & Politics, 1930–1950*. New York: Monthly Review Press, 1979; New Press, 2001.

———. *The New Chinatown*. New York: Hill and Wang, 1987.

———. *Forbidden Workers: Illegal Chinese Immigrants and American Labor*. New York: The New Press, 1997.

Kwong, Peter, and Dusanka Miscevia. *Chinese America: The Untold Story of America's Oldest Community*. New York: New Press, 2005.

LaFargue, Thomas E. *China's First Hundred: Educational Mission Students in the United States 1872–1881*. Pullman: Washington State University Press, 1987.

Lai, Him Mark. *Becoming Chinese Americans: A History of Communities and Institutions*. Walnut Creek, Calif.: Altamira Press, 2004.

———. *The Chinese of America 1780–1980: An Illustrated History & Catalog of the Exhibition*. San Francisco: Chinese American Organization, 1980.

Lampton, David M., Joyce A. Madancy, and Kristen M. Williams. *A Relationship Restored: Trends in U.S.-China Educational Exchanges, 1978–1984*. Washington, D.C.: National Academy Press, 1986.

Langston, Maxine McKinney. "Helping the Generations Build a Bridge towards Each Other—The Chinese Methodist Center Corporation (CMCC), an Outreach Ministry in New York City's Chinatown, Offers a Dynamic Center and Purpose for Children, Youth and Adults." *Engage/Social Action*. Washington, D.C.: Board of Church and Society, United Methodist Church, Vol. 11, No. 4, April 1983, 52–55.

Lankevich, George J. *New York City: A Short History*. New York: New York University Press, 2002.

Lash, Joseph. *Roosevelt and Churchill*. New York: Norton, 1976.

Lau, Estelle. *Paper Families: Identity, Immigration Administration and Chinese Exclusion*. Durham, N.C.: Duke University Press, 2006.

Lee, Calvin. *Chinatown, USA*. New York: Doubleday & Company, Inc., 1965.

Lee, Erika. *At America's Gates: Chinese Immigration during the Exclusion Era, 1882–1945*. Chapel Hill: University of North Carolina Press, 2003.

Lee, Joann Faung Jean. *Asian American Experiences in the United States: Oral History of the First Generation to the Fourth Generation Americans from China, the Philippines, Japan, India and Pacific Islands*. Jefferson, N.C.: McFarland, 1991.

Lee, Josephine Tsui Yueh. *New York City's Chinese Community*. Charleston, S.C.: Arcadia Publisher, 2007.

Lee, Robert G. *Orientals: Asian American in Popular Culture*. Philadelphia: Temple University Press, 1999.

Leong, Gor Yun. *Chinatown Inside Out*. New York: B. Mussey, 1936.

Lien, Pei-te. *The Political Participation of Asian Americans: Voting Behavior in South California*. New York: Garland Pub., 1997.

Lin, Jan. *Reconstructing Chinatown: Ethnic Enclave, Global Change*. Minneapolis: University of Minnesota Press, 1998.

Ling, Huping. *Chinese St. Louis: From Enclave to Cultural Community*. Philadelphia: Temple University Press, 2004.

Lingeman, Richard. *Don't You Know There Is a War On? The Home Front, 1941–1945*. Second ed. New York: Avalon Publishing Group, 2003.

Link, Arthur S. *Progressivism*. Arlington Heights, Ill.: Harlan Davidson, Inc., 1983.

Louice, Vivian. *Compelled to Excel: Immigration, Education, and Opportunity among Chinese Americans*. Stanford, Calif.: Stanford University Press, 2004.

Lubove, Roy. *The Progressives and the Slums: Tenement House Reforms in New York City, 1890–1917*. Pittsburgh: University of Pittsburgh Press, 1962.

Ma, L. Eve Armentrout. *Revolutionaries, Monarchists & Chinatowns: Chinese Politics in the Americas & the 1911 Revolution*. Honolulu: Hawaii University Press, 1990.

Maffi, Mario. *Gateway to the Promised Land Ethnic Cultures on New York's Lower East Side*. New York: New York University Press, 1995.

Mann, Arthur. *La Guardia Comes to Power 1933*. New York: J.B. Lippincott Company, 1965.

Mao, Luming. *Reading Chinese Fortune Cookie: The Making of Chinese American Rhetoric*. Logan: Utah State University Press, 2006.

Mark, Diane Mei Lin, and Ginger Chih. *A Place Called Chinese America*. Dubuque, Iowa: Kendall Hunt Pub. Co., 1982.

Martin, John. "Chinatown." *The Commonwealth*, Nov. 9, 1932.

McClain, Paula D., and Joseph Stewart Jr. *"Can We All Get Along?": Racial and Ethnic Minorities in American Politics*. New York: Westview Press, 1995.

McCunn, Ruthanne Lum. *Chinese American Portraits: Personal Histories 1828–1988*. San Francisco: Chronicle Books, 1988.

———. *Wooden Fish Songs*. New York: A Lume Book, 1996.

McElvanine, Robert. *The Great Depression: America, 1929–1941*. New York: Times Books, 1984.

Mckee, Delber L. *Chinese Exclusion versus the Open Door Policy 1900–1906: Clashes over China Policy in the Roosevelt Era*. Detroit: Wayne State University Press, 1977, 1986.

Mcnickle, Chris. *To Be Mayor of New York*. New York: Columbia University Press, 1992.

Meng, Chih. *Chinese American Understanding: A Sixty-Year Search by Chih Meng*. New York: China Institute in America, 1981.

Miller, John J. *The Unmaking of Americans: How Multiculturalism Has Undermined the Assimilation Ethic*. New York: The Free Press, 1998.

Miller, Stuart Creighton. *The Unwelcome Immigrants: The American Image of the Chinese 1785–1882*. Berkeley and Los Angeles: University of California, 1969.

Min, Pyong Gap, ed. *Asian Americans: Contemporary Trends and Issues*. Thousand Oaks, Calif.: Sage Publications, 1995.

Min, Pyong Gap, and Rose Kim, ed. *Struggle for Ethnic Identity Narratives by Asian American Professionals*. London and New Delhi: AltaMira Press, 1999.

Miranda, Edward, and Ino J. Rossi. *New York City's Italians: Census Characteristics at a Glance*. New York: Italian-American Center for Urban Affairs, Inc., 1976.

Mollenkopf, John Hull, ed. *Power, Culture, and Place: Essays on New York City*. New York: Russell Sage Foundation, 1988.

Moon, Krysten R. *Yellowface: Creating the Chinese in American Popular Music and Performances, 1850s–1920s*. New Brunswick, N.J.: Rutgers University Press, 2005.

Morrison, Joan, and Charlotte Fox Zabusky. *American Mosaic: The Immigrant Experience in the Words of Those Who Lived It*. New York: E. P. Dutton, 1980.

Moy, James S. *Marginal Sights: Staging the Chinese in America*. Iowa City: University of Iowa Press, 1993.

Mulzac, Hugh. *A Star to Steer By*. New York: International Publishers, 1963.

Muller, Thomas. *Immigrants and the American City*. New York: New York University Press, 1993.

Muse, Erica A. *The Evangelical Church in Boston's Chinatown: A Discourse of Language, Gender and Identity*. New York: Routledge, 2005.

Nelson, Donald. *Arsenal of Democracy*. New York: Harcourt Brace and Company, 1946.

Ng, Franklin. *Asian American: Re-conceptualizing Cultures, History, and Politics*. New York: Routledge, 2002.

Okihiro, Gary Y. *Margins and Mainstreams: Asians in American History and Culture*. Seattle: University of Washington Press, 1994.

Olson, James Stuart. *The Ethnic Dimension in American History*. New York: St Martin's Press, 1979.

Palmar, Albert W. *Oriental in American Life*. New York: Friendship Press, reprinted in 1972.

Pan, Lynn. *Sons of the Yellow Emperor: A History of the Chinese Diaspora*. New York: Kodansha International, 1994.

Park, Henry. "Review Essay in Asian Americans: An Interpretive History by Sucheng Chan." *Journal of Contemporary Asia* 25, No. 2, 1995, 284–87.

Perlmutter, Philip. *The Dynamics of American Ethic, Religious, and Racial Group Life*. Westport, Conn.: Praeger, 1996.

Pfaelzer, Jean. *Driven Out: The Forgotten War against Chinese Americans*. New York: Random House, 2007.

Polenberg, Richard. *War and Society: The United States, 1941–1945*. Philadelphia: Lippincott, 1972.

Prange, Gordon W. *At Dawn We Slept*. New York: McGraw-Hill, 1982.

Rauch, Basil. *Roosevelt from Munich to Pearl Harbor*. New York: Creative Age Press, 1950.

Rauchway, Eric. *The Refuge of Affections: Family and American Reform Politics*. New York: Columbia University Press, 2001.

Reed, Ishmael, ed. *Multi America: Essays on Cultural Wars and Cultural Peace*. New York: Viking, 1997.

Reimers, David. *Still the Golden Door: The Third World Comes to America*. Second ed. New York: Columbia University Press, 1992.

Reitano, Joanne R. *The Restless City: A Short History of New York from Colonial Times to the Present*. New York: Routledge, 2006.

Reynold, David. *The Creation of the Anglo-American Alliance: 1937–1941*. Chapel Hill: University of North Carolina Press, 1982.

Rhea, Joseph Tilden. *Race Pride and the American Identity*. Cambridge, Mass.: Harvard University Press, 1997.

Riggs, Fred W. *Pressures on Congress: A Study of the Repeal of Chinese Exclusion*. Westport, Conn.: Greenwood Press, Publishers, 1950.

Ringer, Benjamin B., and Elinor R. Lawless. *Race-Ethnicity and Society*. New York: Routledge, 1989.

Rittenhouse, Caroline Smith, ed. *Like Good Steel: The China Letters of Margaret Bailey Speer, North China, 1925–1943*. Berwyn, Penn.: The Round Table Press, 1994.

Rosenwaike, Ira. *Population History of New York City*. Syracuse, N.Y.: Syracuse University Press, 1972.

Rosenzweig, Roy. *Eight Hours for What We Will: Workers and Leisure in an Industrial City, 1870–1920*. Cambridge: Cambridge University Press, 1983.

Saxton, Alexander. *The Indispensable Enemy: Labor & the Anti-Chinese Movement in California*. Los Angeles: University of California Press, 1977.

Seward, George F. *Chinese Immigration in Its Social and Economical Aspects*. New York: Charles Scribner's Sons, 1881, 1970.

Siu, Paul C. P. *The Chinese Laundryman: A Study of Social Isolation*. New York: New York University Press, 1953, 1987.

Smith, D. Anthony. *The Ethnic Origins of Nations*. Oxford: Blackwell, 1986.

Spence, Jonathan C. *The Gate of Heavenly Peace: The Chinese and Their Revolution 1895–1980*. New York: Penguin Books, 1982.

———. *The Search for Modern China*. New York and London: W.W. Norton and Company, 1990.

Steinhorn, Leonard, and Barbara Diggs-Brown. *By the Color of Our Skin: The Illusion of Integration and the Reality of Race*. New York: A Dutton Book, 1999.

Sung, Betty Lee. *Mountain of Gold: The Story of the Chinese in America*. New York: Macmillan Company, 1967.

———. *The Story of the Chinese in America—Their Struggle for Survival, Acceptance, and Full Participation In American Life from the Gold Rush Days to the Present*. New York: Collier Books, 1967.

Takaki, Ronald. *Strangers from a Different Shore: A History of Asian Americans*. Boston: Little, Brown and Company, 1989.

———. *A Different Mirror—A History of Multicultural America*, Boston: Little, Brown and Company, 1993.

———. *Ethnic Islands and the Emergence of Urban Chinese Americans*. New York: Chelsea House, 1994.

———. *Spacious Dreams: The First Wave of Asian Immigration*. New York: Chelsea House, 1994.

———. *Democracy and Race: Asian Americans and World War II*. New York: Chelsea House, 1995.

———. *Strangers at the Gates: Asian American Immigration after 1965*. New York: Chelsea House, 1995.

Tan, Thomas Tsu-wee. *Your Chinese Roots: The Overseas Chinese Story*. Union City, Calif.: Heilan International, Inc., 1953, 1986.

Tchen, John Kuo Wei. "New York Chinese: The Nineteenth-Century Pre-Chinatown Settlement." *Chinese America: History and Perspectives* 4, 1990, 157–92.

Terkel, Studs. *The Hard Times: An Oral History of the Great Depression*. New York: Pantheon Books, 1970.

Tsai, Shih-shan Henry. *China and the Overseas Chinese in the United States: 1868–1911*. Fayetteville: University of Arkansas Press, 1983.

———. *The Chinese Experience in America*. Bloomington: Indiana University Press, 1986.

Underhill, Robert. *FDR and Harry: Unparalleled Lives*. Westport, Conn.: Praeger, 1996.

Walling, George W. *Recollection of a New York Chief of Police, An Official Record of 38 Years as Patrol, Detective, Captain, Inspector and Chief of the New York Police*. New York: Caxton Book Concern Limited, 1887.

Wang, Guanhua. *In Search of Justice: The 1905–1906 Chinese Anti-American Boycott*. Cambridge, Mass.: Harvard University Press, 2001.

Wang, Xinyang. "Economic Opportunity, Artisan Leadership, and Immigrant Workers' Labor Militancy: Italian and Chinese Immigrant Workers in New York City, 1890–1970." *Labor History* 37, No. 4, Fall 1996, 480–99.

Wang, Y. C. *Chinese Intellectuals and the West 1872–1949*. Chapel Hill: University of North Carolina Press, 1966.

Wheeler, W. Reginald, Henry King, and Alexander B. Davidson. *The Foreign Student in America: A Study by the Commission on Survey of Foreign Students in the United States of America, under the Auspices of the Friendly Relations Committees of the Young Men's Christian Association and the Young Women's Christian Association*. New York: Association Press, 1925.

Wilentz, Sean. *Chants Democratic: New York City and the Rise of the American Working Class, 1788–1850*. New York: Oxford University Press, 1984.

Wohlstetter, Roberta. *Pearl Harbor: Warning and Decision*. Stanford, Calif.: Stanford University Press, 1962.

Wong, Bernard P. *The Chinese in Silicon Valley, Globalization, Social Networks, and Ethnic Identity*. Lanham, Md.: Rowman & Littlefield, 2006.

Wong, K. Scott. *Americans First: Chinese Americans and the Second World War*. Cambridge, Mass.: Harvard University Press, 2005.

Wong, K. Scott, and Sucheng Chan. *Claiming America: Constructing Chinese American Identities during the Exclusion Era.* Philadelphia: Temple University Press, 1998.

Wong, Wayne Hung. *American Paper Son: A Chinese Immigrant in the Midwest.* Urbana and Chicago: University of Illinois Press, 2006.

Wood, Forrest. *The Arrogance of Faith: Christianity and Race in America from the Colonial Era to the Twentieth Century.* New York: Knopf, 1990.

Wray, Harry, ed. *Pearl Harbor Reexamined: Prologue to the Pacific.* Honolulu: University of Hawaii, 1990.

Wyman, David. *The Abandonment of the Jews: America and the Holocaust, 1941–1945.* New York: Pantheon Books, 1984.

Wytrawal, Joseph A. *Poles in American History and Tradition.* Detroit: Endurance Press, 1969.

Yen, Le Espiritu. *Asian American Women and Men: Labor, Laws and Love.* The Gender Lens Series. London: Sage Publications, 1997.

Yu, Renqiu. *"To Save China, to Save Ourselves": The Chinese Hand Laundry Alliance of New York.* Philadelphia: Temple University Press, 1992.

Yuan, D. Y. *Chinese-American Population.* Hong Kong: UEA Press Ltd, 1988.

Yung, Judy. *Unbound Voices: A Documentary History of Chinese Women in San Francisco.* Berkeley: University of California Press, 1999.

Yung, Judy, Gordon H. Chang, and Him Mark Lai, ed. *Chinese American Voices: From the Gold Rush to the Present.* Berkeley: University of California Press, 2006.

Zhao, Jianli. *Strangers in the City: The Atlanta Chinese, Their Community, and Stories of Their Lives.* New York: Routledge, 2002.

Zhou, Min. *Chinatown: The Socioeconomic Potential of an Urban Enclave.* Philadelphia: Temple University Press, 1992.

Zhu, Liping. *Ethnic Oasis: The Chinese in the Black Hills.* Pierre: South Dakota State Historical Society Press, 2004.

Conference Papers

The Chinese American Experience: Papers from the Second National Conference on Chinese American Studies, 1984.

Dissertations, Theses, and Research Papers

Carrs, Nancy. "The Early Historical Evolution of Chinatown, New York City." Research Paper, Chinatown History Museum, 1980.

Chan, Kim Man. "Mandarins in America: The Early Chinese Ministers to the United States, 1878–1907." Ph.D. Dissertation, University of Hawaii, 1981.

Chen, Chin-yu. "San Francisco's Chinatown: A Socio-Economic and Cultural History, 1850–1882." Ph.D. Dissertation, University of Idaho, 1992.

Chen, Helen. "Chinese Immigration into the United States: An Analysis of Changes in Immigration Policies." Ph.D. Dissertation, Brandies University, 1980.

Chen, Hsian-shui. "Chinatown No More: Changing Patterns of Chinese Organization in Queens, New York City." Ph.D. Dissertation, City University of New York, 1990.

Chen, Hsuan Julia. "The Chinese Coming in New York, 1920–1940." Ph.D. Dissertation, American University, 1941.

Chen, Yong. "China in America: A Cultural Study of Chinese San Francisco: 1850–1943." Ph.D. Dissertation, Cornell University, 1993.

Forman, Allan. "Celestial Gotham." Research Paper, Chinatown Historical Museum.

Gyory, Andrew. "Rolling in the Dirt: The Origins of the Chinese Exclusion Act and the Politics of Racism, 1870–1882." Ph.D. Dissertation, University of Massachusetts, 1991.

Hao, Peter Te Yuan. "An Analysis of Certain Learning Difficulties of Chinese Students in New York City." Doctoral Dissertation, 1955.

Huang, Hsiao-ping. "Chinese Merchant Background and Experience in Hawaii under the Monarchy." Ph.D. Dissertation, University of Hawaii, 1989.

Leon Azofeifa, Moises Guillermo. "Chinese Immigrants on the Atlantic Coast of Costa Rica: The Economic Adaptation of an Asian Minority in a Pluralistic Society." Ph.D. Dissertation, Tulane University, 1987.

Lin, Jan Chien. "Capital and Community in Urban Change: Chinatown: New York City." Ph.D. Dissertation, New School for Social Research, 1991.

Loew, Peter. "The Development of an Intentional Ministry in a Bilingual Chinese Church in Brooklyn, New York." Ph.D. Dissertation, The Eastern Baptist Theological Seminary, 1990.

Mar, Donald Warren. "Chinese Immigrants and the Ethnic Labor Market." Ph.D. Dissertation, University of California, Berkeley, 1985.

McCullough, Kenneth Bruce. "America's Back Door: Indirect International Immigration via Mexico to the United States from 1875–1940." Ph.D. Dissertation, Texas A & M University, 1992.

McGlinn, Lawrence Alan. "Institutions and Individuals: Space and Power among Chinese in the Northeastern United States, 1870–1920." Ph.D. Dissertation, Pennsylvania State University, 1992.

Ng, Wing Chung. "Ethnicity and Community: Southern Chinese Immigrants and Descendants in Vancouver, 1945–1980." Ph.D. Dissertation, University of British Columbia, 1993.

Salyer, Lucy Elizabeth. "Guarding the 'White Man's Frontier': Courts, Politics, and the Regulation of Immigration, 1891–1924." Ph.D. Dissertation, University of California, Berkeley, 1989.

Tsai, Shih-shan Henry. "Reaction to Exclusion: Ch'ing Attitudes toward Overseas Chinese in the United States, 1848–1908." Ph.D. Dissertation, University of Oregon, 1970.

Wang, Xinyan. "Tradition, Assimilation and Response to Homelands Politics: A Comparative Study of Italian and Chinese Immigrants in New York City, 1890–1965." Ph.D. Dissertation, Yale University, 1988.

Wong, Kevin Scott. "Encountering the Other: Chinese Immigration and Its Impact on Chinese and American World Views, 1875–1905." Ph.D. Dissertation, University of Michigan, 1992.

Ye, Weili. *Crossing the Cultures: The Experience of Chinese Students in the U.S.A. 1900–1925*. Ph.D. Dissertation, University of Michigan, 1991.

Yu, Li-hua. "Chinese Immigrants in Idaho." Ph.D. Dissertation, Bowling State University, 1991.

Yu, Sui-wen. "A Guidance Program for Chinese Youth in the Chinese Christian Center NYC." Ph.D. Dissertation, Teachers College, Columbia University, 1940.

Zhang, Qingsong. "Dragon in the Land of the Eagle: The Exclusion of Chinese From U.S. Citizenship, 1848–1943." Ph.D. Dissertation, University of Virginia, 1994.

Zhou, Min. "The Enclave Economy and Immigrant Incorporation in New York City's Chinatown." Ph.D. Dissertation, State University of New York at Albany, 1989.

Index